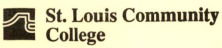

SUCCESSFUL SCHOOLS FOR YOUNG ADOLESCENTS

SUCCESSFUL SCHOOLS FOR YOUNG ADOLESCENTS

JOAN LIPSITZ

Transaction Books
New Brunswick (U.S.A.) and London (U.K.)

Library of Congress Catalog Number: 83–9139
ISBN 0–87855–487–4 (cloth); ISBN 0–87855–947–7 (pbk.)
Printed in the United States of America

Library of Congress Cataloging in Publication Data

Lipsitz, Joan.
  Successful schools for young adolescents.

  Bibliography: p.
  Includes index.
  1. Education, Secondary—United States—Aims and objectives. 2.
Middle schools—United States—Evaluation. 3. Middle schools—United
States—Case studies. I. Title.
LB1623.L56 1983   373.73   83–9139
ISBN 0–87855–487–4
ISBN 0–87855–947–7 (pbk.)

Seventh Printing, 1987

To M., who made it possible.

Contents

Part III   Recurrent Themes in Successful Middle-Grade Schools

Acknowledgments

Being a good observer and analyst means knowing what questions to ask. If we were better at asking questions, we would have many more answers in education. I have been deeply affected by the questions of the following people, to whom I am very grateful:

Terry Saario, as always; at the National Institute of Education (NIE), Bruce Haslam, Mike Cohen, and Saul Yanofsky; at the Center for Early Adolescence, Gayle Dorman and Leah Lefstein. Their questions are heard throughout this book. The following people generously responded to requests for help at the outset of the study: Walter Allen, John Arnold, Mary K. Chelton, Frances Coe, James P. Comer, M.D., Larry Cuban, William A. Daniel, Jr., M.D., Nancy Doda, Thomas Gatewood, Judith Gillespie, Adele Hofmann, M.D., Frances Hooks, Charity James, Michael James, Susan Kaeser, The Honorable Orm Ketcham, Marya Levinson, Eliot Levinson, John Lounsbury, Anne Petersen, Edith Phelps, Joan Schine, Irving Sigel, Ted Sizer, Karl Stauber, Mason Thomas, Neal Thomas, and Paul Ylvisaker.

Andy Dobelstein generously helped me work my way out of a central quandary, when I thought I had finished and failed. Bill Kerewsky, Mary Haywood Metz, Fritz Mulhauser, and Terry Saario wrote lengthy critiques that, while both daunting and buoying my spirits, improved the text.

My colleagues at the Center for Early Adolescence were always ready to run to the library, type from impenetrable drafts, negotiate between two incompatible bureaucracies, arrange complex travel itineraries, and listen to my stories. For these gifts I am grateful to Suzanne Rucker, David Sheaves, Ruth Thomas, and especially to Ernie Quade.

In order to gather qualitative data through observation, one becomes a participant observer. It is impossible to spend time observing schools without having some effect on them, if only by virtue of the questions the observer asks. The nature of the questions frames in unusual ways the terms in which people think about their work. The presence of an observer impels some people to communicate among themselves about grievances long held silent. Sometimes the observations of the visitor lead to a reconsideration of the fundamental purposes of day-to-day practices.

For allowing me to be an obtrusive observer in the lives of their schools, I am grateful beyond even the extent of my admiration to the principals of all the schools I visited, and in particular to the four described in this book: Wilma Parrish of Western Middle School in Alamance County, North Carolina; Thomas Washington of Region 7 Middle School (The Dorothy L. Fisher Magnet Middle School) in Detroit, Michigan; Terry Brooks of the Samuel V. Noe Middle School in Louisville, Kentucky; and Cary Bell and Bonne Sue Adams of the Shoreham–Wading River Middle School in Shoreham, New York. Thanks also to Hattie Scott of the Carolina Friends School in Durham, North Carolina; Bill Kerewsky of Harper's Choice Middle School in Columbia, Maryland; John Quinn and Walter Kurtzman of the Alexander Burger Intermediate School in the Bronx, New York; Harry Stanfield of East Cary Junior High School in Cary, North Carolina; and Donald Vineburg of Ocean Intermediate School in Ocean Township, New Jersey.

In each school, people's hospitality spilled over beyond the school day and the demands of professional courtesy. In particular, I am thankful for the hospitality of Charlene Davis and Linda Perky of the Noe Middle School, Diane Fleming of the Detroit Public Schools, and especially Winnie Pardo of the Shoreham–Wading River Middle School.

I am grateful to the University of North Carolina for agreeing to release 50 percent of my time so that I could accept the Intergovernmental Personnel Act assignment to NIE. The work on which this publication is based was performed pursuant to Contract Number NIE-P-81-0120 of the National Institute of Education. It does not necessarily reflect the views of that agency.

This study would not have been attempted had it not been initiated by Bruce Haslam, who tolerated and brought clarity to my periodic confusion. He bears no responsibility, nor does anyone else at NIE, for the failures in this book, but much credit is due him for many of its insights.

My last and deepest thanks go to my children: to Annie, whose telephone conversations filled motel rooms with warmth and encouragement, and to Jonathan, who never once asked me to stop despite my many weeks away from home. His pride in me was completely unanticipated, typical of the gifts with which adolescents sustain their parents.

Preface

From September 1980 through August 1981 I was on assignment to the National Institute of Education as a research associate under the Intergovernmental Personnel Act to identify and examine "effective" middle-grade schools that "foster healthy social development." This book is the visible product of that study. It rests, both because of the assignment and my strong personal conviction, on the central assumption that school effectiveness and developmental responsiveness are inextricably intertwined.

The impetus to accept the assignment came from an outburst several years ago. I was coordinating a series of regional conferences on early adolescence for the Ford Foundation and the Mary Reynolds Babcock Foundation. At the 1977 Mid-Atlantic Conference, one participant declared in disgust: "I'm sick and tired of hearing what doesn't work. I know what doesn't work. Tell me what works or I'm going to go and watch television." He watched a lot of television.

Since then I have asked junior high and middle-school principals, "Is your school a good school?" Many have a great deal of trouble articulating what a good school for young adolescents is, even when they believe they have one. After a good bit of rambling and gesturing, they fall back almost predictably to: "You just have to come and see my school."

I have tried to do that; there is no substitute for it. But it is so costly in terms of finances, time, and personal energy as to be beyond the reach of most school personnel and policy setters, the very people who need to travel around the country looking at successful middle-grade schools. I have tried to write a book that helps people "see" four of the schools I visited. On paper, no school comes alive in all its diverse energies, sounds, moods, colors, relationships, sagas—in all those aspects of community life that give each school its distinct personality. I apologize to these schools, each of whose unique excellence in the face of powerful pressures toward mediocrity I have failed to capture as vividly and effortlessly as a visit does.

Nonetheless, the attempt is important. Teachers and principals are defeated daily by this age group, whose refusal to remain malleable children occasions dismay among adults. The intermediate level is the least prestigious in the entire continuum of schooling. Our most frightening horror stories, along with statistics to back them up, come from our junior high schools. From test scores as well as rates of absenteeism, suspension, vandalism, and assault, we appear to have ample evidence that young adolescents and their schools are failing each other.

There are, however, schools in which young people and adults live and learn together in an atmosphere not only of civility but mutual concern. This study began with an attempt to answer one question: how do public schools for young adolescents deal with the developmental diversity of the age group? This question seemed key to answering the plea, "what works?" As I proceeded, the question was expanded to include what "school effectiveness" means for this age group. I was struck by the limitations of some of the current school effectiveness literature. I worried that, as in so many other areas concerning early adolescence, the conclusions from school effectiveness studies pertaining to the early elementary grades would be applied unexamined to the middle grades.

I began asking questions that took me well beyond the scope of the current literature: what do we expect of middle-grade schools in terms of safety, comportment, and achievement? How does a middle-grade school win acceptance within the context of the local community and its expectations? How do these schools function in response to unresolved public policy issues like desegregation, sex equity, and mainstreaming the handicapped? And always, how do schools respond to the developmental diversity of early adolescent students?

It is tempting to refer to this book as a school effectiveness study and thereby quietly to expand the definition of "effectiveness." I have chosen instead to use a different term to signal readers more blatantly that they are being asked to become engaged in a broader analysis of schools that work. Therefore, I refer to the schools as "successful." My intent is not to introduce a new, marginal distinction into the literature, just to alert others to the necessary complexity of the undertaking.

In America we have a system of schooling created by many more pressures than trying to provide the best educational environment for children and youth. Given that the system now exists, is hard to change, and is suffering from a growing lack of enthusiasm about free public education for every child in America, it is urgent that we look at ways in which some schools achieve and maintain educational excellence. In reference to early adolescence in particular, we should be able to progress from a dismal picture of schooling to a rethinking of how we can create productive educational and social environments for 10- to 14-year-olds that maintain community support. Some schools are succeeding brilliantly in teaching young adolescents, while many others are bankrupt. What can be learned from success? I began by looking for characteristics shared by good schools for young adolescents. I ended by looking at the diverse ways in which excellence is attained in middle-grade schools.

Part I
EXPANDING THE DEFINITION OF EFFECTIVENESS

1

A Framework for Examining Successful Middle-Grade Schools

General Expectations

What is a good school for young adolescents? What do we expect of such schools? What is special about young adolescents that makes good schooling at this level so difficult to achieve? At the root of the difficulty in schooling for young adolescents are massive individual differences in their development. The challenge is to design a program for such variability that also meets parental expectations about academic learning and socialization. Compounding the difficulties are public policy questions that help shape the context in which schools function. The most powerful of these public debates at present is over the tradeoffs necessary to achieve both quality and equality in public education, a debate that generates questions we must answer before we lose our remarkable and essential commitment to public schooling for every child in America. Schools respond to these policy questions daily, whether or not their principals and teachers consciously react to them. They also respond, successfully or otherwise, to the unprecedented variability in growth that is characteristic of early adolescent development.

There is a growing body of literature on effective schools that addresses children in particular social contexts but ignores child development. On the other hand, there is a growing body of literature on schools for young adolescents that addresses the demands of adolescent development but ignores social contexts. This book attempts to open a wide-angle lens through which we can look at schools for 10- to 14-year-olds, including all three perspectives: adolescent development, social contexts, and public policy concerns.

3

Effective Schools

Every major study of effective schools has concluded that adult expectations, school climate, and especially the nature of school leadership are powerful determinants of student outcomes. In 1971, Weber reported on four schools where inner-city elementary school children were learning to read. All four, while using different reading programs and instructional techniques, had principals who were involved in setting instructional goals and strategies, staff members who held high expectations for their students, and an orderly yet pleasant atmosphere. In addition, all four placed strong emphasis on the acquisition of basic reading skills and closely monitored student progress in acquiring those skills.[1] Similarly, Edmonds has reported that effective urban schools are characterized by a strong principal; clear academic goals with an emphasis on basic skills instruction; a well-defined testing program; a clean, secure, serious environment; and high expectations for students expressed in positive relationships between professional staff and students.[2]

It is difficult to simultaneously conclude that schools make no difference in achievement and that student achievement is consistently declining. Surely the genetic pool or family background of American students has not declined so rapidly that either explains the 20-year decline in student achievement. We, therefore, operate on the assumption that there may be some explanation for the level of student achievement in the nature of the schools. [Wilbur B. Brookover, "Effective Secondary Schools."]

Edmond's work, like that of almost all investigators in that body of research now being called the "effective schools literature," defines an effective school as "one in which the children of the poor are at least as well prepared in basic skills as the children of the middle class."[3] In this literature, effective schools are held to two criteria: a high mean level of student achievement on standardized tests, and movement toward social equity as seen in the attenuation of the relationship between student background and performance.[4] Effective schools research suggests that there are instructionally effective schools that considerably reduce this relationship.

The research looks at a specific population of children—urban, Black, in elementary schools—with limited outcomes in mind: scores on standardized reading and arithmetic tests. Its implications for diverse populations of older students, for diverse settings—rural and suburban, as well as urban—and for less limited outcomes can only be suggestive. Also, because the research is cross-sectional, we cannot obtain from it information about the schools' historical bases, which may be crucial to understanding their effectiveness.

Michael Rutter and his colleagues, in a study of effective inner-city secondary schools in London, have expanded the scope of effective schools studies by looking at more varied outcomes. What, they asked, does the public expect of schools? It expects good comportment, high attendance, success in public exams, low delinquency rates outside of school, and success in future employment. Using four of these measures (employment one year after leaving school is a long-term outcome still being studied), Rutter and his colleagues found large and statistically significant differences among secondary schools: "In short, it appears that in a part of inner London known to be disadvantaged in numerous ways, some schools were better able than others to foster good behavior and attainments."[5]

These investigators asked: "Do a child's experiences at school have any effect; does it matter which school he goes to; and which are the features of school that matter?" They concluded that "the research findings provide a clear 'yes' in response to the first two questions. Schools do indeed have an important impact on children's development and it does matter which school a child attends."[6] Rutter suggests that, in answer to the third question, "Which are the features of school that matter," the picture is less clear but intriguing. No one system of school organization showed overriding advantages. What did correlate with desired outcomes were:

- high levels of rewards and praise;
- pleasant and comfortable school conditions for students;
- ample opportunities for students to take responsibility and participate in running their school;
- an academic emphasis set by the school staff;
- consensus among staff members about curricular expectations, school norms, and discipline.[7]

The importance of these separate school processes, according to Rutter, may be in their combined contribution to the "ethos" of the school as a whole.[8] Rutter et al., perhaps because they were looking at older students than those studied by Edmonds and Weber, were concerned with how the values and norms of the school come to be accepted by its students. Researchers, just like school officials and parents, must question the means and extent to which adolescents, a less pliable group to work with than students in the early elementary grades, accept adults' values and norms. In other words, the issue of adolescent socialization becomes central. Rutter and his associates studied schools as social organizations. They found that students' behavior and academic success are considerably influenced by the internal life of the school.

This book addresses that internal life, which results from the interplay of people, organizational structure, activities, and history. It addresses the lives of successful schools specifically designed for young adolescents, a population of students whose diversity imposes special challenges on schools that are to date unexplored in the effective schools literature.

Early Adolescence and the Purposes of Schooling

It is the central bias of this book that to succeed with young adolescents, schools must be responsive to their developmental needs. The imperatives of early adolescent development are too compelling to be overlooked or denied. Unfortunately, early adolescence is a time in life about which we suffer from an embarrassing lack of knowledge. The middle-school years span pre- and early adolescence. Our tendency, as Cohen and Frank point out, is to extend our knowledge about "middle childhood" upward and adolescence downward to mask our ignorance.[9] It is in this state of ignorance that we define schooling for an age group experiencing the dramatic conjunction of rapid biological, social, emotional, and cognitive changes.

Biologically, early adolescence is marked by a characteristic growth spurt, the appearance of secondary sex characteristics, and the onset of puberty. The rate of growth during early adolescence is second only to that in infancy. From then on, there is no time in life that rivals early adolescence for rapidity of growth—or for self-consciousness about it. Records indicate that the onset of puberty has occurred four months earlier every decade since 1840. Even if, as it now appears, this trend has stopped and the age of menarche (first menstrual period) remains approximately twelve and a half, young adolescents are biologically more than four years older than adolescents in the mid–nineteenth century, for whom the average age of menarche was seventeen. Biologically, today's young adolescents are approximately two years in advance of the young people for whom the first junior high schools in America were established. They are capable of reproduction at what to many adults seems a shockingly early age. Socially, however, we consider them younger than their grandparents and give them fewer outlets for responsible social behavior. Yet the early onset of puberty imposes responsibility for their sexual behavior at a much younger age than was required of their grandparents. They are at once socially younger and biologically older.[10]

This paradox creates one of the central tensions in schools for young adolescents. Schools are called upon to establish programs for students at different levels of social and physical development in communities that accept neither their social competence nor their biological precocity.

In conjunction but not necessarily in synchrony with physical changes, significant psychological changes are occurring. The psychosocial tasks of adolescence include forming a conscious sense of individual uniqueness and solidarity with group ideals. The resolution of these tasks is determined in large measure by what precedes adolescence and will determine much of what follows.[11] The events of adolescence are part of a continuum, not isolated phenomena. The challenge to schools is to work with people in an age group who have in many ways been isolated from the rest of the age span and to work with them at a time when they seek to extend their personal autonomy from adults and simultaneously to identify with them.

Adolescence is, first of all, a matter of biology—an intrinsic development process in a physiologic sense. It is also a matter of psychology insofar as it involves the resolution of internal issues around self and others. Finally, it is a matter of social experience, or rather of social context and cultural definition. [John Demos in *The Turbulent Years,* ed. John Scanlon.]

Schools are peculiar social agencies, charged by society with socializing youth into that society while excluding them from it. Their essence is artifice: they are surrogate societies. In these institutions, teachers and administrators substitute for other adults as young adolescents act out their ambivalence about attachment to adults and one another, about their new areas of social and intellectual competence, about their bodies and feelings —about their changing but familiar selves. In such settings, young adolescents attempt to explore the challenges of developmental tasks such as forming a sense of identity, commitment to group ideals, personal autonomy, and increasingly intimate relationships.

It is the avowed purpose of schools to enhance the power of students' intellect. There is considerable controversy about the quality of those powers during early adolescence. Piagetians hold that during adolescence, if at all, a qualitative shift occurs in cognition that enables human beings to reason abstractly. This development, the shift from concrete to formal operations, makes possible propositional thinking, considering ideas contrary to fact, reasoning with hypotheses involving multiple variables, appreciating the elegance of a mathematical theorem, the subtlety of a poetic metaphor, the power of political ideology. It makes possible projecting oneself into the future and thereby accepting the necessity of preventive behavior. It allows the examination of values accepted without question during childhood. It makes personally accessible such concepts as "the greater good," "the social fabric," "the ends justify the means," "civil disobedience," "give me liberty or give me death," "$E = MC^2$," "to be or not to be," and "the cradle of civilization."

Not all researchers agree about whether cognitive development is characterized by quantitative growth only or in addition by qualitative shifts.

There is far less agreement about when such a shift to formal operations occurs, if indeed a shift occurs, and whether it is possible via proper instruction to hasten the shift to hypothetical reasoning. At the heart of the central purpose of schooling, then, is a controversy about how abstract a curriculum for this age group should be and whether instruction can profitably be directed toward accommodating and even stimulating qualitative shifts in cognition. The controversy has direct bearing on curricular decisions being made at the middle-grade level, assuming that they are made thoughtfully and with concern for how adolescents learn.

Were this a raging controversy, middle-grade schooling would be in excellent condition. Professionals would be attending to the interdependent nature of development and learning. Whatever the outcome of the debate, curricular and instructional purposes would be based on an articulated philosophy of development. Such scrutiny of purpose and practice does not characterize schools for young adolescents.[12]

I remember what I devoutly wished as a parent: that there would be at least one faculty/staff person in a school to whom my child could relate; that there be at least one classroom/school experience that would give my child a feeling of inspiration and success; and that there be at least one learning experience that could try my child's soul without overwhelming odds that he/she would be emotionally crippled as a result. [Paul Ylvisaker, Harvard University, letter to author, October 27, 1980.]

As unsure as middle-grade schools are of their academic purposes, they are even less assured about their role in the socialization of children to adulthood. This confusion derives in part from the numerous outcomes the public expects from schools. As Metz says: "Americans have unrealistic expectations of public schools. The accomplishments they expect are dazzling in ambition and variety. Public schools should give every child a sound grasp of the three R's, foster creativity, impart a thorough knowledge of world history, literature and art, train minds in the scientific method of inquiry, offer vocational training, develop problem-solving ability, foster imagination, develop independence, impart skills of social interaction with adults and peers, and support good moral character. My list is not exhaustive."[13] Not at all. And schools are expected to produce these results equally well with members of diverse cultural groups and with an age group itself characterized by broad developmental diversity.

No further discussion would be warranted if all schools failed to meet these ambitious expectations. The fact is that some schools for young adolescents are remarkably successful in taking on all comers, developing in an initially inchoate group an energetic sense of community on adults' terms, and fostering creativity, social ease, and intellectual growth.

Developmentally Appropriate Schools

At the outset of this study, letters were sent to close to one hundred leading researchers and practitioners in diverse fields that relate to early adolescent development and schooling. Each respondent was asked to nominate schools for visitation and answer the question: "What are five characteristics of effective schools for young adolescents?" It is surprising that few respondents to this question devoted more than one or two of their five answers to academics; they focused on developmental appropriateness. In part, this choice reflects a belief among some that the middle-grade years are not years for vigorous intellectual pursuits. In part, it reflects a confusion about the academic purposes of middle and junior high schools. The extensiveness of the combined lists of characteristics is an indication of the numerous expectations held for schools and also of a need for dialogue. It is in the process of discussing schools that we sort, categorize, and refine our expectations. Lacking this process, the expectations are numerous and diffuse.

Respondents' emphasis on personal and social development is an acknowledgement of the compelling needs of young adolescents that less effective schools ignore or attempt to combat. As Rutter says, "schools have a choice in the norms they select."[14] Successful schools for young adolescents choose to become environments that promote social development. They assume social development to include a multitude of characteristics: self-discipline, industriousness, respect for authority, perseverance, patience, honesty, the ability to work toward goals, a sense of respect for self and others, assertiveness, enthusiasm and interest in learning, confidence, the ability to function in a peer group, individuality, communication skills, generosity toward others, empathy, flexibility, trust, the ability to work with others and alone, an awareness about and concern for larger social issues, the ability to define one's sex role and racial role, the ability to derive strength from oneself, others, the arts, sports, knowledge, beautiful things . . .

What is clear from this "laundry list" is that the outcomes that successful schools for young adolescents expect to effect encompass attitudes and behavior as well as teachable skills. The desired outcomes are expectations about social development. The norms selected are weighted more toward communal than individual qualities. To be developmentally appropriate is to be responsive to the individual needs of rapidly changing individuals in a group setting. The Center for Early Adolescence's Middle Grades Assessment Program has identified seven categories of needs that are addressed in the structure and programs of schools responsive to the social development of young adolescents:

- competence and achievement;
- self-exploration and definition;
- social interaction with peers and adults;
- physical activity;
- meaningful participation in school and community;
- routine, limits, and structure;
- diversity.[15]

These seven areas summarize the lists of developmental needs generated by people who address the questions: What is an effective school for young adolescents? What does it mean to be developmentally appropriate? They are seven areas of expectation, and schools that are developmentally appropriate can be expected to have high expectations for themselves in these areas.

Methodology

Using the typology of seven needs helps to corral disorganized thinking about demands for developmental responsiveness made on schools and that schools make on themselves. Developmental responsiveness, however, cannot by itself account for school success. It must be examined in terms of the social and historical context in which each school thrives.

What is a good school for young adolescents? There is public consensus that it is a safe and orderly school where students, at a minimum, continue to learn to read, write, and compute. There is growing agreement, although by no means unanimous, that it is a school that takes seriously what is known about early adolescent development. In addition, a good school for young adolescents, like any social institution, must be acknowledged as a legitimate social agency by its constituency. Finally, it must either successfully resolve, ward off, or be untouched by the major schooling conflicts about which there is currently little public consensus. These schools are referred to here as "successful."

A distinction is being made here between effective and successful schools. Effective schools, as defined in the research literature, are safe, orderly schools where poor children, as well as middle-class children, perform reasonably well academically, as indicated by standardized measures of academic achievement. Effectiveness is the least we should expect of schools.

Successful schools are effective; they also meet more than minimal expectations. They are safe, orderly schools where students and adults want to be. The comportment and achievement of their students and teachers meet parental expectations. The schools are acknowledged by their local communities to be legitimate public agencies for the socialization of their children. As such they become, over a period of years, stable public institutions that have earned community support. Successful schools also cope well with divisive national controversies in public education that impinge on them from outside the local community. The following criteria form a framework for identifying and observing successful middle-grade schools:

1. they measure up to a set of "threshold" criteria related to safety, comportment, and achievement;
2. they respond appropriately to the developmental levels of students;
3. they pursue competence in learning;
4. they have won acceptance within the context of the local community and its expectations;
5. they function well in response to or despite unresolved national policy issues.

The unit of analysis in this descriptive and interpretive study is the school. Excellent programs can be found in terrible schools. It is possible that the accretion of good programs in weak school structures further weakens rather than strengthens schools. Also, children attend schools, not individual programs. The nature of their school experience is not merely the sum of seven or eight individual periods, departments, or curricula. If schooling for young adolescents is to improve, the school must be the unit of change. As such, it is the arena for observation in this study.

The threshold criteria were set in response to a personal concern that the current literature on middle schools, which stresses early adolescent development, is disconnected from major societal concerns about school safety, discipline, and student achievement. The criteria encourage the observer to hold schools to a set of at least minimal expectations for all students. The literature on school climate and effective schools, as well as the results of public opinion polls, yield entry criteria that are readily observable school outcomes. They are referred to here as "nonnegotiables" because they served as a rigid first line of criteria for school selection:

1. scores on standardized achievement tests at, above, or approaching the district or county mean;
2. low absentee rates among students and staff;
3. a low incidence of vandalism and victimization;
4. few or no destructive graffiti;
5. low suspension rates;
6. parental satisfaction;
7. a reputation for excellence.

The majority of these indices reflect the absence of negatives in a school. While they are not indicators of excellence, they provide some assurance about a limited range of achievement, social behavior, and tranquility.

Three criteria were not used. First, low staff turnover was rejected as an indication of staff satisfaction and internal stability because of "reductions in force" or "excessing"; that is, teacher layoffs mandated by the central office. (As the study progressed, it became clear that this entry criterion would have been easily met by the schools visited. Staff turnover was extremely low.) Second, rates of student participation in extracurricular activities were rejected as an indication of school satisfaction and success because, as a result of budget cuts or metropolitan busing, some schools mandate 100 percent participation by incorporating those activities into the school day. Thus, a common definition of "extracurricular activities" is breaking down. Third, teacher satisfaction was rejected as a threshold criterion because it was feared that the most thoughtful teachers would express more ambivalent attitudes toward their schools than the least thoughtful would. A good teacher is rarely satisfied. (As the study progressed, it became clear that teacher satisfaction, as an aggregate category, is very high in these successful schools, even though in particular areas of school performance there may be dissatisfaction. The adoption of teacher satisfaction as an entry criterion would not have changed the results of the school selection process.)

The first nonnegotiable relating to test scores is controversial. First, standardized achievement tests are extremely limited, some say limiting, sources of information about learning. Second, norms are set so that half the student population will perform below the mean. Third, many believe that one can look at the catchment areas for a school (how many students are receiving free lunches?) and predict its performance on standardized tests. The standard, it is therefore argued, should be a comparison among comparable schools, not all schools within a district or county.

All these objections are well taken; but they can lead to opposite conclusions. If the tests are limited, then at the very least schools should measure up to the limited outcomes demanded by them. Those that do measure up have something to teach those that cannot. At the heart of this controversy is an expectation that schools will strive to be equitable. Absolute scales are helpful in ensuring that the same minimal standards are upheld for the poor as for the middle class. While using students' progress as a measure of school effectiveness is important, it is not sufficient unless we abandon our goal to improve school equity by seeking outcomes relatively untied to race or social class. Some schools perform beyond the level predicted on the basis of their student population. Again, they have something to teach those that do not. A guiding question in this investigation has been: what can we learn from success? The achievement test criterion was therefore chosen as a nonnegotiable outcome that all schools selected for case studies met.

The second threshold criterion, low absentee rates, presents a problem: what does "low" mean? The national daily absenteeism rate is 8 percent, but rates of 30 percent in urban secondary schools are not uncommon. Medical authorities say that illness should account for 4 percent.[16] Absence rates vary from state to state. The Citizens' Council for Ohio Schools reports average 1978–79 rates of 12 percent in big city districts, with 15 percent absence rates in junior high schools. (The most dramatic change in attendance occurs between the elementary and junior high levels.) Junior highs in smaller districts (15,000–30,000) had absence rates of 10 percent.[17] South Carolina reports average attendance rates for 1978–79 of 94 percent for all schools, the highest being 96.4 percent and the lowest 91.7 percent.[18] For the purposes of this study, "low" absenteeism was defined as no more than the 8 percent combined national rate. This criterion was met by all the schools visited. "Low" teacher absenteeism was defined as rates below the teachers' contractual number of allowable absences. Again, the criterion was easily met.

The definition of "low" for the third criterion, a low incidence of vandalism and victimization, was sought in *The Safe School Study,* which found that the risks of violence to persons are highest in junior high schools, especially in large communities. In a typical month, 12.4 percent of junior high students are victims of reported personal theft and 2.1 percent of attack.[19] Nineteen percent of junior highs nationwide report five or more monthly incidents against the school (especially property destruction), against persons, or victimless crimes. On a per-school basis, a little more than one offense is reported to the police by a school every two months. Two or three other offenses are known to the principal but unreported.[20]

There is no rational way to set a definition of "low" in this context. To parents, "low" means none. To school officials, "low" means under the average for similar schools. For the purposes of this study, "low" was initially defined as under the national average, a faulty criterion that gives rural schools a lot of leeway and urban schools none whatsoever. The struggle to define was dropped as it became clear that in the successful schools visited, "low" approximated parental expectations of no violence or vandalism.

The fourth threshold criterion, few or no graffiti, is an indirect indication of school pride and student acceptance of school norms. While graffiti may be exuberant expressions of individual creativity, they are more often private or group acts of misbehavior that indicate a lack of connectedness with the values of the school. It was not necessary to define what "few" means because of the absence of graffiti in the schools visited.

Criteria 2–4 are indicators of what some school observers refer to as "good character." As one school critic writes: "I have never seen an official document issued by any school which said the school was indifferent to student character. . . . Discipline is simply the layman term for character."[21] Criteria 2–4 are indicators, albeit weak, of the discipline or character of students. The fifth criterion, regarding suspension rates, provides an indication of schools' responses to lack of discipline.

In 1972–73, according to an Office of Civil Rights study, 9 percent of elementary students and 8 percent of secondary students in surveyed districts were suspended at least once. Nationally, 4.2 percent of all students were suspended. Black secondary students were suspended twice as frequently as White.[22] The rates appear to remain constant across the years. For the purposes of this study, a rate under the national average of 4.2 percent was established as "low," since middle-grade schools are neither elementary nor secondary. Because of extremely few cases of out-of-school suspensions in the schools visited, the criterion was superfluous.

Parental satisfaction, the sixth entry criterion, is a catch-all category. It can be assumed that parents will be dissatisfied with schools in which their children's achievement does not approximate parental expectations, in which the atmosphere is not conducive to learning and interpersonal harmony, and in which they are not reasonably hopeful about their children's academic and personal preparation for the future. At the least, parental satisfaction indicates an absence of negatives. It may not indicate pleasure, but it does indicate that the schools are perceived as more helpful than hindering. Again, this is a minimal expectation for schools. Three of the four schools selected for case studies had extremely high levels of parental satisfaction; the fourth, what can best be characterized as a mixture of tacit approval and indifference. All four schools selected met the sixth threshold criterion.

The seventh criterion, a general reputation for excellence, was ascertained in part through the nomination process for the schools to be visited and then by interviews with community leaders, school board members, superintendents of schools, other principals in the same district, parents, students, and in some cases, hotel reservation clerks, bellhops, taxi drivers, and restaurateurs. None of the schools visited has an extensive national reputation as certain American senior high schools do. Only two of the schools were recommended by more than one person in the initial phase of this study, which speaks more to the lack of importance attached to intermediate schooling in this country than to the quality of the schools. Within each of their communities the schools have extensive reputations for being "good schools" that people are happy to send their children to, wish they could send their children to, wish more schools in the district would emulate, and/or recommend as models of excellence for other districts to consider. Although not without controversy, these schools are deeply appreciated in their communities. Each is reputed to be excellent.

There is one final point to be made about school outcomes and threshold criteria. Negative outcomes are easy to identify, so it is easy to select their absence as criteria. The positives to look for are elusive. Adopted as a positive nonnegotiable criterion was a readily observable phenomenon of infrequent occurrence in many schools: joy. If a bias of this study is that an ultimate outcome should be healthy development, then laughter, vitality, interest, smiles, and other indications of pleasure are reasonable expectations for schools. Some school critics ask: what is pervasive and permanent among human beings? And answer, discipline and character.[23] This study insists that joy is also pervasive.

In gathering data about social indicators for policy analysis, social scientists select happiness in marriage as a subjective indication of well-being. Likewise, in the lives of children and adolescents, happy experiences in school are central to well-being and should be so recognized by policy setters, practitioners, and researchers. At first the selection of joy as a threshold criterion was tentative, perhaps timid; however, the schools themselves were testimony to the fact that this is an obtainable school effect. Joy was added as an eighth nonnegotiable criterion after the first set of visits to successful schools.

The findings of this research show that school climate may have a mediating effect upon school achievement. However, the way in which a given climate is developed and the way in which students, teachers and principals become socialized in it are questions which cannot be answered through our statistical analysis. [Wilbur B. Brookover et al., "Elementary School Social Climate and School Achievement."]

The selection of minimal threshold criteria and the questions later asked in each school were informed by a review of the literature on school effectiveness, school climate, school organization, poverty and schooling outcomes, ecological school studies, and early adolescent development. In addition, the nomination process yielded entry criteria and highlighted areas of concern to be pursued later in school observations and interviews. Many respondents, however, either refrained from nominating a school or recommended only private schools. Many people assume that there are no excellent public middle-grade schools. There is also no lore about junior high schools that would lead people to recommend them sight unseen, based on reputation, as they would senior highs. The public schools nominated were, with one exception, middle schools rather than junior highs. Only two received more than one nomination. No school received more than three nominations.

It was hoped that from the literature search, the questioning process, and an initial series of visits to schools, a range of school types would be identified for further study as to developmental appropriateness in specific community contexts. This range might include paramilitary, high technology, experiential, developmentally grouped, and other strongly defined school types. The selection of these schools would be controlled for achievement and security by means of the "nonnegotiables." Perhaps more time devoted to gathering recommendations and to making initial visits would have resulted in such a mix. The schools recommended are all on the same continuum between a basic skills orientation and experiential learning, although each is in a different place on that continuum and is strongly defined as to that place.

Initial two-day visits were made to a dozen recommended schools. Selections from among these twelve were made on the basis of geographic distribution, type of community (urban, suburban, rural, and suburban-rural), their programmatic responses to the seven needs areas, and their success in meeting the nonnegotiable threshold criteria. Final selection was determined by the schools' "stories," their inherent interest, and their applicability to other schools' experiences.

Impressionistic case studies were conducted during seven days of observation in each of four schools in an attempt to capture the personalities of the schools, their histories, goals, work processes, organizational structures, and environmental contexts. Each case study was structured by nine categories for observation and discussion:

1. *purposes, goals, definitions:* the items ask what the underlying rationale or purpose of the school is;
2. *school climate:* the items attend to norms, beliefs, responsiveness to developmental needs, academic purposefulness, learning and behavioral expectations, socialization for discipline and order, working conditions, and the physical setting;
3. *organization:* the items attend to staff organization, graded or multiaged organization, scheduling, grouping, open or contained classroom structure, and responsiveness to the nature of the school's clientele;
4. *curriculum:* items attend to issues of curricular balance, articulation with elementary and senior high schools, and thoughtfulness about adaptation to the nature of the school population;
5. *instructional practices:* items attend to the work process, how objectives are identified and accepted, student choice, allocation of time, rewards, and assessment;

6. *leadership:* the items address the principal as leader, how authority is established and norms are set, and the principal's role as interpreter of the school for the community;
7. *the community context:* items address the external pressures that impinge on the school, its history, the role of parents in the school, and the school's response to its local context, as reported by the principal, superintendent, school board members, community leaders, and parents;
8. *public policy questions:* items address the school's response to desegregation, P.L. 94–142, which mandates mainstreaming handicapped students into the regular classroom or in the least restrictive setting possible, and Title IX, which requires that girls receive services equal to those provided to boys;
9. *self-evaluation:* items address ways in which schools scrutinize their practices and hold themselves accountable. (For further elaboration of the question items, see Appendix A.)

Some of the questions are easily replicable, especially those concerning the nonnegotiable criteria. It is also possible to point to responses by principals, teachers, students, parents, and community leaders as supporting evidence for what is reported here, should the reader be concerned that the observer went totally native. But much of what follows comes from personal observation of the ebb and flow of events in the lives of schools. The writer is the instrument for data collection. As such, the interpretations are necessarily subjective.

The discussion of each school is also strongly influenced by the respondents' interest in particular questions, some of which drew many responses and were of great interest, others of which were confusing or irrelevant. Questions that were particularly fascinating to respondents in each school revolved around the principal ("What would happen if the principal left?" "Does school excellence all come down to the principal?"); school climate ("How does this school feel?" "Why do people obey rules?"); the community context ("What were the intentions that influenced the original decisions about the school?" "What gives it 'staying power'?" "Would this school work anywhere?"); and public policy questions ("Are there things boys do that girls shouldn't, don't, or won't?" "Is it possible to have quality schools that also provide equal access to all?"). Because these questions drew numerous animated responses, their answers are heavily weighted in the case studies that follow.

Also, because of the powerful history and leadership style of each school, equal weight cannot and should not be given to each of the nine categories for observation. In fact, in one case study (Region 7 Middle School) no attempt is made to isolate public policy questions from the fabric of the discussion, because the school's very existence is a response to a once strong and now waning commitment to social equity.

Because each school is unique, the information is organized to capture what is most important about each one. The intent to compare the schools does not drive the development of the case studies; rather, the intent to let the schools speak for themselves does. Each of the four schools has struggled to define "developmental appropriateness" in practice. The aims of the case studies were to capture the nature and results of that struggle in four communities; to broaden the scope of explorations in the area of school effectiveness; to broaden areas of consensus about what constitutes positive learning environments for young adolescents; and to focus public attention on successful schools.

Notes

1. George Weber, *Inner-City Children Can Be Taught to Read: Four Successful Schools* (Washington, D.C.: Council for Basic Education, 1971).

2. Ronald R. Edmonds, "Some Schools Work and More Can," *Social Policy* 9 (March-April 1979): 28–32.

3. Ibid., p. 28.

4. Research on Instruction Team, National Institute of Education, "Instructionally Effective Schools: Research Area Plan" (mimeographed, n.d.): 3.

5. Michael Rutter et al., *Fifteen Thousand Hours: Secondary Schools and Their Effects on Children* (Cambridge, Mass.: Harvard University Press, 1979): 93.

6. Ibid., p. 1.

7. Michael Rutter, "School Influences on Children's Behavior and Development," *Pediatrics* 65 (February 1980): 208–20.

8. Rutter et al., p. 183.

9. Donald Cohen and Richard Frank, "Preadolescence: A Critical Phase of Biological and Psychological Development," in *Mental Health in Children,* vol. 1, ed. D.V. Siva (Westbury, N.Y.: PJD, 1975).

10. Joan Scheff Lipsitz, "Adolescent Psychosexual Development," in *Adolescent Pregnancy: Perspectives for the Health Professional,* ed. Peggy B. Smith and David M. Mumford (Boston, Mass.: G.K. Hall, 1980): 2–3. For a review of physical development during early adolescence, see especially William A. Daniel, Jr., *Adolescents in Health and Disease* (St. Louis, Mo.: C.V. Mosley, 1977); Melvin M. Grumbach, Gilman D. Grave, and Frances E. Mayer (eds.), *The Control of the Onset of Puberty* (New York: Wiley, 1974); Jerome Kagan et al.,

12–16: Early Adolescence (New York: Norton, 1972); James Tanner, *Growth at Adolescence* (Oxford: Blackwell, 1962).

11. Erik Erikson, *Identity, Youth, and Crisis* (New York: Norton, 1968).
12. For further discussion see Joan Scheff Lipsitz, "The Age Group," in *Toward Adolescence: The Middle School Years. The Seventy-ninth Yearbook of the National Society for the Study of Education,* part 1 (Chicago, Ill.: University of Chicago Press, 1980): 7–31.
13. Mary Haywood Metz, *Classrooms and Corridors: The Crisis of Authority in Desegregated Secondary Schools* (Berkeley, Cal.: University of California Press, 1978): 3.
14. Rutter et al., p. 187.
15. Gayle Dorman, *Middle Grades Assessment Program* (Chapel Hill, N.C.: Center for Early Adolescence, University of North Carolina, 1981).
16. Chrissie Bamber, *Student and Teacher Absenteeism,* Phi Delta Kappa Fastback no. 126 (Bloomington, Ind.: Phi Delta Kappa Educational Foundation, 1979): 9.
17. Citizens' Council for Ohio Schools (Cleveland, Ohio: news release, January 5, 1979).
18. Division of Administration and Planning, *Rankings of the Counties and School Districts of South Carolina, 1978–79* (Columbia: South Carolina Department of Education, March 1980): 78–79.
19. National Institute of Education, *Violent Schools-Safe Schools: The Safe School Study Report to the Congress,* vol. 1 (Washington, D.C.: U.S. Government Printing Office, January 1978): iii, 61.
20. Ibid., p. 43.
21. Edward A. Wynne, *Looking at Schools: Good, Bad, and Indifferent* (Lexington, Mass.: Heath, 1980): 72.
22. Susan C. Kaeser, "Suspension in School Discipline," *Education and Urban Society* 2 (August 1979): 469. See also Joan McCarthy First and M. Hayes Mizell, *Everybody's Business: A Book about School Discipline* (Columbia, S.C.: Southeastern Public Education Program, 1980).
23. Wynne, p. 216.

Part II

CASE STUDIES OF SUCCESSFUL MIDDLE-GRADE SCHOOLS

2

An Introduction to the Schools

In the famous opening line of *Anna Karenina,* Tolstoy announces: "Happy families are all alike; every unhappy family is unhappy in its own way." The reverse is true of schools. While not "all alike," unhappy schools are often so similar that observers constantly record their deadening sameness. Happy schools have distinct personalities; they achieve clear definition in the midst of confusion about schooling for young adolescents.

As of December 1979 there were 34 different grade combinations that attempted to encompass the middle grades. But a few examples are 7–9, 7–12, 6–8, 5–8, and K–8.[1] There is no consensus about where young adolescents should be in school, much less about what the schools should be doing. No other level of public education for minors is so poorly defined. Teacher education for this age group is in a state of flux, as are certification standards. Added to this institutionalized chaos is the personal dismay all too often experienced by teachers who work with the age group, some of whom have been prepared to teach secondary level courses in specific subject areas, with little or no background in child development, while others have been prepared to teach elementary school students and have few, if any, areas of academic expertise.

The four schools selected for case studies are all middle schools. Three have grades 6–8, and one emphatically insists on being a 5–8 school. This selection in no way implies that these particular grade organizations are inherently superior to others. What one can infer is that a diverse group of people who are asked to be thoughtful about developmental responsiveness are most likely to nominate middle or intermediate schools. The task that the successful schools described in this report have mastered is to be institutionally and personally responsive to the developmental diversity of the early adolescent age group. They are positive environments for early adolescent social and academic development.

The case studies that follow are of four schools in 1980–81. Western Middle School in Alamance County, North Carolina, is an orderly, quiet school filled with constant excitement, in a conservative community that insists on discipline, order, and decent test scores. It is a school that attempts to optimize what is best about middle-grade schooling in America, and succeeds. Detroit, Michigan's Region 7 Middle School is a magnet school created by court order as part of Detroit's school desegregation plan. With a totally inadequate budget and building, it serves predominantly inner-city students creatively and well. While optimizing what is acceptable to a hostile regional school board, it also departs from the predictable in middle-grade schooling insofar as budget, building, and Board tolerance will allow. In the present (and still coming) hard fiscal times, Region 7 Middle School is an example of how to achieve excellence on a shoestring. The Noe Middle School in Louisville, Kentucky, has over 1,000 students from predominantly working-class homes in a large, open-plan school. The school was created by court order, staffed by court order, students are bused by court order, and the principal was assigned, along with many handicapped, gifted, and delinquent students, by court order. One cannot reasonably expect this to be a successful school, but it is. Through brilliant organization that departs from most models, it is becoming one of the outstanding schools in Louisville, and the only one of its type. The Shoreham–Wading River Middle School in Shoreham, Long Island (N.Y.) is an example of what creative policy setters, administrators, and staff can do with a lot of money, energy, and community participation. On the continuum of excellence from optimizing what is best about American schooling to redefining it, Shoreham–Wading River has gone furthest toward redefinition.

Western Middle School says to us: "Look at what can be done to meet the needs of students in a stable community that values back-to-basics and law-and-order schooling." Region 7 Middle school says: "Look at what can be done with inadequate and dwindling budgets and Board support in an obsolete building." Noe Middle School says: "Look at what can be done when everything in the external world is going against you. If we can do it, anyone can." Shoreham–Wading River Middle School says: "This is what you can do in a middle-class community with as much money as you need, dynamic leadership, and a hand-picked staff."

Goodlad and Klein ask: "Is some stereotype of schooling so built into our culture that it virtually shapes the entire enterprise, discouraging or even destroying deviations from it?"[2] These schools attest to the fact that the answer, in some outstanding cases, is no. They can be added to our repertoire of examples of the diverse ways in which thoughtful and creative people deviate from the stereotype of mediocrity and distress in American middle-grade schooling and create distinct and distinctive school communities.

Notes

1. Market Data Retrieval reports that as of December 21, 1979, there were 4,004 junior high schools (7–9); 3,662 comprehensive schools (7–12); 3,070 middle schools (6–8); 2,628 schools grades 7–8, 1,024 middle schools (5–8); and 1,315 elementary schools (1–8). There were 19,650 schools for young adolescents other than K–6 or 1–6 elementary schools.
2. John I. Goodlad and M. Frances Klein and Associates, *Behind the Classroom Door* (Belmont, Cal.: Wadsworth, 1970): 91.

3

"Proud Country"

Western Middle School
Alamance County, North Carolina

Question: Do you like this school?
Answer (sixth-graders): No, we don't like it. We love *it!*

The lights are off in the corridors to save energy. Everything is peaceful. There are open cubbies instead of locked lockers. There is no theft. Students walk quietly in the corridors. "Why?" they are asked. "So as not to disturb the media center," they answer, which is self-evident to them but not to the visitor, who is left wondering, "But why? What makes them so concerned about the needs of others?"

There has been one "incident" today. A girl has reported to the assistant principal that a boy has shown her marijuana stashed away in his pocket. She is upset because she is being a stool pigeon, but she is concerned about him and her school. She does not want drugs in Western Middle School. The marijuana turns out to be a plug of chewing tobacco. The assistant principal talks to the boy.

In the cafeteria, Blacks and Whites are sitting at tables together. A White cafeteria worker carries a tray for a black student on crutches. He thanks her warmly. "You're welcome, honey."

An eighth-grader knocks tentatively on the principal's door. It is rarely closed, and he is not sure what to do. The principal, Wilma Parrish, jumps up, apologizing profusely to him because she has forgotten to get him his lunch. He has been assigned to in-school suspension for skipping school to go to the swimming hole. She asks him whether he wants ketchup on his hamburger. "Yes, ma'am." Mustard? "Yes, ma'am." Relish? "Yes, ma'am." She runs to get the lunch. He calls after her: "Could I have an extra pickle?" "Of course!" The principal explains that she wants school to be so inviting that he will never skip again. She settles him back down in the suspension room with his food and a hug.

A visitor asks 21 sixth-graders if there is a single word that characterizes their school. They shout out in unison: "Proud!"

Near the end of the day, the principal suddenly exclaims to a visitor: "Do you want to see the world's largest T-shirt?" and begins pulling endless yards of cotton knit out of a wicker basket. It is a Fruit-of-the-Loom shirt, specially made to hang in a regional bank office. One could drive a car into it. "What are you going to do with it?" she is asked. "I'm going to go have fun!" She wants all the students in one team to put their heads through the neck so that she can take their class picture. There is ample room.

Western Middle School is an orderly and vibrant school. The colorful modern building, erected in 1978, looks brand new except for one stain on the carpeting that drives the principal wild. She wants perfection. The 741 students are divided into four units or "houses." The sixth-grade house is green, the seventh is blue, eighth is peach, and a house with all three grades, dubbed "The Outhouse" by its students, is orange. The open cubbies are color-coordinated and very neat. That is the way the principal wants it. The "media center" is really a center. The four houses radiate out from the media center, which forms their architectural and symbolic hub. (There are no library fines in this school. "We *want* our students to read.")

In the other half of the school building are the music room, the gymnasium, and the home economics, occupations, and business labs, radiating, again symbolically, from the cafeteria. (This school has the best school lunch, bar none, of any school its numerous visitors have ever been in. Everything, says the principal, must be "inviting.") Joining the two halves of the school, in the strongest architectural statement of all because of the quality of the school's leadership, are the school offices: the reception area, teachers' work room, guidance office, assistant principal's office, and most importantly, the principal's office.

The Community

School architecture is important in Alamance County. In an angry backlash against "open education," the community spent one and a half years arguing about this school building and revising the architect's plans, thereby making their statement about the kind of school philosophy they would support. Prior to building the school, the Board of Education, having made serious mistakes in imposing open-plan schools on the county, authorized the naming of a steering committee, which was assigned the responsibility for developing specifications for the school. Thirty-four people were named to the committee, including ten faculty representatives, ten advisory council members, ten PTA representatives from other county schools, a member of the Board of Education, two central office administrators, and a representative from the State Department of Public Instruction. When the school board began thinking a school would never be built, representatives finally settled on a ratio of 60 percent open to 40 percent closed, a compromise resulting in a design that is much more contained than the county schools built in the 1960s, but still too open for some parents' comfort. Nonetheless, it is their school, and they have a strong sense of ownership in it.

The Alamance County school district is just outside Burlington, North Carolina. It is a stable, conservative, mostly rural area of factory workers, farm workers, professionals, small businessmen, and teachers at Elon College. Western Middle School is in the western zone of the county. Over 70 percent of the parents own their own houses. Approximately one-third make more than $20,000 in combined income; one-fifth between $16,000 and $20,000; one-fifth between $12,000 and $16,000; over 15 percent earn between $5,000 and $12,000 a year. The rest earn below $5,000. Seventy percent of the students live with both their parents; 14 percent live with their mothers only and 3 percent with their fathers only; 8 percent live with their mother and a stepfather. Some children live with their grandparents or foster parents, and some live in Elon Home for Children, a residential care facility for dependent, neglected, and court-referred children. As many parents finished college or have advanced degrees as have an eighth-grade education or less: 10 percent of the mothers and around 15 percent of the fathers. Half the mothers and 40 percent of the fathers finished high school and attended a technical school. Their aspirations for their children are high.

Members of the staff do not feel they have anything in particular to overcome in working with these students. Their own family backgrounds are quite similar. Many teachers were born and bred in the county. (The inbred nature of the faculty is, in one case, quite literal. While researching his family tree, a White teacher discovered that he and a Black teacher on the staff were cousins.)

Yes, this is a good school. Everyone says the building does it, but you can do the same thing in any building with the correct staff. Schools aren't doomed by socioeconomic status, the way people say. People live up to the level expected of them. The teachers expect a lot. They invite the children to learn. They expect a lot of the children. They expect a lot of the parents, also, and the parents rise to that level and support the school. If parents aren't involved elsewhere in the county, it's because they aren't asked. The impetus isn't there. Here, everyone pulls together and meets the school's high expectations. [A Western Middle School parent]

There is one very small pocket of extreme poverty whose backwardness is of concern to the staff. Up until about ten years ago, it was called "Tent City." It had no indoor plumbing, only wells and outhouses. Families lived in tents or, at best, cardboard houses. Federal funding has since provided standard housing. The other group of children requiring some special attention, according to teachers, are the children from the Elon Home. Otherwise, teachers are extremely comfortable with the students and their parents.

Meeting the Nonnegotiables

The school meets all but one of the nonnegotiable threshold criteria with ease. Students score above national norms on the California Achievement Tests in reading, but not math. In 1980, sixth-graders (the only grade at this level tested by the county) scored in the 54th percentile in reading, higher than the average of students countywide (51st) and statewide (50th). They scored in the 49th percentile in math, slightly lower than the statewide average of 61st and lower than the countywide average, 54th. These scores were higher than the previous year's, which was the school's first year. The principal is at a loss to explain the math scores but is making an all-out effort to improve the performance. The scores of Black students are higher in this school than in other schools in the county.

Average daily attendance is between 97 and 98 percent. The principal has been known to get in her car and go to students' homes to pull them into school. She also has a reward system for high attendance. Mostly, though, students attend because their parents believe they should and because the instruction is so exciting that they want to attend.

Two students were suspended from school in 1979–80, a far lower rate than in similar schools in the district. There was one incident of vandalism in 1979–80, a lower incidence than in similar schools in the district. Students are proud of being in the new building that their parents paid $2.5 million to build. They went from abused buildings that were falling apart to this beautiful school in which the principal's mania for cleanliness and neatness has become a school legend. The students see her helping the janitors, picking up paper, and straightening chairs as she moves rapidly about the school. There are constant reminders over the intercom about keeping the school beautiful. There have also been incentives like popcorn on a Friday afternoon for the class with the highest student council rating for cleanliness.

Parental satisfaction with the school is high. The principal knows this because she polled parents, asking questions about their aspirations for their children and their satisfaction with the school program. Almost 85 percent said the school is meeting the educational needs of their children "extremely well" or "well"; almost 14 percent said "fairly well"; 1.5 percent said "poorly" or "very poorly." Ninety percent rated the school as "excellent" or "good"; no one said "very poor." In rating the difficulty of their children's work, 80 percent said it was "just right," 8 percent said "too hard," and 4 percent said it was "too easy."

Parents are willing to take time off from their jobs to speak to a visitor about the school, a sign of both their enthusiasm and the power of a request from the principal. They, as well as others who happen to be delivering or picking up a student, are boosters for Western Middle. They are clear about what the school expects from their children: "To do their best and behave well." Parents are clear about how they judge the school's effectiveness: the children are eager to attend; they cannot wait to leave elementary school and get to the Middle School; they are close to their teachers; their test scores are "high"; their behavior is good; they are happy. The parents praise the administration's communication with them. Any complaint is handled immediately. "It can't fester. Natural complainers have nothing to complain about." (The School Board chairman confirms this. He gets no angry late-night telephone calls about Western Middle.) Parents are pleased with the Community Advisory Council, a group of parents representing a cross-section of the school's students who consult with the principal about the school. They find the principal "very open." The school, they say, is right for this age group because of its personal atmosphere, because its size is small enough that the teachers know the students, because of the exploratory program, the high level of student involvement, the excitement of the instructional program, the dances, and a curriculum that prepares students for high school "scholastically and emotionally."

Excitement and comportment are two competing values at Western Middle. Comportment must always win. A first impression of the school can leave an observer concerned that the students are constrained and subdued. The school makes a quiet statement; it can take a while to hear it. The school meets the last nonnegotiable criterion, joy, if by joy one means quiet pleasure rather than uncontained emotion, smiles rather than laughter, and gratification rather than open delight.

Leadership

When Charity James, a British observer, visited American schools in the early 1970s, she was struck by the first message school environments convey: "I was overwhelmed by an accumulation of those corridors with built-in lockers—so unchildlike, and speaking only of power and possession," like Tennyson's description of a grande dame, "icily regular, faultily faultless, splendidly null."[1] There are no lockers in the halls of Western Middle. Mrs. Parrish will not have them. They are ugly, take up wall space that should proclaim the creativity of children, and bespeak a lack of trust. She insisted on the colorful cubbies that serve as movable room dividers in classrooms. Mrs. Parrish chose the comfortable furniture in the reception area, the carpeting, the desks and chairs. She pored over the architect's plans for the building and made changes along with the parents and other steering committee members. Her hand is in everything, her mark everywhere. She is a dynamic and powerful principal. For many people in Alamance County, her name is synonymous with Western Middle School.

Wilma Parrish was a principal of a K–8 elementary school before her assignment as the first principal of Western Middle. Prior to being a principal, she taught grades 6 and 8, was a GT (gifted and talented) teacher, and a basketball coach. "There is no subject here I can't teach," she says, and her teachers know it. She refers to the students as "my children," who must be kept "busy, learning, and happy." She is extremely proud of her teachers and lets them know it daily: "Mrs. Parrish tells us all the time how great we and the kids are." She is constantly referred to in the school. As one teacher says: "Mrs. Parrish is the core of the school. She is the instigator of everything good in the school."

My central conclusion from my years at the Martin Luther King School and my reading of the new research is that the principal's role is central to almost everything. For teachers to be optimally productive and feel part of an effective school team, there must be dynamic, omnipresent, humane educational leadership at the school building level. [Kimbrough Marshall, "How Effective is Our School?"]

When asked what would happen if the principal left, a seventh-grader answers, "The school would fall apart." A parent takes a long pause, as if thinking the unthinkable, and then says, "I'd hate to think of it." The School Board chairman says she is dedicated and untiring, setting high standards that the staff follows. But the school is like a winning athletic team with a winning tradition, he says. It will survive her retirement, when that day comes, "the way a winning team survives a change in coaches."

Mrs. Parrish loves middle-school children, and she insists that they are vulnerable people with sensitive emotions who must never be embarrassed. "They are adults today, children tomorrow. They need understanding, not harshness or permissiveness. They need respect." She sees working with this age group as "a calling." When she was an elementary school principal, she would go to Tent City to help students with their homework at night. Her husband, who accompanied her, would put on work clothes "so they wouldn't be embarrassed." She did this as much for the teachers as the children, "to project to them that these are important people who need encouragement." Mrs. Parrish's missionary zeal about children in troubled environments took her all the way to court in a fight against the Department of Social Services. She wanted to adopt a student, a nine-year-old foster child whose home life lacked stability. He had many problems but also promise that she saw and believed in. The Department of Social Services said she was too old. As one parent says, "You don't mess with Wilma Parrish." She took the county to court and won a David vs. Goliath battle.

The stories about her involvement abound: Mrs. Parrish collecting food and clothing for the needy; the cafeteria making food for a student's funeral, the parents asking her to deliver the eulogy; Mrs. Parrish arranging for a student to move to Florida to be raised by an aunt instead of a well-meaning but overwhelmed, alcoholic father. She is a dynamo, constantly in the classrooms, praising and teaching ("I like Mrs. Parrish when she teaches— she's fun," says a seventh-grader), straightening furniture, making things just a tad neater and cleaner, inspecting students' dissection of frogs, tapping her foot to the band's music, savoring the cafeteria food. Nothing changes when she enters a classroom: her presence is a permanent condition.

Mrs. Parrish cajoles and praises a staff of 39 teachers, 30 female and 9 male, 4 Black and 1 Oriental, two with secondary training and the rest with either elementary or middle-school certification. Special personnel include an assistant principal, a guidance counselor, a music teacher, four teachers for exceptional children, a half-time speech teacher, a librarian, a home-school coordinator, and a part-time nurse.

Mrs. Parrish is a stickler for setting and meeting objectives. She prepares thoroughly before launching a new campaign with her staff. Having decided that her next goal is to get the entire school organized around interdisciplinary teams in thematic units, she has written a position paper for her staff: "Middle-School Goals and Earmarks." She cites goals recently adopted by the National Middle School Association as prerequisite for a good middle school, and then William Alexander's "earmarks of a good middle school": a comprehensive curriculum plan, a home base advisory plan, a continuous progress arrangement, a variety of instructional approaches, many exploratory activities, adequate health and physical education, and team planning/teaching. "Let us now interest ourselves with the last of these earmarks, team planning/teaching," she writes. She cites the literature on teaming, outlining each level of responsibility from the principal on down. "It is the responsibility of the principal, as instructional leader of the school, to initiate the interim steps essential for a cooperative program that will involve the entire staff in team planning and team teaching." The trumpet has sounded.

Mrs. Parrish would like to adopt other goals, like extending the advisor/advisee program throughout the school and integrating the arts into the core curriculum. She will begin work on the latter through a summer in-service workshop. She is more hesitant about the former: "I wouldn't want to shove it on everyone." She is working toward other things, which she rattles off easily. She wants more in-service workshops for parents on raising young adolescent children ("So much is undone when they get home"); she wants to extend the intramural athletic program; she wants to extend the nature trail that students have built so that life sciences courses can be held almost totally outside; she wants to build an obstacle course like the one they use in a nearby park, to teach self-confidence and interdependence. ("It shows students how dependent everyone is on each other, how difficult and important it is to carry out a group task—but support is available if we accept it.")

The Alamance County School System has no middle-school specialist. No one in the central office defines what is developmentally appropriate for the age group. The superintendent assumes that principals know what a middle school should be from training and prior experience. In the hiring process, five people interview prospective candidates for principalships: usually an assistant superintendent, a principal of one of the middle schools, another principal from the system, a curriculum specialist, and a teacher or assistant principal. According to the superintendent, they look for qualities that have never been written down but are generally accepted, especially "extreme love for children," professional expertise, and "attitude as much as anything else."

What sustains me? The schools. When things get crazy, I leave the central office and visit a school. The stars get back in their orbits, and things look right again. [Superintendent of schools, Alamance County.]

After that, it is up to the principal to define and implement middle-school education. Decisions are made at the school building level where they belong. Mrs. Parrish makes them with assurance. She is a woman in control.

She is ahead of and behind her teachers, leading and prodding. Her estimate that she spends 35 percent of her time supervising instructional staff and 30 percent on long-range curriculum planning appears accurate. The teachers perceive her as more ambitious and positive about the students than they are. They assume that she expects not only more than they do, but more than she actually does. She emerges a bit larger than life in their estimates of her expectations.

Mrs. Parrish has accomplished a few feats that live up to the teachers' image of her. When a new and excellent teacher was "riffed" (reduced in force, or laid off), Mrs. Parrish helped her obtain a new position. On the other hand, the significantly less dedicated of her classroom teachers have come to know the results of not meeting her standards. In such cases, riffed probationary teachers stay riffed, and tenured but inadequate teachers know that tenure means exactly what it is legally supposed to mean: they will be fairly evaluated and then dismissed through proper due process. In one instance, a tenured teacher resigned because the pressure from Mrs. Parrish to perform became too great, the rewards too few. In another instance, a teacher with twenty-three years' experience who had become incompetent was fired. One way or another, the message from the principal to achieve excellence in the classroom is clear. Her adept handling of such cases has not gone unnoticed, either by the teachers or the central office. Mrs. Parrish, by reputation as well as by action, has exercised considerable control over the hiring and firing of her staff.

Her influence is felt by the parents as well, albeit less directly. The parents' advisory council, with her help, coordinated a back-to-school program for the parents on a Saturday morning, with all the teachers present, to experience the environment their children were in. Parents were given buttons proclaiming: "I went back to school for my child." They received diplomas. One parent says: "We don't want the love to stop in the morning or learning to stop in the evening." Mrs. Parrish adds: "We don't want the love to stop in the evening—when the children go home."

Among her peers, Mrs. Parrish is acknowledged as a leader. Alamance County schools are divided into four zones. Some schools used to get more funds from the "nonparticipating budget" (for capital improvements) than others. She suggested that allocations from the central office go to zones, not schools, and that the principals within the zones then submit requests. Her suggestion was accepted. Priorities are now set within each zone.

Every year Mrs. Parrish forms a committee within the school to allocate the "participating budget" (discretionary) of $20 per child, to be used for library books, instructional materials, audio-visual supplies, masking tape, and the like. There is always a representative from each house, the special services areas, and the media center. Teachers do not see this as being a delegation of power to them. So far as many of them are concerned, they have no budgetary discretion nor need it: "I turn in my list of needs and I get most of what I ask for." They feel well attended to.

You don't get frowning in this school. [A Western Middle School teacher]

The leadership style establishes favorable work conditions for the teachers. There are no teacher union members in the school, although anger about two issues has led to union membership in other schools in the county. A supplemental tax (for more personnel, especially a librarian and music teacher in every school) was voted down by the citizens, although backed by the school board. Teachers were angry and the union made headway in other schools. Also, teachers wanted assurances from the board that riffed teachers would be rehired, even if probationary and with mediocre evaluations. The principals fought against this agreement and won. The teachers were furious. The union made more headway, but not in this school. Teachers are too satisfied to break with the antiunion feelings of their community.

I couldn't think of a better place to teach. You could bury me in this school. [A Western Middle School teacher]

The staff is mature and experienced. Forty percent have taught for ten or more years, 36 percent for five to nine years. It is not a highly credentialed staff because state law does not require Masters' degrees. Two-thirds of the staff have less than an M.A., one-quarter the M.A. or some work beyond, and the rest have B.A.'s only. The overwhelming number are very happy they were assigned to this school and like the setting they are in, which they identify as a predominantly (81 percent) White school with children from a cross-section of society. They see the school as successful in its academic and socialization goals, although they want it to improve. They see most of the students as being work-oriented and trying hard. They feel very responsible for their students' progress and are grateful for the parental support they receive. They are satisfied with social relations among the teachers, between students and teachers, with teacher autonomy and teacher evaluation procedures. While feelings are more scattered about teacher-administration relations, participation in decision making, and recognition of teacher achievement, only a small minority expresses dissatisfaction in these areas. Most teachers agree with their colleague who says, "It's the best place I've ever worked."

They like the building, although several would like more doors so the students could be more exuberant. They like teaching in blocks so they can get closer to the students and have few time limitations. They like not teaching in blocks, if they are in contained classrooms, because their personal teaching preference has been honored by the principal. They appreciate being with cooperative, sharing colleagues who have positive attitudes about students. They have the freedom to be comfortable. They are assigned to grade levels and to contained classrooms, two-teacher teams, or other team arrangements according to their personal interests, strengths, and styles. They cite this policy as one of the most outstanding accomplishments of Mrs. Parrish's leadership. They like having a principal who will grab a ditto from their hands and say, "Don't waste your time doing that," as she leaves to run the ditto off for them. One teacher looked at a school closer to her home in an attempt to reduce her 30-minute commutation to five minutes. Her decision not to change baffled her husband. "This school gives me what I need: satisfaction and contact with people. Mrs. Parrish likes what I do, and that makes all the difference."

Since teachers do not function in departments, there is no structure for departmental meetings. There is also no set structure for house meetings. Decisions are made primarily on a one-to-one basis between Mrs. Parrish and individual teachers or team members. Hers is an individualized style of leadership that protects the teachers from many of the major pressures that occur in other schools. Mrs. Parrish creates a safe environment in which she says, in effect: "Just go into your classroom and teach as well as I know you can. I'll take care of the rest." The teachers appear quite unreflective about schooling issues. For instance, it is not possible to engage them in a discussion about whether they sacrifice academic quality for developmental responsiveness. They are at a loss to explain the school's success in meeting the threshold criteria. They are inarticulate about how teachers from two elementary schools were successfully merged into one faculty. (Mrs. Parrish argues that they are not unreflective. Rather, she says academic quality vs. developmental responsiveness is *not* an issue because it has been resolved by means of a balanced curriculum.)

There is only one unresolved conflict that some teachers are bitter about. They feel isolated in the four separate houses. Teachers who were colleagues in their previous school do not get to see each other during the school day. They want a teachers' lounge to meet in at the end of the day. It is the only area of dissatisfaction teachers discuss, and they do so with great hesitancy. The teachers deeply appreciate the highly individualized style of leadership because it affirms and institutionalizes their teaching preferences in the school's organization. This same style also isolates them. It is a tradeoff the teachers have not recognized.

The staff feels that major decisions about middle-grade schooling are history. Fights over open schooling that ripped the community apart are over, the school is built, and teachers are teaching. While everyone does not sit down together to make decisions about the school, most feel that "we are all pulling in the same direction." They take a good deal for granted because they are encouraged to. Mrs. Parrish has inherited, chosen, and nurtured dedicated teachers who love children and want to do their best. She sets the school's agenda, its tone, its standards. They teach.

Purposes, Goals, and Definitions

There is remarkable consensus about the purposes and goals of Western Middle School. According to two-thirds of the faculty and the principal, its primary responsibility is to teach academic subjects. Its second major responsibility is to enhance personal growth and development. One-third of the faculty, while citing the same two goals, put them in reverse order. The principal cites a double set of purposes as the number one responsibility, teaching academics and enhancing self-concept. Teachers tend to see enhancing self-concept as an objective they set as a means for meeting their instructional goals.

What is the goal of this school? To have every teacher, first of all, and every student feel that no matter who the student is, he or she has the same opportunity to learn and is invited to learn. [A Western Middle School parent]

The word *inviting* is heard often in Western Middle. "Inviting school success" is cited in discussions about the school's purposes. It is a tag term from a workshop that had a profound effect on school staff and parents. (The workshop is based on William W. Purkey's book, *Inviting School Success.*[2]) The title has become part of their collective ideology, as terms often do when they provide a vocabulary for what a school staff has been doing well but inarticulately. It provides a handle for their ideas. Western Middle School aims to be an inviting school, from its instructional program to its lunches. Children are invited to enter, to join, and to succeed. "Invitational learning" is a motif that permeates discussions about school purposes and practices. It provides a common frame of reference and vocabulary. It binds together and lends continuity from discussion to discussion.

There is considerably more consensus about the school's definition than in most intermediate schools. Western Middle School is, according to Mrs. Parrish, definitely an elementary school in tone and moving toward "the middle-school philosophy." It is not, under any circumstances, a secondary school, which loses too much of "the motherly touch," is too random in its student-teacher relationships, and too abstract and subject-oriented in its curriculum. She would rather hire a teacher certified at the elementary or middle-school level, one who knows that "if you're a good teacher, you can learn a new subject." Most teachers agree that it is an elementary school. A few say it is a mixture of both elementary and secondary, "like the students." Parents see the middle school as starting secondary school earlier rather than extending elementary school, but starting it gradually and in a protected, warm environment. Students, who refer to themselves as "junior teenagers" or "young adults," like to think of Western Middle as a secondary school that is getting them ready for high school. They feel too old to be in elementary school. Significantly, though perceptions vary, all feel their needs are being met.

Mrs. Parrish has compiled a list of components of middle schools from several education texts: (1) teachers who are child- vs. subject-centered; (2) a curriculum that emphasizes skills and exploration; (3) a block schedule rather than fragmented periods; (4) an interdisciplinary team organization; (5) an advisory relationship between students and teachers; (6) teachers organized in teams rather than departments or single classrooms; and (7) students in multiaged rather than chronologically aged groups. The school has adopted the first three and is working toward the fourth and fifth. The sixth, team teaching, is less resourceful than Western Middle's organization, which gives teachers, students, and parents options ranging from the single classroom to the four-person team. The seventh, multiage grouping, will never happen in the core curricular subjects, even in "The Outhouse," because of community opposition. It is part of the philosophy of the school to be as responsive to the community's mandate as to the students' academic and developmental needs.

Responsiveness to developmental needs is part of the rationale of the school. Mrs. Parrish worries about what happens that "turns kids off around fourth grade. They came in so excited in the early years. By sixth, they're turned off and new expectations are being added." Being responsive means, first, developing a program to make them comfortable and excited: "Love them, hug them, praise them, excite them." Second, develop a school that is compassionate and understanding. Third, develop rules to protect and enhance life and negative sanctions for breaking them that are not harmful. Fourth, emphasize the social aspect in everything, from instructional units that bring friends together to scheduling and grouping that "makes sure buddies are together. Don't separate friends. That is their life!"

Where there is greatest consensus among school, family, and community (the major socializers of these youngsters) on appropriate aims, values, and activities, one will find schools to be doing a more effective job of educating early adolescents. I would think. The reason is readily apparent; the youngsters would be consistently receiving the same messages and reinforcement patterns in each of these areas. [Walter Allen, Center for Afroamerican and African Studies, University of Michigan, letter to author, October 21, 1980.]

There is countywide consensus about the school's priorities. In developing a statement of beliefs and objectives for the school system, the superintendent found a high degree of agreement in the professional staff and the general public about the goals and even their priorities. The overwhelming first priority is to develop self-concept in all students. The second is to develop communication skills, and the third computational skills. As a result, Western Middle School's emphasis on being an inviting school that stresses social development as well as academics is part of a general congruence of opinion and sentiment.

School Organization

The organization of Western Middle School reflects its definition, goals, and purposes. There are two self-contained classes, one in sixth grade and one in eighth. There are several two-teacher teams, and one four-teacher team. Some teachers teach blocks of subjects within a team, others teach two subjects. This unique organizational plan makes possible a finely tuned responsiveness to the teaching and learning styles of teachers and students, as well as to the social maturity of members of this diverse, highly variable age group. A great deal of thought goes into the placement of students in houses. Teachers make recommendations to achieve the right balance of structure and freedom for each child. Mrs. Parrish spends much of the summer on the floor of her office, surrounded by students' folders, to achieve a balance of male and female, Black and White, and a range of ability and maturity, to fill parents' requests, schedule band and special education students, and to keep buddies together.

The process for arriving at the organization of the school day depends on the individual houses. Each house has four hours for reading, language arts, math, social studies, and science. The four academic teachers make decisions about grouping and scheduling within those four hours. In some cases, teachers also make decisions about what they teach. For instance, in one house four teachers decided they all wanted to teach reading classes, instead of its being taught by the one teacher who was assigned to be the reading teacher. They told Mrs. Parrish that this was their intention. "She trusts us to make decisions in our house." The role students play also varies from house to house. In the seventh-grade team in "The Outhouse," students have a great deal of say in rule-setting for the room. They also help set the daily schedule.

"The Outhouse" has the most varied organizational structure of the four houses: a self-contained special education class, a seventh-grade team, a sixth-grade team, and two eighth-grade blocks consisting of two teachers who do not team. One teaches a contained language arts/social studies block and the other math/science, and they switch students. Several teachers in "The Outhouse" feel that the school organization does not adequately address the issue of vast developmental diversity in the age group. They would like grade-level groupings in the core curriculum and multiage grouping in other school offerings. They worked on this plan for "The Outhouse" one summer but could not overcome scheduling conflicts with the rest of the school. Some teachers are not comfortable with the idea. They must come to see it as an alternative to the present organization before Mrs. Parrish will discuss it as a schoolwide option.

School Climate

The school's atmosphere is the epitome of descriptions of effective schools: "Orderly without being rigid, quiet without being oppressive, and generally conducive to the instructional business at hand."[3] When asked how the school "feels," students say "proud," "comfortable"; parents say "comfortable," "not tense," "orderly." The building is neat and clean, with paperbacks everywhere. Students have built a reading loft in one corridor to augment the already comfortable library furniture. Their class work is displayed throughout the school. The school feels very spacious and personal. One wonders if there really are 741 students in it. There are no graffiti, no bells, and little noise. The school feels friendly, calm, and contained. Its many visitors are absorbed into the purposefulness of the day, unnoticed.

Good schools have a collective identity. Their members invoke group symbols in defining themselves.[4] There are many symbols that students, teachers, and parents might select for Western Middle: the lights off in the halls, the absence of locked lockers, the biracial groups lunching together in the cafeteria—none of these is mentioned. Students and teachers are surprised that they are noteworthy. They take them for granted, seeing nothing unusual in them that requires explanation. The principal's prized rock collection is on display near the front door. It might serve as a symbol of the safety, trust, and sharing in this school, and also of her indomitable drive to make every school practice and every inch of space educational. No one mentions the rocks. For students, teachers, and the principal, the symbol is pride: they are, simply, the best school in the county, and they intend to be even better.

Socialization means good behavior in Western Middle School. How is order kept? Why do students accept the values and expectations of the school? One teacher says: "We tell the kids, and they're responsive." This answer echoes the simplicity of students' response to: "Why are you quiet in the halls?" "So as not to disturb the media center."

Students know what is expected of them: "Good behavior. Do the best you can. Treat the school right. Have your work done. Play when it's okay to play." They see socialization as being the major effort of the school: "What are five characteristics of a good middle school?" "Cooperation, good behavior, discipline, being on the level, good teachers who give you a good education."

Question: What's special about this school?

Answer: We respect it. [A Western Middle School student]

It is difficult for people within the school to account for the apparent ease with which Western Middle and its students achieve accord. The fabric of the school community appears to have been woven out of whole cloth. Background is an important factor. Students are in school for reasons important to them: "Our neighbor can't read or write"; "to stay off welfare"; "to get off the farm"; "to go to college." They, their principal, and most of their teachers come from a stable community where people adhere to family, church, and school as enduring institutions of deep personal importance. School climate is also important. Students live daily in a school that rewards them for their courtesies: a student gets up to fill the classroom stapler, and his teacher comments, "Thank you, Curtis, that was very generous." They are surrounded by caring: a teacher writes "I love you" twice on a test. A student asks if "I love you" is a test question. "No, but answer me back." There is a constant bustle of activity, making boredom and idleness close to obsolete in this school. Dance, plays, chorus and band productions, arts and crafts, special theme weeks in houses, field trips, sports events ("interscholastic sports provide incentives for some students you wouldn't hold otherwise, and it brings the parents in," says the principal), special visitors, assemblies—the school is constantly hopping with activity.

We are flexible in our expectations about behavior—flexible but unyielding. [A Western Middle School teacher]

Order is also achieved because students are valued. They flourish in a school where teachers' expectations for learning and good comportment are high. "I say to my students: 'Maybe I'm expecting too much of you, but if so, you'll have to live up to it.' " Students say they do. They feel pressured about discipline ("cleanliness, sportsmanship, pride, knowing right from wrong") but not "about brains" ("just do your absolute best"). Rules are consistent and firm. Students agree that there are not many rules, "but if you break them, you die." The rules are unequivocal. Returning high-school students say high school is easier academically and more difficult socially.

The superintendent says discipline is self-imposed at Western Middle. "They carry themselves in an orderly, respectful manner toward one another and adults. They have come through good elementary schools and good home situations, in large measure, where there is respect, order, and a high emphasis on good education." Even so, to account for the school's success in socializing students into the values of the school, he says: "That can be answered in two words: Wilma Parrish." She, and therefore her staff, "preach, practice, admonish. She starts with the idea that that's the way it ought to be, and sets expectations high."

They're not leaving an environment of love at home and coming to a school where people don't care. It's the same environment of love. [A Western Middle School parent]

Mrs. Parrish has parents come into school the first week of the new school year to meet with teachers about expectations, grades, and sharing information. She sends "happygrams" to students about their work. She checks over 700 report cards and encloses notes about how proud she is to see progress. She gives awards for citizenship, for the outstanding student in each house, for sportsmanship, and special awards in band, chorus, and sports, as well as reading, science, math, and social studies. It is a large "incentives package" that she sees as being appropriate for the age group. Most important is the personal touch—"you must get the child with you before you can offer or impart anything."

In some middle schools, the socialization process is enhanced by an advisor-advisee program. At Western Middle, students talk a lot about their guidance counselor. They cite him as one of the good things about the school. When they have problems or questions, they do not hesitate to talk to him. The school has a traditional guidance advisory system that works well for most of its students. A teacher advisor-advisee system functions—but not with equal effectiveness—in all four houses. Students do not mention it as a significant aspect of school life. In the one house where time is set aside for advisor-advisee meetings, discussions about rules, responsibilities, and opportunities in the home reinforce traditional social values, for instance, against divorce and in favor of obedience to parents.

School socialization does not involve only students; teachers must also accept the norms of the school. New teachers are socialized into the values and practices of the school by the principal, assistant principal, other teachers, and the school's reputation. They hear about this school "all the time" in the community. They know they are entering "a school with a tradition of excellence to be kept up," says a new teacher who came from "a school where rules are not enforced. I knew before I walked in here that the school is the best in the county." So do most of the students.

There is another aspect of school socialization referred to only by some students, their parents, and the assistant principal. Paddling is legal in

North Carolina. The U.S. Supreme Court has upheld its legality, ruling against those who challenged a law that forbids local school districts to ban corporal punishment in their schools. In a state that finally managed, in 1980, to pass a law allowing local option about selling liquor by the drink, there is no local option about corporal punishment. When students are asked: "How do you learn the rules in this school?" invariably a boy in the group answers, "You get paddled." "Why do you obey rules?" "I'd get killed." "How?" "Paddled" (by the assistant principal or by parents). In most schools there is a subculture of students who do not acquiesce to the norms of the school. In Western Middle School, there is a subculture of students and parents who accept the norms but rely on negative sanctions for their reinforcement. Whether this minority approach is part of the "whole cloth" of the school culture or a fault in the fabric to be ripped out and rewoven depends on which parent or school administrator is speaking.

Curriculum and Instruction

Curriculum and instruction are the heart of Western Middle School's program. While this is usually assumed to be true of any school, it is not necessarily the case even in successful schools. The fireworks that happen outside of class or the "hidden curriculum" may provide the special definition and excitement of a school that motivates everyone to attend school and attend to classwork.

The principal is in charge of curriculum. There are systemwide curricular guides and resources that include teaching hints for every curricular area at every grade level, "to keep everyone on the same highway, if not in the same lane," according to the superintendent of schools. Teachers devised the curriculum guides, teaching guides, and teaching materials. According to the superintendent, "we've got some of the weirdest on earth, but they developed them." Teachers say they often rely on the guides, whose key word is "flexibility."

The school's three distinct curricular divisions are standard for middle schools. The core subject areas of language arts and reading, social studies, science and health, and mathematics (there are no foreign language classes) form the first division, called "Curriculum" at Western Middle. "Unified Arts" is the second, consisting of physical education, career education (including vocational and industrial education), band, and music. The third division, called "Exploratory," is an offering for all students not taking band. During Exploratory, teachers offer short courses ranging from macramé or weight lifting to metrics or the novel. Exploratory and Unified Arts form one block. The rest of the day is devoted to Curriculum, the other block. While the school's curricular organization seems radical to some parents, it is now quite standard, with its three divisions and two time blocks, "A-Day" and "B-Day" to alternate P.E. and careers, and ability grouping in reading and math. Parents in this community want to know at what time their children are learning "the basics." They can be assured that there is a specific, unchanging, and uninterrupted time during which their children are learning math and reading.

An academic emphasis is created by high teacher expectations for academic performance, an inviolable four-hour block of time for Curriculum, with no interruptions for any reason, and a principal who seems to be always in the classroom, giving resources to teachers, helping write up plans for children with special needs, praising students' work, and, if necessary, teaching demonstration lessons.

Some parents object to the Exploratory program. They find it strange to see teachers and students sitting on the floor, painting, writing, or making Christmas ornaments, relating in an informal and relaxed manner. That is not "basic," they say. Mrs. Parrish disagrees emphatically. "No way! We've never gotten away from basics. Exploratory is learning! That's the inviting part. Career exploration is basic. Art and music are basic." She will not choose between "back to basics" and developmental responsiveness. Exploratory is a daily commitment made to both teachers and students. Teachers get to teach something of their choice that is special to them and that they want to share with students. It enriches a school program that, even without Exploratory, meets curricular experts' criteria for excellence: it is balanced between organized knowledge, personal development, and continued learning of skills; continuity is provided; it is flexible; individualization is provided.[5] Exploratory adds diversity, informality, and, when the personality of the teacher and the area being explored encourage it, a good deal of fun.

A teacher from another school said to me that a middle school is a holding ground. This school is a learning experience. The students get to try out everything. [A Western Middle School parent]

The artistic products of students in Exploratory decorate the halls of the school. For a school without a formal art program, there is a surprising amount of graphic art in the school, because of Exploratory. In one Exploratory class, artists from the county art program visit the school and teach students. Exploratory also enables teachers to introduce areas that are rarely discussed in middle schools. For instance, one class learns about the county's services, like the rape and crisis center, alcohol and substance abuse prevention, and suicide prevention (the county's suicide rate is 5 percent higher than the national average). People from county service programs visit the school to meet with the class. Students see a film from a nearby technical college explaining the differences between criminal, civil, and juvenile court cases. Students go out to observe court sessions (the judge interrupts the proceedings to explain what is going on).

They visit the minimum security prison unit in the county. It is a hot, sunny day. Prisoners are staring at the visitors, playing basketball, lying on their gray beds, watching television, buying soft drinks at a snack bar. Three prisoners are talking to the students about how they wound up in prison. It is tense. One student says: "I guess this is a stupid question, but why did you do it?" Her directness makes everyone fearful. The inmate appreciates the question, smiles, and delves into himself. Everyone relaxes. Later, the students seem restless. An inmate stands up to his full height of over six feet, glares at them, and in a deep bass voice says threateningly: "I don't want to make this into 'Scared Straight,' but I don't think you are taking us seriously." The students stiffen. Soon they do what they know the inmates cannot do: they wait at the locked gate, walk out when it is finally opened for them, and get on the familiar school bus to go home.

Western Middle School is not rich in clubs and other extracurricular activities. Students can join the band, chorus, student government, the school newspaper, intramural sports, and, in the seventh and eighth grades, interscholastic sports, cheerleaders, and spirit squad. The richness comes from Exploratory and from the special excitement that characterizes the instruction in some of the classrooms.

The key word teachers use when talking about their classes is "excitement." "Mrs. Parrish doesn't mind what you try so long as you're enthusiastic. She likes very different, exciting things. She wants to see excited faces. She gives me ideas." As for incentives to experiment, "Mrs. Parrish loves it!" Mrs. Parrish makes it clear to the teachers that she admires seeing different things going on at the same time in one room, with teachers moving around among students and helping ("sitting down to work with students is the only time teachers should sit"). Her ideal is the interdisciplinary, thematic unit.

It was very much easier to be a good teacher in some schools than it was in others. The overall ethos of the school seemed to provide support and a context which facilitated good teaching. Teaching performance is a function of the school environment as well as of personal qualities. [Rutter et al., *Fifteen Thousand Hours.*]

Circus Week in the Outhouse Gang's sixth-grade team wins not only Mrs. Parrish's admiration but a good deal of local press coverage. The culmination of a week's work is a trip to the circus in Greensboro. Teachers work nights and throughout the previous weekend to plan and decorate for the week. Students entering their classrooms on Monday find its entrance transformed into a circus tent's opening. The class is divided into three rings for the week. Math lessons on estimation and measurement become "popcorn math": "Before we start popping corn, estimate the longest distance any single kernel will go; estimate how many kernels of corn will land in your section of the table; what fraction of the total number landed in each section? Measure the distance from the center of the nearest kernel to the popper and the kernel farthest from the popper, in metrics." "You have created a new brand of popcorn. Create a new box for it, a character to sell it, and a jingle that will make it a best seller in the country; actually build the boxes." Language arts revolves around circus themes: " 'If I were in the circus. . .' Hand in your essay with a picture of your favorite thing in the circus"; "Would I rather be a grain of corn or a popcorn popper?" On one bulletin board, a grammar poster with a four-car train proclaims: "The circus train knows four kinds of sentences: declarative, interrogative, imperative, exclamatory." On another, a balloon is attached to a sign—"Measure me: how long is the string on this balloon?" Clown masks made by the students decorate much of the wall space. After lunch on one child's last day at Western Middle, clown-shaped and decorated cakes, made by one of the two team teachers, are served during a going-away party. The child's picture is taken holding one of the cakes, to be added to a collection of pictures of students and teachers dressed up like clowns. In a session on mime, students pick slips of paper from a bowl with adjectives like "sad," "lovely," "happy" written on them, and then mime the emotion for the class to guess. A dart board game is really a lesson in geography. The teachers read circus stories during storytime.

The curriculum's first concern is to arouse enthusiasm in students, to motivate them, to involve them in learning. The school takes the central problem of the underachiever, whether its source lies in cultural deprivation, emotional disturbance, or in a more academic area, to be his apathy toward education. The first task is thus to excite him, and only afterward to remedy the skill deficiencies that are symptomatic of his problem. ["Elements of a Proposal to Establish an Advancement School in Philadelphia," in Saul Yanofsky, *A Report on the External Programs of the Pennsylvania Advancement School.*]

Many of these students have never been to the circus before. After the three-ring circus in Greensboro, the teachers are exhausted. Mrs. Parrish is delighted, not only with the teachers but herself. She has managed to get a father to allow his son to go to the circus even though his report card was disappointing. It takes separate calls to both the mother and the father, an offer to pay for the circus ticket, and an explanation that Circus Week is Curriculum, before the father yields.

The students seem unfazed by all this excitement. The emphasis in the school is on teachers' inventiveness and energies, not necessarily on students'. Mrs. Parrish pushes hard for teacher creativity. That encouragement is not always passed along by the teachers to the students. It is possible for students to passively accept the excitement the way they passively accept content in many schools. Their teachers come up with superb ideas in Curriculum and Exploratory, which the students do not appear to see as unusual or noteworthy. One wonders if next year a four-ring circus will be required to impress them. Not one student mentions the special events of the week, like the field trip to the correctional unit, Circus Week, or a special concert for Black History Week. They mention nothing about major events of previous weeks. The events appear to be more major in the lives of the school staff than of their students, who with great seriousness discuss achievement and comportment, not excitement. Parents say it is different at home.

All instruction is not high in dramatic intensity. Quiet excellence is observable on a daily basis. A teacher holds up a laminated picture from a magazine during a lesson on fractions. A man is holding a large fish. The question superimposed on the picture tells us the weights of the fish when caught and when dressed, and asks what fraction was lost. The class works together on the problem until everyone is clear about procedure. Then each student picks a laminated picture and works on the question attached. They talk quietly together or ask the teacher for help. When they have solved some very clever problems, the teacher challenges them to make up their own. They dive into a pile of roughly cut-out magazine pictures, not laminated and with no problems written on them, and begin to make up fraction "word problems" for other students in the class to solve. They try them out on one another. It is hard at first to account for their high level of interest in this assignment. They appear to be completely gripped by the challenge. The next day the teacher and class choose several of the problems to be placed in her file for next year's students. The pictures will be laminated, the problems attached, and their names written on the sheet. The students are deeply engaged because they are part of a tradition. Later in the day, several of them tell older students: "I worked on your problem today." Next year, someone will tell *them*. It is a technically brilliant lesson.

A team of two seventh-grade teachers have begun a lesson on China. There are many "stations" around the room with various tasks for students to complete. As a treat at the end of the unit, the team will go to a local Chinese restaurant. Students are working in groups at the stations, in a large armchair that dominates an informal meeting area in one corner, and in the hallway. The room is filled with the equipment of a rich, teacher-made elementary school environment, replete with gerbils, an aquarium, a corner with an anatomy display, and a reading area. On a bulletin board are posters and pamphlets about China. Students' work is displayed around the room. The noise level is pleasant and productive as students talk and work together and receive help from the teachers. The tasks are adapted to varying levels of ability and interest. Few of them require rote learning; most are creative and questioning. After 25 minutes, a timer goes off and students change stations. The transition seems effortless. The self-selected and constantly shifting groups remain interracial, friendly, and mutually supportive. There is almost no monitoring of behavior. Teachers check work and offer encouragement but ask not to be called over too frequently. They encourage independent work. They are warm, task-oriented, and well prepared.

Mrs. Parrish enters the room. She is constantly on the move, talking, asking, helping, and praising. She loves the strong emphasis on active learning in this team. The timer goes off. It is time to regroup. Students receive high praise from one of the teachers for switching from the centers to their seats so smoothly. During story time, as a student reads a story set in China to the class, a Black girl sits down on the same chair with a White girl, to whisper in her ear. A White boy and Black girl whisper together over something they are reading. The teachers say nothing. Later, they will insist that there is nothing outstanding or unusual about the afternoon and will be surprised to be contradicted.

While the tone of the school is relaxed and teachers feel relatively unharried, considerable energy is spent battling wasted time. Gaining even several minutes of additional "time on task" per hour demands the constant effort of exerting powerful pressure against inertia. At Western Middle School one senses the constant drive against the undertow, to do more and more, and then even more. Mrs. Parrish pushes for productive use of time. She also wants to see more talking among students, working together, helping each other, moving around the room. She wants students selecting their own seats. She wants teachers working with an entire class less frequently. In practice, most teachers usually work with the class as a whole on the same lesson and one-quarter of them say they seldom allow students to talk to each other, move around the room without permission, or select their own seats. What is clear, though, is that school policy is an important factor in determining curricular objectives and instructional practices. One suspects that the 25 percent figure will decrease over time. Instruction at Western Middle School is predominantly of high technical quality. The underpinning rationale for teachers' methodology comes not from them, but from Mrs. Parrish, who believes that school success lies more in instruction than in school organization. She has assuaged the community in her insistence that good teachers, not teaming or self-contained classrooms, make good schools. She puts her major daily effort into improving instruction. Some of the teachers, who seem completely unperturbed about the process of learning and the development of young adolescents, have mastered teaching techniques that result in cameos of instructional excellence day after day.

Developmental Responsiveness

There is a reasonably high level of responsiveness to the developmental needs of young adolescents at Western Middle School. The most striking area of responsiveness is the school's emphasis on diversity. To accommodate individual maturity levels, the school offers an unusually diverse organizational structure. Programmatically, there are always many different things going on during a school day, with the various pursuits of Exploratory, 200 different activity units in fifteen career clusters, sports, special theme weeks like Circus Week, and schoolwide special events like concerts during Black History Week and an annual international festival.

There is not great diversity among the adults in the school. This staff is not a collection of strong, individualistic personalities loosely drawn together by a benign, mediating principal. It is a staff of homogeneous, like-minded people, the large majority of whom adhere to a dominant principal's definitions of personal integrity and instructional excellence. Also striking is the school's emphasis on young adolescents' need for structure and clear limits. Sometimes this emphasis can become overbearing, at which point Mrs. Parrish "takes it down, tone by tone." She is appalled if a student is made the object of ridicule by an adult—"I will not have my students humiliated." Structure and limits are set in order to allow students to grow, not to thwart their growth. These are subjective terms, set in the context of a defining community that appreciates strict discipline.

Young adolescents have a powerful need for competence and achievement. Schools usually offer two routes for success: academics and athletics. Western Middle offers a third, which is its most important and attainable by almost every student: considerate behavior. A visitor enters a classroom and a student, unprodded, offers a chair. It is a small gesture, but in the lives of schools it is a major achievement. When Western Middle School students go on trips, for instance a social studies class's trip to Washington, D.C., their decorum is noted everywhere. On their return, they are highly praised by parents and school staff for this success. It is an area of achievement with high standards but no exclusivity.

Young adolescents' need for social interaction with their peers is met even before school begins by the principal's effort to keep friends together in their house assignments. Students say they get to be with friends in the cafeteria, where all students from each grade eat together, and, to varying degrees, in the houses and their classes. Since they are controlled so much of the day, Mrs. Parrish encourages them to go outside during lunch, unsupervised, to run around and be together.

Students at Western Middle School do not have many opportunities to interact with a diverse group of adults from outside the school. The absence of such interactions results in part from an almost total lack of emphasis on opportunities for meaningful participation in their community. While there is a high level of involvement in adult-sponsored activities in school, there are no opportunities for community service. Responsibility within the school, aside from student council, is on an ad hoc basis. Students help Mrs. Parrish sweep up. Under the direction of two highly energetic teachers, they built a nature trail for science. When it came time to move into the new school building, books were never boxed away. Students carried eight to ten books apiece, rode the buses, and put the books on the shelves in the new school. This is typical of the rather automatic but unstructured integration of students into the upkeep of the school. Western Middle School could, in the same spirit, sponsor a youth participation program in the community with little institutional strain.

Because PE is offered every other day, students say they do not get as much physical activity as they would like. They move around a lot in most Curriculum classes, in Exploratory, in Careers, outside after lunch, and, in some classes, when they get to go to the library after their work is completed. ("The library is comfy.") The students in the band who also happen to be in the minority of classes where students are discouraged from leaving their seats have little chance for the physical activity that their growing bodies need.

The need for self-exploration and self-definition is intense during early adolescence. Western Middle School is not an extremely intellectual environment. People do not spend time together exploring or playing with ideas. The emphasis is on facts, skills, and activities. Self-exploration and definition, therefore, are not intellectual pursuits. They occur by means of self-testing in the various curricular and extracurricular areas, in creative expression, in counseling with the school counselor, in talks with the principal, and with groups of peers. The tone of the school encourages the personal investment of students that is a prerequisite for self-discovery.

We believe that our middle school should have a student-centered program dedicated to the purpose of proving each student's worth. We also believe that to survive in today's society an individual must be able to use the basic tools of communication and reasoning. The responsibility of learning should be inspired by the parents, encouraged by the teacher, and ultimately accepted by the students. It is our aim to develop each child's humanness as well as his skills and help him become aware of the importance of developing character, sound morals, and a positive attitude. And finally, it is our desire to encourage students to learn to think for themselves and accept individual responsibility as they choose their own goals in life and work toward achieving them. [Western Middle School, Student Information Folder, 1980–81.]

One aspect of curricular commitment to self-understanding is stunning in its candor, thoroughness, and ease. Sex education is part of science. Only one child's parent has refused to grant permission for his child to take part in the program. Teachers incorporate sex education into their classes. For instance, a seventh-grade teacher reads to her Life Science class from Marion Howard's *Only Human,* a sensitive book about teenage mothers that was recommended by the guidance counselor. In another class on the same day, a county health nurse teaches anatomy and sexual reproduction to girls, while the guidance counselor teaches the boys.

It is the fourth day that the nurse, a very young woman, is meeting with the girls. She starts answering the questions they have been writing down and putting in a question box. They have already received a lot of instruction on reproductive "plumbing." The questions are as varied in their maturity and fearfulness as the girls are: "How do you get your body regulated?" "Do you have to have intercourse several times to get pregnant?" "If you have sex with a guy and are on your way to having a baby and you turn around and have sex with another guy—what happens? Does the baby die?" "When you are about to have a baby and not fully developed and you are smoking and drinking, would that baby die?" "What happens if you have your period two times in one month?" "Is having a baby the closest you can come to death?"

The nurse is reassuring about bodies regulating themselves. She gives a clear message, via a true story about a thirteen-year-old mother, that they should stay in school and be teenagers. Her answers are straightforward and factual. She is unflappable. No one is testing her limits; they are asking to have their fears assuaged. These questions are on their minds as they play outside after lunch, walk quietly through the halls, and work diligently over fractions. It is hard for an adult to integrate the images of these different selves that have been revealed. As if enacting the various ages these young people juggle, a girl in the classroom listens intently as the nurse answers her question, all the while holding a stuffed monkey, her favorite toy.

There has never been a furor over sex education at Western Middle School. The superintendent does not know how to account for that, saying only: "It's just low key." Perhaps a school that has otherwise won its community's trust can meet its students' needs for information and self-definition. There are schools in communities that pride themselves on their liberal politics and on child-rearing philosophies that would not dare offer such candid and informative sex education classes. True to form, teachers at Western Middle School see nothing unusual about their Life Science classes. Labels like "liberal" and "conservative" peel away in a successful school.

The Community and Public Policy Issues

The rhetoric that surrounds a school is important. Whether or not it accurately reflects school philosophy, practices, and outcomes, it helps determine them. In Alamance County, there is remarkable agreement between rhetoric and practice. While some parents would like a school with egg-crate architecture, bells, and changing classes every forty-five minutes, stricter discipline and higher morals ("there is a general decline in morals in society—some teachers don't set a good example"), they are, as the superintendent says, "all on the same highway." The school is at the center of community life. Perhaps because of its secure sense of identity, the community has not been wracked with conflict over major public policy decisions. The school has been left in peace to deal with sex equity, mainstreaming the handicapped, and desegregation. Almost nothing is said about the first two of these issues.

Why is it a good school? Everyone is pulling for the same thing. Schools are better off in a rural setting because farmers are sweating. They want their kids to get an education and get a better job. The children have learned how to work, to apply themselves. This is a Christian community that holds onto old values: the work ethic, help your neighbor, support your school. Parents are willing to sacrifice money and labor for the school. They want the school to succeed. And behind every good school there's a good community. [Alamance County School Board chairman]

The music teacher gives a guitar concert commemorating Black History Week, tracing the influence of Blacks on the blues, spirituals, minstrel music, boogie, jazz, and rhythm and blues. As he prepares to sing "Take This Hammer," he asks: "How many of you guys have ever split wood?" There is an outcry from several girls. He restates the question with a smile. The principal is talking to a visitor about her high expectations for the students "to perform to the best of your ability. We have pride that we're here to learn academics. Also, to have high morals, to be a somebody, someone who cares for himself and makes himself a man." She pauses, adds, "and a woman, of course," and then continues pell mell with her credo. Both sexes have full access to all school offerings. There are no readily observable signs of sexism in classroom instruction and management. Parents, students, and school staff exhibit a heightened awareness about sex discrimination. Title IX is alive and well in Western Middle School.

I didn't mind the cooking, but I wasn't too pleased about my son sewing. But he enjoyed it, found it relaxing. And he took pride in his cross-stitch. [A Western Middle School parent]

Educable mentally retarded and learning disabled (LD) students receive special services. The community has put no pressure on the school for any other services under P.L. 94–142 or North Carolina's even stricter law on schooling for "children with special needs." Educable mentally retarded (EMR) students are mainstreamed in homeroom, Exploratory, and Unified Arts. They have either one or two hours of special instruction a day, according to their needs. LD students are in special classes most of the morning. They receive, among other services, specialized reading instruction at least once and often two times daily with a reading teacher. Teachers are proud to point out that there is little attention paid to students who go for special instruction, since careful scheduling allows them to leave when band students also leave. Sensitivity to the feelings of mainstreamed students involves no hoopla. Predictably, the staff does its job and finds it commonplace to do so.

A good bit more is said about desegregation. It was 1963 when the first Black student attended a White school in Alamance County, at Western High School. There still is not total agreement about the role of the community during the early days of desegregation. Some White teachers and parents say that the school did not stand alone because "we work with them and play with them" and because "the churches did not teach hate." Integration was not started only in the schools, according to this view. It was communitywide. Other teachers and parents say that the school did what no one else could or can do. Churches were and are segregated. Recreation teams like midget league were desegregated well after schools were.

Yes, we have lost quality because of desegregation, but still, we must bring on the equality. It makes me sick to my stomach when I think of the attitude we took on minorities in my childhood. The federal government has been right in its intent. We needed it. It took time while we adjusted to bringing the races together. But quality is coming back with adjustment and forgetting. There is still some tension at the high school. But these at Western Middle are kids who've never known anything else. I don't care if we lost 100 SAT points to get my child friendly with Blacks. If we lost quality as measured by 100 points, it doesn't matter. [Alamance County School Board chairman]

At present, Black parents say they feel comfortable in the school. White parents acknowledge that "Blacks are achievers," and their achievement has helped eliminate tensions. Blacks are perceived by White parents as being as hard-working as Whites. Parents reject arguments about socioeconomic differences between Whites and Blacks. There are, they insist, as many deprived Whites as Blacks in the school. Teachers say that there are as many unmotivated Whites as Blacks, and add that television and Little League get in the way of academics more than desegregation ever did. The children see one another outside of school. "Kids pull tobacco and drive tractors, Black and White together." The superintendent says his son, who is a high-school student, is an only child, "but we have two sons, and one is Black. They met in school."

We haven't lost, when you take the total and look at it. If Whites were pulled down, they didn't have enough stamina. Aren't we strong enough to take care of ourselves and help someone else? Blacks were not given equal opportunities. We created that. We let it go divided too long. It was a sin. It was wrong. The churches are segregated. Where's our religion? If it is a sacrifice, I feel good about it. And for those students and teachers who weren't ready, the principal just has to pick up the slack. [Wilma Parrish, principal, Western Middle School.]

Several White teachers acknowledge residual race problems, for instance, in attitudes toward seeing a Black boy becoming close with a White girl in school. But it is a personal problem, they add. They agree that quality has been lost in schooling because of pressures toward equality, as if parroting truisms they hear all the time. But when asked if they have lost quality in their classrooms, they contradict themselves and insist that they have not. "Our job is harder. There has not been an actual decline in quality. It's just harder to get it." The unresolved residual problem that many White administrators, parents, and teachers refer to is unqualified Black staff. No one sees children as "unqualified."

In elementary school when Blacks were first brought in, the White children perceived them as slower. As they migrated to Mrs. Parrish's loving arms, the children changed their perceptions. [A Western Middle School parent]

Conclusion

Is Western Middle School one-of-a-kind or is it replicable? Every school is unique in the particular mix of history and people that makes its personality. Everyone who knows Western Middle feels that the community is central to its definition and well-being. It is also impossible not to be struck by the happy conjunction of principal, students, parents, staff, and building.

One teacher says that the school could, nonetheless, work anywhere. Despite what she sees as its unique student body and community, the schedule and program could be adopted elsewhere, and these are, in her view, what makes the school work so well on a day-to-day basis. She points especially to joint planning time for teachers in houses and to the Exploratory program. Another teacher argues that the history of the school is unique. The community fought hard for this school after learning from their mistakes with others. The success of the school is very dependent on the people in the school zone, the staff, and the building. But, she says, "consistency of expectation *is* replicable, even though there is a unique combination of history, community, and building. This is the lesson for other schools."

Mrs. Parrish says that while the building is in their favor, the middle school concept was new to a wary community. She and the former assistant principal attended summer school to study about curricular philosophy and practice and about adolescent self-concept. They then bombarded the teachers with what they had learned. They practiced run-throughs of schedules. They worked incessantly on students' folders in making assignments to houses. Anyone, she says, can do what they did, with a united faculty, complete readiness on day one, and constant questioning: "How can we be the best? How can we make it inviting? Anyone can do all this."

Western Middle School is a successful school. It produces, to use Tomlinson's prescription, "motivated and efficient work in its students, which is undoubtedly the single most powerful treatment we could devise to raise both the level of achievement and the functional ability of the child."[6] The school reduces distractions while increasing excitement for learning. It is a place that rejects dichotomies and insists on both basics and exploration, both decorum and developmental responsiveness. It responds to the diversity of the age group it serves by means of its organizational structure, varied programs, and instructional techniques. It has gained wide community support while also responding successfully to the massive external pressures for change that have overwhelmed many other schools, both Southern and Northern.

The school would lose its character if there were so sizable a subculture of students rejecting its values that the power of its consonance were lost. It would lose its staying power if a new principal were to allow its program and organization to outstrip community tolerance. It would lose its importance as an example for others if community pressure, a change in leadership, or changed hiring practices led to a decreased emphasis on creating a positive environment for adolescent social development.

While it has unresolved issues and small tensions, Western Middle

School is as happy a school as one is likely to find. There is consensus about the major issues that affect the lives of young people. Western Middle School is a middle-of-the-road school. As such, it has a great deal to teach other schools. Its staff is not moving far away from standard definitions of schooling in America. They are committed to many characteristics of the traditional graded school. Mrs. Parrish says they want to make even better what is already good in schooling, not to redefine it. "Do it better. Find new ways, but don't throw away the old. There are good, tried and true things. Optimize them."

Few schools can replicate the special congruence of principal, staff, students, community, and building. What is not unique, and therefore of great import, are things all schools can control: attitudes about students; expectations for students, parents, staff, and principal; energy; organizational ingenuity; and a coherent philosophy of how young adolescents grow and learn that pervades every aspect of school life.

Notes

1. Charity James, *Beyond Customs: An Educator's Journey* (New York: Schocken, 1974): 27.
2. William W. Purkey, *Inviting School Success* (Belmont, Cal.: Wadsworth, 1978).
3. Ronald R. Edmonds, "Some Schools Work and More Can," *Social Policy* 9 (March-April 1979): 32.
4. Fred. M. Newmann, "Research Prospectus: The Potential for Generating Collective Identity in Secondary Schools: Implications of Research on Adolescence" (Madison, Wis.: mimeographed, April 1980): 1–2.
5. William M. Alexander and Ronald P. Kealy, "From Junior High School to Middle School," in *The Middle School: Selected Readings on an Emerging School Program,* ed. Louis G. Romano, Nicholas P. Georgiady, and James Heald (Chicago, Ill.: Nelson-Hall, 1973): 17–18.
6. Tommy M. Tomlinson, "Student Ability, Student Background, and Student Achievement: Another Look at Life in Effective Schools" (paper presented at Conference on Effective Schools sponsored by the Office of Minority Education, Educational Testing Service, New York, May 27–29, 1980): 20.

4

A Parable for Hard Times

Region 7 Middle School
(The Dorothy L. Fisher Magnet Middle School)
Detroit, Michigan

*If I had the money, I'd try to make more schools like ours. We
have a better chance to learn. We really experience what we learn.*
— *A Region 7 Middle School seventh-grader*

No one is neutral about Region 7 Middle School. People are either
fighting for it or trying to destroy it. The middle school was started with
the noblest of purposes: to develop an integrated magnet school responsive
to parental opinion, early adolescent development, and individual learning
needs. Its story evokes deep admiration and anger.

The logo of Region 7 Middle School, designed by a student in 1971,
symbolizes all races working together in unity in the school. From outside
a circle containing the number 7, four children's hands reach inward toward
one another, seeking connectedness. Students still identify with it because,
they say, the school lives up to its symbol. The middle school was begun
in 1971 in response to a court order to establish eight magnet middle
schools, one in each of Detroit's eight decentralized school regions, as part
of a citywide plan for school desegregation. Parents signed up their children
for the school in the spring of 1971, even before the school was assigned
a building. The driving force behind defining the purposes of the middle
school and its unique organizational structure, the hiring of a specially
qualified staff, the involvement of parents, and the recruitment of students
to the school, was Dorothy Fisher, the school's first principal.

The history of the middle school has been a counterpoint of remarkable
social and academic successes and political defeats. In 1975 the regional
school board attempted to change Region 7 Middle School from a school
with grades 5–8 to a 6–8 school. Parents formed the Committee to Keep

Our 5th Grade, and won. In 1977 the board ruled that magnet schools must have the same staffing as all other city schools, changing the staff/student ratio from 1:25 to 1:35. Further budget cuts led to a drastically revamped program, with cutbacks in educational opportunities and services. In a move ostensibly to save money, the regional board transferred Region 7 Middle School from the large facility it was in, a former Catholic high school (St. David's), to an old, run-down, and very small elementary school building. Parents petitioned the regional and central boards, and lost. They petitioned again when the decision was made to reopen St. David's as an administrative annex to the regional office. It was hard for parents to understand how a building that was too expensive to run for 525 students was not too expensive to run for 29 administrators. They lost again. The enrollment at the middle school was cut to 420 students, taught by twelve teachers, one librarian, a remedial reading specialist, and a guidance counselor. The school lost its assistant principal, career counselor, media center, and reading and math lab, among other positions and services.

Miss Fisher retired in February 1978 in protest, refusing to be a party to hurting children. She had been with the Detroit school system for 34 years, ten as a teacher, ten as an assistant principal, and fourteen as a principal. The attempt to make the school conform to other schools' standards had, in her opinion, ended its alternative nature.

Thomas Washington, formerly assistant principal, became the principal of Region 7 Middle School. The school's parents fought for him and won. A product of the ghetto and poor schooling, later a graduate of the University of Michigan and a pilot in the navy, Mr. Washington felt that it was still possible to teach the school's children. "Education is a matter of attitude. Some students can still learn, even in the worst facilities and homes." He wanted to find them and instill in them and their parents a positive attitude about learning. "To Miss Fisher, this was a terrible thing to happen to kids. Coming from nothing, anything was good to me."

St. David's had what the building that now houses the school lacks: science facilities, a huge auditorium-gymnasium, a larger lunch room, large home economics and industrial arts rooms, a math lab, a media center that could hold all the school's books, adequate counseling rooms, and classrooms large enough to accommodate 35 middle-school students without crowding. It also had the requisite number of children to qualify for ESEA Title I funds for reading and career counseling, but the children—and hence the funds—were also lost in the move. The staff of Region 7 Middle School adapted to the loss of students, staff, and money, but the hope of returning to St. David's remained a powerful motivator. In February 1981, the regional school board reopened St. David's as a school building. Parents from the middle school once again petitioned and once again lost. The building went to the constituency of the regional board chairperson whose neighborhood pressured hard for the school as an alternative to busing.

Until new statistics were released in March 1981, giving the dubious distinction to Miami, Detroit had the highest homicide rate in the nation. Unemployment soared. The city schools were 82 percent Black. Twenty thousand students were bused in 1979–80 in Region 7, the second highest number of students bused per region in the city.

The 420 students in the middle school transfer from fifteen feeder elementary schools and six other middle schools. There were 516 applicants for 133 slots in 1980. They applied through a meticulous lottery procedure run by a community selection committee. The committee selects on a first come, first served basis, maintaining an equal male/female ratio and accepting no more than ten children from any one school. The Black/White ratio set by the court was 50/50. It was later changed to 60/40, then to 70/30. (As of June 1981, several months after the observations reported in this chapter, the ratio was changed to 80/20.) Some parents interpret the changes as further attempts to scuttle the school. Others say that, with the continued decrease of White students in the city schools, a 50/50 or 60/40 ratio is politically unfeasible. Just as the middle school was resented for having originally had a lower student/staff ratio, it has been attacked for luring White students from other middle schools. The fact is, however, that the majority of those White students enter Region 7 Middle School from private schools and return to private schools after eighth grade. They are not a pool of students available to the schools in the region.

Purposes, Goals, and Definitions

Every year the principal visits the feeder schools to describe the school and its goals to prospective students. The school stands for something and it makes strong statements, both in words and practice, about its purposes. The goals were developed by a planning committee of staff, parents, and students in 1971, and are reaffirmed by each year's Planning Committee. The school seeks "meaningful integration; continuous growth in skills and extension of interest; student self-direction; instruction by all staff based on needed skills; use of regional and city resources as part of schooling experiences; community and home involvement; an atmosphere of helping, caring, and freedom with responsibility; our goal is to help students learn to live in today's world, as well as make a living." These goals are based on seven foundations:

- Everyone learns best if successful. We provide individualized learning and pacing for SUCCESS!

- We teach what is needed, not just "one subject." All skills are involved in all rooms.
- We work WITH the non-performers to MODIFY their attitudes and work, to find some way to teach them.
- Learning is fun and exciting. We help them find this out.
- We organize to give constant experiences in SELF-DIRECTION so students develop this skill.
- We organize to offer CHANGE to students who need and desire variety at their age level.
- We plan so that study and work assignments and CONTACTS come from STUDENT needs . . . within each classroom.[1]

In a report written by Dorothy Fisher with parents and students, "It Can Be Done: The Five-Year Story of an Integrated, Innovative Alternative Middle School," the alternative nature of the school is defined as "an option based on interests and educational ideas." The report stresses the school's "unique organizational plan," less use of regular texts, a new reporting system developed by students and parents, and the optional nature of the school: parents apply. There is also a strong emphasis on pre- and early adolescent development. The middle school should be concerned with the development of "self-confident, self-directing, and interested young people who can accept challenges, direct their own studies, help others cooperatively, and make intelligent decisions about themselves and their world in high school and beyond."[2]

Dear new Region 7 Middle School student:

Welcome to Region 7 Middle School. You will find our school to be a unique approach to secondary education designed to offer a program to attract an integrated student body in grades 5–8. The school focuses on the personal growth of students, individual class selections, and independent study opportunities.

Region 7 Middle School was organized by court order in 1971 to be integrated, innovative, and a "magnet" for Region 7 students in grades 5–8.
. . .

Some students will face the challenge of adjustment to new teachers, new teaching methods, and meeting great educational responsibilities. Students most successful in our school are those who develop the skill of thinking for themselves and who develop the skill of self-responsibility. Students will also have many opportunities to express individuality and demonstrate a spirit of cooperation. [Thomas A. Washington, principal, "Region 7 Middle School Handbook."]

Students are very articulate about the school's goals. Because they and their parents have chosen the school, because of the constant battles to lose as little as possible, and because Mr. Washington and his staff constantly reiterate the school's goals, they are very articulate about what the school stands for. First and foremost, they discuss integration; second, they stress that it is a place where they get to choose classes and speak their minds; third, they describe at length how it has become a place where people learn as much as possible in as many settings as possible.

School Organization

Despite a political and financial maelstrom that should make the school dysfunctional, Region 7 Middle School is an achieving school living out its original dream. It is a harmonious, integrated school that is constantly walking away with honors. In one week in March 1981, for instance, the school triumphed in three different competitions. The Future Homemakers of America Club took three first-place prizes and one second place in a citywide competition with Detroit Public Schools middle and high schools. The Equations Team (mathematics) won a trophy in a statewide competition at Eastern Michigan University. The school had two winners in the Metropolitan Science Fair. The display case in the front hall is filled with trophies from students' academic successes. All three of these triumphs are the direct result of an organizational plan that encourages independent and group study based on personal interest and energies. When students are asked why the school is a good school, they list, without fail, its safety and IST (independent study time).

An outsider has to learn a new language to understand the school's organization and schedule. Teachers are divided into "sets," teams of three or four teachers. Each student is assigned to a set for one session of approximately nine weeks. At the end of the session, the student moves on to another set of teachers. Each day, Monday through Thursday, students attend four classes in their set and then may choose one independent class, or IST, from among the classes offered by the set's teachers. Friday, the regular schedule is completely dropped, and students select all their classes from among a rich array offered by the entire school staff, including administrators. This schoolwide IST, or SWIST, is the highlight of every week. Students say they can tolerate just about anything Monday through Thursday "because of Fridays." The mini-courses are offered based on student and teacher interest. Although there is a lot of continuity, SWIST electives change weekly and students sign up weekly. This schedule continues through four sessions. The fifth, during the last three or four weeks of school, is SWIST every day, all day. The only requirement is that students, who sign up for electives, which last the entire session, must choose at least one language arts and one math course, and either science or social studies.

This organization has varied over the years as differing learning needs have been identified and as the staff has been reduced (in 1980–81 the school had only twelve teachers, one librarian, and one guidance counselor). The staff and students engage in a good deal of healthy argument about "the best plan." In 1979 the school had four sessions, three of eleven weeks' duration and the last of six weeks'. In 1980 the school switched to four nine-week sessions and a fifth of three weeks' duration. The purpose of the switch was to allow for greater variety and interest. Some teachers feel nine weeks are too few for the intensity of instruction they require. At the end of school year 1980–81, the decision was made to extend the school day by one period, to extend sessions to eleven weeks, and with additional staff because of the longer school day, to reorganize the faculty into three sets of five teachers. An innovation of school year 1980–81, mandatory independent study time, was dropped to allow for an increased emphasis on science and social studies. Mandatory independent study time was a plan for increasing individualized emphasis on reading and math. For a maximum of three times a week students were assigned to homogeneous groups for special instruction. The science and social studies teachers strongly opposed this schedule change. As with all school policies, it was reconsidered by the entire staff at the year's end.

The schedule allows for a certain amount of flexibility. For instance, a set of teachers can offer a double class of any subject or can rotate classes so that students get a subject twice in one day. All classes except mandatory independent study time are heterogeneously grouped. Some electives like Advanced Scrabble, Money and Banking Club, and Equations Team, have prerequisites. All independent study and fifth-session classes are multiaged, allowing for a great deal of interaction among a broader variety of students and between students and teachers. The variety of courses is remarkable. There are 110 offerings in fifth session, and because of a Monday-Wednesday-Friday, Tuesday-Thursday schedule, each student takes ten of them. The school "uses the excitement of change and variety to stimulate learning," as its literature says. It also allows students to choose not only their courses but their favorite teachers in all independent study classes, acknowledging that, as Miss Fisher said, "we learn for those we like."

We believe middle schools must serve students at a particular stage in their development. The organization, curriculum, and policies of middle schools should serve the particular needs of their pre- and early adolescents. Middle schools should USE their knowledge of the psychological stages to HELP students learn. And so, we used our understanding of our students to determine our organization and procedures! This has been one of the reasons our unique procedures have worked these five years—they were not done just to be "different" but . . . because we were answering some of the basic needs of students at this stage. It is important to have reasons for what a school does. [Dorothy Fisher, "It Can Be Done."]

The underlying assumption of this complex organization is that because of the nature of early adolescent development, especially a desire for increased freedom, middle-school students will learn more if they can express their interests by making responsible choices. The numerous awards that students won during the second week of March 1981 were all the result of classes and clubs that students freely elected.

Curriculum and Instruction

Staff energies are expended more creatively in the independent course structure than in the standard curriculum. While there is considerable joint planning by sets at the beginning of each session and some block scheduling in one set, and while teachers meet for parent-student-teacher conferences as a set, there is no team teaching and very little interdisciplinary instruction. Teachers identify more with disciplines and departments than with their sets. No one pushes hard for organizational innovation or instructional variety within the core curriculum. Several teachers would like more interdisciplinary team teaching and have selected that as a personal goal for future improvement. The genius of the school, however, is expressed in its organizational vitality outside the core curriculum.

Natural resources are oil, iron, copper, coal. They have some cork tree there. . . . Important water bodie are the Mediternean Sea and the Atlantic Ocean. Algeria is one of the finet deset in Africa [sic]. [Student report on bulletin board, fifth grade social studies, Region 7 Middle School.]

The core curriculum in Region 7 Middle School is a program reduced to bare bones by loss of staff, budget cuts, a commitment to basic skills in language arts and mathematics, and the emphasis on independent study courses. Many middle schools in Detroit offer science only once or twice weekly. Students at Region 7 Middle School receive more than the required amount of science instruction because of electives. In the core curricular classes, however, they get the equivalent of two hours per week, concentrated in one eight- or nine-week session. Students take only four courses at a time in concentrated time periods, an approach to curriculum that both Miss Fisher and Mr. Washington support because of its intensity, the resulting emphasis on efficient use of time, and the change and variety of subjects and teachers it allows from session to session. Math and language arts "get the lion's share" of instructional time because they are "the backbone of the school," according to Mr. Washington. Students enter the school deficient in reading and computation. Their classes at the middle school are designed to make them proficient in both areas, both because of the inherent importance of these skills and because "those are the city's priorities"—only 2 percent of the standardized tests relate to social studies and science. In a typical 1979 schedule, with three sessions of eleven weeks, science and social studies were taken for only one session. Language arts and math were taken three times. The schedule was the same for all four grades:

Session	Classes
1	IST, language arts, math, science, vocal music
2	IST, language arts, math, social studies, home economics
3	IST, language arts, arts and crafts, math, PE

In the 1980 schedule, with four sessions, two of eight and two of nine weeks' duration, students took three courses at a time and independent study. Mandatory independent study time (MIST) was introduced three times weekly. Once again, social studies and science were offered in one session only:

Session	Classes
1	language arts, math, today's living, IST, MIST, or repeat of one class
2	language arts, math, music, IST, MIST, or repeat of one class
3	language arts, science, gym, IST, MIST, or repeat of one class
4	social studies, math, art, IST, MIST, or repeat of one class

Reducing class time even further is the instrumental music program, an elective that meets only twice weekly for a total of 100 minutes a week in Detroit. Approximately one-quarter of the school's students are pulled out of class for instrumental music and are responsible for making up class work during IST on those days. There is no flexibility in scheduling because the school is assigned the teacher only two half days per week. The same is true for speech, remedial reading, and special services for learning-disabled students. The external constraints on the program are considerable. The school is meeting the curricular requirements of the city in this stripped-down program.

Curriculum and instruction at Region 7 Middle School are as varied in quality as in any standard school. Students in art make pottery, African masks, and molas (a folk art form from Panama) that would be considered triumphs even in schools with excellent facilities. In contrast, language arts tends toward uninspired ditto sheets on parts of speech and spelling tests on Thursdays.

Years back in a very interesting book, *How to Survive in Your Native Land,* James Herndon described his years of teaching language skills in a junior high school. He comments about the young people that he worked with: "I had these kids for 45 minutes each day and we struggled with reading and language. And about the time that I thought we might be getting somewhere, the kids had to leave to go to social studies class, which they couldn't pass because their language skills were so low. And then they went to math class which they couldn't pass because their language skills were so low." And then he framed the question, "Why is it that we don't just spend a lot of time getting the language to the point where they can do those other things?" He then pursued that further saying, "How in the world did this school ever get like this anyway? How did we ever get to the point where we decided that every single child in the seventh grade needed eight subjects all 45 minutes long and they had to occur in that pattern?" And as he says, "I researched that problem, I talked to people; I read lots of books; I interviewed everybody in town; and what I found out was that none of the people involved in that decision had been around for the last fifty years. In fact, the last one who participated in the decision died 42 years ago."

I think all of us get into patterns that we no longer understand and no longer have any emotional ties to. We just sort of go about our job as usual. I think the junior high school more than any other segment of our schooling is the place where we really do need to begin to step back again and ask once more: What is it that we're about? What is it that these young people are about? And, how do we begin to match those things more productively? [Vito Perrone, *Proceedings.*]

Language arts teachers are required by the Detroit School System to spend at least twenty minutes two times weekly on Detroit Objective Referenced Tests (DORT), a management system designed to standardize reading instruction citywide in an attempt to deal with the mobility of students in the schools and their poor reading ability. DORT contains pretests, diagnostic profile sheets for individual student progress, lesson plans and materials to gear instruction to individual skill needs, and record-keeping forms for communicating to parents, administrators, and the students' receiving teachers. The materials for middle-school students begin with literal comprehension and become more advanced, step by step, stressing four major skill categories: detail, vocabulary, inference, and generalization (which alone has 29 subcategories). While some teachers say that it is an excellent system, others say that "the patient is dead before you learn to use it." It is mandatory in a system attempting to deal with a highly transient student population.

Some classes in Region 7 Middle School respond to its particular clientele in equally direct but also creative ways. For instance home economics, or Today's Living, teaches clothes washing, ironing, and minor repairs of laundry machines. Students bring laundry from home and learn to sort, wash, dry, fold, and iron their clothes. They learn to sew from patterns and from their own designs. They learn to prepare meals. When they are proficient, they invite their parents to school and prepare a meal for them. It is a very popular class.

Whatever the subject, there is considerable emphasis on thinking and questioning. It is the administrative style in the school to challenge students to solve their problems by thinking through alternatives to their behavior. Likewise, most teachers stress curiosity and inquiry. Eighth-grade students say they have been pressed to be creative and curious: "They like us to think first."

In science, for instance, a totally individualized approach devised by the teacher and approved by the district supervisor presents students with choices of activities in anatomy, botany, ecology, energy, geology, machines, matter, waves, weather, and zoology. Activities are geared to different levels of difficulty. Students can choose their products as well as subjects: they may perform experiments, write reports, prepare graphics, or build special projects. The teacher keeps track of students' strengths and weaknesses in classifying, organizing, and applying information, and generalizing and synthesizing experiences. The students' evaluation forms report to parents every session on these skills, as well as on the work habits that every teacher in the school reports about: following directions, listening, completing assignments, making good use of class time, working well independently, doing work that shows conscious effort, asking for help when needed, being self-disciplined. (Students like the school's evaluation form "because it tells us our strengths and weaknesses rather than labeling us with a grade.") The science teacher insists that it is impossible to teach the same science principles to everyone at once in this age group without alienating them. "I try to appeal to their natural curiosity."

There are striking instances of that appeal in math, Today's Living, and social studies. For the most part, the appeal to the curious is made in the special interest classes or "activity curriculum," as IST, SWIST, and the 5th session are called. Friday's electives include Scrabble, Equations, Future Homemakers of America, gymnastics, football (for boys only, which is currently the hottest issue among students in the school), swimming at a nearby pool, chess club, literature club, Taster's Choice (students tasted the sesame candy, halvah, for the first time, as well as many other ethnic dishes), art union, photo club, *Hotline 7* (the school newspaper), creative writers' club, fashion show, student council, junior weight watchers, story hour, natural dyes, working with rational numbers, spelling bees, library staff, reading vacation maps, African folk tales, glee club, crocheting, speed typing, problem solving, animal study, map and globe skills, and scores more. The special interest classes change with student and teacher interest and student need. They compete successfully in the marketplace of the student sign-up process or are dropped.

One course of special interest to advanced math students is the Money and Banking Club. With the help of the National Bank of Detroit, the club runs a savings account in which all students can deposit 50¢ a week, earn interest, and can borrow up to $1 at 5.5 percent interest, with one month to pay. The club has a loan officer who manages these transactions. An official from the bank teaches students how to keep the books, audit accounts, compute interest rates, and maintain checking accounts. Students work with real money in conjunction with a real bank.

In addition to these electives, the school has a Theme Day every month. The student council nominates the theme for the day, which is approved by the principal. The entire school then participates in such events as UN Day, Color Day, Film Day, and Ethnic Day.

In preparation for 5th session the school holds a pep rally. The principal gives a rousing introductory talk about the uniqueness of 5th session ("we are the only school in the country with these classes") and teachers give a "big sell" promotion for their classes. Students then enter a lottery for course selection. Because no grades are given, teachers are not held to their areas of credentialing by the school system. The 110 offerings are as varied as possible: The Russian Alphabet, Civilization of Mesa Verde, Scrabble (the teacher is swamped with requests), Advanced Scrabble, Tennis (Mr. Washington brings his motorhome to transport ten students to free city courts), I Love a Mystery, Gymnastics, Physical Fitness and Grooming, Decathlon, Softball, Modern Dance, Making Your Own Science Games, Color and Textiles, Photo Club, Woodshop, Writing Music, Piano, Latin, Needle Art, The Bakery, Weight Loss Clinic, Fashion Show Projects, Relax and Read, The Book Worm, Caligraphy, Probability and Statistics, Bookkeeping and Accounting, Typing Relays, Metrics, Oceanography, Medieval England, Poetry (Yours and Theirs), Grammar Workshop, Computer Math, Backgammon, Special Help with Basic Math. . .

Tastes! It's not a matter of their tastes! We can't suit their tastes; we're here to teach them the tastes to have suited! [Teacher quoted in Metz, *Classrooms and Corridors.*]

The curriculum of Region 7 Middle School consists of basic skills classes, the special interest program, and as many additional activities as Mr. Washington decides the school can afford financially and can afford to impose on the staff. The school budget cannot support these extra activities. Personal sacrifice by administrators and staff, parents' contributions, and the proceeds of candy sales constitute a supplementary source of funding for a camping trip, ski trip, swimming, tennis, and the numerous other new experiences that Mr. Washington wants inner-city children to have. These activities pull students out of class, leading to the major source of conflict in the school. Several staff members feel that pull-out programs are detrimental to the students' education because there is already so little time for instruction in their disciplines. Other teachers, with Mr. Washington's strong agreement, refuse to assign greater importance to a science class than to a camping trip that, among many other life skills, teaches ecology to the students. It is a vigorous conflict among people who want inner-city children to have the most effective middle-school program possible, but whose values about effectiveness differ.

In April 1981 the Money and Banking Club went on a trip to a money museum; the Dance Club went to Wayne State University to make a presentation as part of a dance workshop for middle- and high-school students; and the Future Homemakers of America went to a statewide conference. The home economics teacher alone planned the trip to the statewide FHA conference, a fashion show for the Ethnic Festival, a health program, and a fashion class show, all in April and May. Most teachers can list three or four things they are doing and working on simultaneously. The February 1981 issue of *Hotline 7* discusses February's activities: the Region 7 Math Fair, where the school took second place and three honorable mentions, and a student drama production derived from *Roots;* March's activities: a trip by 44 students to their future high school, a trip to Eastern Michigan University of 10 students for the Michigan League of Academic Games Super Tournament, a camping trip that 79 sixth- and seventh-graders went on, and a motivational workshop on self-image for 30 students; and in April: Ethnic Night, featuring Afro-American, Polish, German, French, Mexican, Japanese, and Indian food, fashions, and dances representing the ethnic backgrounds of students in the school, and a schoolwide spelling bee. The list is only a sampling of special events. As one teacher says: "This staff will do just about anything for kids. We are always going and doing. It is hard sometimes to be tolerant with so many things going on and the kids leaving."

During these special events teachers and students learn collaboratively. After visiting junior high and middle schools in America, Charity James observed: "I must say that it is honest personal interaction which I found most seriously lacking in many schools."[3] During a seventeen-hour bus ride to Georgia for an Equations Team competition or on a five-day camping trip, students and teachers form the gentle, honest relationships that are characteristic of this school.

Outside Detroit, the Proud Lake Recreation Area has dormitories for students who go on five-day camping trips for outdoor education. No Detroit school had ever studied there before 1981. A trip had been planned by the school for the previous year, but permission was granted by the regional office only three days before the scheduled departure date, making the trip logistically impossible. The planning process, initiated by a teacher at the middle school, began again in September 1980. Proud Lake was worried because "Detroit is coming." Expecting a bunch of ruffians at best, the management set up as many controls as possible, effectively blocking the trip. Having received clearance for the trip from the regional office but not Proud Lake, Mr. Washington took his case all the way to the governor's office, protesting the barriers being constructed because of the social make-up of the group. The governor's office called Proud Lake and the trip was on. Because the regional superintendent did not allow Mr. Washington to stay all week with the campers, he commuted daily after school and spent evenings and the weekend with them. The cost was $30 per student. Parents donated $600 for the bus and sponsored students who could not otherwise afford to go. Proceeds from the school's candy sale were also used.

In preparation for the trip, the staff sent letters home outlining everyone's responsibilities, including cleaning, cooking, serving, and keeping journals. They sent a notice to parents about their plans to eat "family style" from serving bowls on the table and asked them to practice with their children. During the trip, the teachers received help from the Conservation Club. A retired naturalist spent one and a half days with the campers, identifying plants and trees, giving lessons in water purity, and making plaques from bracken. Other members of the club showed students how to train hunting dogs and gave lessons in firearms safety. A taxidermist showed students how to preserve a bird. ("Have you ever stuffed a human?" asked one student.) The management of the Proud Lake Recreation Area gave the group their highest praise. So did the principal and the four teachers who took the students.

It is Thursday morning. The teachers and principal have planned a surprise awards ceremony for the student campers. They have bought trophies for the outstanding campers and want to have a schoolwide assembly to present them and show slides of the trip. The awards ceremony will recognize the outstanding contributions of individual students to the camping experience and will also help recruit students for next year's trip. Mr. Washington had hoped to have 100 students go this year, but many parents were reluctant to permit their children, many of whom had never left home, to go out of Detroit for a week. After this year's successful trip, he expects 100 students to go next year.

At the last minute, teachers learn that the instrumental music teacher must use the auditorium for rehearsals. The awards must be presented in the industrial arts room. No other meeting area is available since the cafeteria must also serve as a gymnasium. The room is barely large enough for the 79 campers, four teachers, and Mr. Washington. It becomes a private affair. The teachers are deeply disappointed. Nonetheless, the meeting is warm and high-spirited. Slides of the trip show teachers and students learning, working, and playing together. Students laugh at their semicomatose faces at breakfast and at Mr. Washington roasting stacks of marshmallows on wire hangers he has brought. They are completely surprised by the trophies, which are given not to the students with the best journals or the ones who were smartest in the outdoor education classes, but to those whose cooperation, service, and general goodwill made the experience of living together so enjoyable. The experience is intense, and there are tears in some eyes. A teacher praises the campers for their mature behavior and for the good questions they asked on the trip. Later, in the afternoon, the slides are shown to the rest of the faculty, amidst a great deal of laughter and congeniality. A trophy is placed in the trophy case for the best all-around camper, with room for many names of campers in years to come. A tradition has begun.

An argument is often made that in middle-class public and private schools, because entry into the opportunity structure of the economy is almost guaranteed, adolescents can be offered a broad variety of experiences that are not necessarily "preparation for life" in adults' eyes. In working-class and lower–middle-class public schools, however, because entry into the opportunity structure is not guaranteed, school experiences are necessarily narrow. Region 7 Middle School argues to the contrary, through its philosophy and practices, that by broadening the experiences offered inner-city children, schools most effectively respond to the special needs of their students.

Many observers would object to the clear dichotomy the school creates between core curriculum, especially reading and math, and special interest classes and activities. The argument of the school is that students cannot be competent in other important aspects of their present and future lives without mastering the basics; therefore the curriculum guarantees them time. It is reasonable that some learning be neither voluntary nor fun. What the school has not done is create a duality between "real learning" and special interest classes. All school activities are "real learning." When students are asked what aspects of school are the most fun, they all point to IST, SWIST, and 5th session. When they are asked when they learn the most, they point to the same classes.

Developmental Responsiveness

Region 7 Middle school is testimony to the fact that a school can embrace the back-to-basics trend in schools and also be responsive to young adolescents' developmental needs. Most striking is the school's organizational and curricular response to young adolescents' need for diversity. The opportunities for a multitude of new experiences every Friday, all 5th session, and during plays, field trips, contests, and other special events, make them extremely tolerant of some humdrum daily instruction, Monday through Thursday. And they always know that if things are going poorly during one session, in two months they will rotate to a new set of teachers and classes. The lottery for school attendance also yields a more diverse peer group than they would have had in the schools to which they were originally assigned.

At the same time, the school offers young adolescents the routine, structure, and limits they need. The rules are clear and unequivocal, enforced with universal evenhandedness and alacrity. The school day is highly structured. While students exercise responsible choice and decision making in signing up for classes, contests, and trips, they do so under constant adult watchfulness, using streamlined and efficient procedures. Limits on behavior are set by adults who, in a small school building, know everyone and see everything. Their emphasis is on preventing crises by constantly challenging students—in the halls during change of classes, in the auditorium at the beginning of the day, in the lunchroom, and in private counseling sessions—to think through their options for behavior. Most important, given adult protection, meaningful choice, and a sense of personal empowerment, students quickly create their own inner limits and controls.

Young adolescents need many routes for achieving a sense of competence and achievement. Region 7 Middle School offers many more opportunities than the usual academics and athletics. In fact, without interscholastic sports, students whose siblings and neighbors have depended on athletics for self-definition are pressed to seek other routes. The variety of classes and activities opens numerous opportunities for mastery. The trophy case and encouragement heard daily attest to the fact that students receive equal praise for excellence in cooperation, artistic creativity, academics, honesty, self-discipline, curiosity, initiative, and leadership.

Students stress that although they do not have opportunities through the school for community service ("The Region 7 board says it's not educational," explains an eighth-grader), they take a great deal of responsibility for school policy. The most dramatically successful petition was initiated by three students in response to a short-lived schedule change that reduced the number of SWIST periods on Fridays. The Student Council is an advisory group to the principal. Their recommendations are taken seriously. Council members also take responsibility for distributing supplies to all students (folders, pencils, pens, papers) at the beginning of each session. Students are especially appreciative of their ability to go to the principal with a complaint about a teacher. As one teacher says admiringly: "The kids feel they have rights and they exercise them." They are encouraged to. Students are also invited to contribute ideas for 5th session classes.

Students fill many jobs in the school, including service in the main office, flag duty, delivering messages (the school has no intercom), checking buses, running a book store, and selling ice cream in the cafeteria. Students apply for jobs and are interviewed and hired by the guidance counselor. They are fired if they do not live up to their responsibilities. The lunchroom job is especially prestigious because it entails handling money. While students do not earn money, they gain real work experience.

Some students say that when they enter contests or make posters that are then hung in the front hall's ad hoc "art gallery," they feel they are taking responsibility for the school. Others point to the wildly successful annual candy sale, when a student body of 420 raises over $5,000 to supplement the reduced budget. Others point to clean-up day, when everyone pitches in to clean the building and school yard. The greatest sense of responsibility comes from making choices in selecting classes.

I'm proud of this school. I'm proud in particular of the students. I want people to know about our school. I have kids who are happy and want to come to school. I have teachers who put in extra time and work together. I have parents who would lie down and die for the school. I want our kids to have every possible tool for them to succeed in life. They may not have all the tangibles, but they will have the one essential intangible, attitude, to learn. [Thomas A. Washington, principal, Region 7 Middle School.]

Mr. Washington stresses maintaining a school climate in which students are allowed, encouraged, and even pressured into taking responsibility. "It's not a difficult age group. The fact that they're not predictable is predictable. Just prepare for it. There is no reason to be surprised by it. They are changing socially and are embarrassed easily. Allow them to provide experiences for themselves, to excel in an area, to be individuals, to plan activities that allow them to be different. Let them be forceful in expressing their likes and dislikes. Have as little regimentation as possible. Let them voice what they want and see it happen. Let them share responsibility in the operation and maintenance of the school." Mr. Washington contrasts this emphasis with a nearby elementary school that has a yellow line down the middle of the hall and demerits for crossing the line during class changes. "Here, students are taught to take responsibility for getting to class on time with no bells and no lines—just do it with consideration."

Students at Region 7 Middle School have ample opportunities for the peer interaction so crucial to their healthy development. Because they can choose many classes voluntarily, they get to be with their friends during electives as well as during "passing," the time between classes in the halls. Some of them say that they are with their friends all through classes: "Most of us are friends in this school." While some students say "there is a lot of girl-boy stuff" in the school, most say that "we wait until we get out of school." Although there are no rules about "contact," students feel it is not appropriate. They sense a sexual taboo from administrators who want them to "leave it at home" and not grow up prematurely, as the adults in the school feel so many ghetto children do. They can relax into being children, learning, and having good times together.

This is the way school should be. The kids are good. School is fun. You get to choose a lot of what you do. It's better than my old school, where everyone fought. No one got along. I obey the rules because I don't want to be sent home. I don't want to miss the fun. [Region 7 Middle School student]

Mr. Washington would like the students to have more access to adults outside the school. While a banker consults with Money and Banking and a communications specialist from a local radio station teaches students to make tapes, many more experiences with adults in the workplace are on his agenda for school improvement. Within the school, while there is no advisor-advisee program, students say they have instant access to the guidance counselor, who is always in the halls during "passing," and they have at least one teacher they feel really knows them and is important to them.

When asked what opportunities they have for self-exploration and self-definition, students give two answers. First, they emphasize, as do their parents, that there is a great deal of respect for divergent opinions in the school. They are encouraged to express themselves, to explore their thoughts and opinions, and to discuss them with adults who are open and not threatened by contradiction. (The emphatic and enthusiastic parental insistence on this encouragement of dissent casts a disquieting light on other schools their children have attended.) Second, students say that counseling about careers and college "helps me think about myself as an individual."

While Title I funds for a careers program have been cut and Michigan has banned sex education courses, the guidance counselor gives informal seminars and counseling sessions in these areas of self-awareness. He teaches both students and parents about what they can expect during adolescence, stressing physical changes, social acceptability in the peer group, dating, and sexuality. He also does small group work with eighth-graders getting ready for high school. Mostly, given a guidance staff of 1 and a student body of 420, he does preventive counseling in the halls, in the auditorium, at the buses, in the lavatory, and during lunch. ("Don't tell kids what to do. They have enough of that at home. Teach them how to solve problems." Students say he does.)

The building was not planned for physical activity, a need during early adolescence that the school cannot be responsive to, to everyone's deep frustration. Small and outmoded, geared to elementary-school children's size and activities, it is completely inappropriate for young adolescents' physical size and perpetual movement. Classrooms are small and inflexible. Three rooms' worth of science equipment is crammed, along with students, into one small classroom. A potter's wheel and kiln are used in a storage closet. Reading kits are stored in a staff lavatory, because scores of library books that cannot fit in the library are displayed in already overcrowded classrooms. There is no room for privacy or for one-on-one student-teacher conferences. Old, dingy classrooms in need of paint resist personalization by teachers and students. The small gymnasium must be turned over to food services during lunchtime. The auditorium is too small to hold the entire student body. Lunchtime and period breaks are therefore noisy by design. Mr. Washington encourages as much expenditure of energies as is safe because of the extreme limitations on movement.

Students have PE only one session a year. SWIST and 5th session offer many supplements to PE to give as many students as possible at least one period per week of physical activity. They cannot rely on extracurricular sports because the Board of Education cut intermural athletics from budgets. In addition, there are no activity buses for after-school intramurals. Some students stay late on Fridays for basketball, if they can arrange transportation. For most students the school day affords few opportunities to be physically expressive.

The Community

Despite its dismal building, Region 7 Middle School is a spirited, zestful place. Students are anything but subdued; they are enthusiastic and friendly. The school's climate is achieved through careful planning for young adolescents in an urban environment. Students at Region 7 Middle School are curious about everything a visitor wears and carries. They ask where a pair of suede boots was bought, compete to borrow a razor-point felt-tipped pen for the day (it is scrupulously returned before dismissal), comment on a velvet jacket, or just stare in well-meaning silence. In gymnastics (Stunts), while four girls wear leotards, tights, and leg warmers, and one boy wears a warm-up suit, the remaining thirty students wear regular street clothes. In the halls students are neatly and simply dressed, some in thin cotton clothes in a nineteen-degree January snowstorm.

The cafeteria serves 190 free lunches to 45 percent of the students. Parents are predominantly factory workers, many suffering from layoffs in the automobile industry. Among the parents are two doctors, several attorneys, five or six ministers, police officers, fire fighters, and city employees. Most of the parents live in depressed areas. Approximately 15 percent attended or graduated from college. Close to half did not graduate from high school.

Because it is a magnet school with an institutional commitment to heterogeneity, Region 7 Middle School is not in an inner-city neighborhood; it is in a residential area with tracts of small private houses and handkerchief-size lawns. Many houses are for sale, some because of "White flight" but most because of factory layoffs. There are few neighborhood children among the students, most of whom are bused from a variety of other neighborhoods serving the fifteen elementary schools and six other middle schools in the region.

The school is small, so the stories of children who are victims of their childhood are widely known. There is the girl who saw her father shoot her mother and then her uncle shoot her father. There is the girl who was sexually abused by her mother as an infant. There is the girl who is living with her grandmother but is wanted by neither the latter nor her mother. Like all other Proud Lake campers, she wrote a letter from camp to her mother. When the mother was called to go to school to pick up the letter, she said that the girl lived with her grandmother. When the grandmother was called, she said: "She wrote the letter to her mother." The girl and the letter remained unclaimed.

Over 50 percent of the students come from single-parent families. Mr. Washington, in whose previous school the figure was 84 percent, has little patience with parents or students who use family status as an excuse for failure of responsibility or achievement: "The bottom line is, if you do not achieve, you do not succeed. You don't get the job, no matter what your excuse is."

School Climate

Region 7 Middle School has established a climate that encourages students to work hard and succeed. When asked how the school feels, one student answered: "It feels smart. We're smart. Look at our test scores." Most students address their answers to another aspect of the school's climate: the safe, energetic environment in which an integrated group of students play, create, and learn together. How does the school feel? "It feels friendly, not scary. The only thing I'm afraid of are the [caged] rats in the science lab!" "We don't need guards or IDs. It's small and the trips and IST help us get to know each other." "It feels enthusiastic. We take part in lots of contests." "It's not like other schools. There's too much fighting there, and police, and you can't give your opinion to the teacher. There's no fighting here. We have a chance to meet people." "It's different, not like other schools. It feels integrated."

Students point to the school's logo as the symbol of the school: "Everyone working together." Students, parents, teachers, and administrators all identify the biracial student body and staff as the core of the school. They fear that once again the ratio of Black to White will be raised and they will lose their identity. Every activity in the school must be integrated, every square in square dancing, table in the lunchroom, study group in classrooms, everything. When the principal sees several instances of single-race groupings in classrooms, he puts a notice up on the teachers' bulletin board: "If we let it happen, we're perpetuating it."

There is another striking symbol of the school's norms. In this old, deprived school—70 percent Black, predominantly poor, with students whose siblings and friends go to, and who themselves have gone and may return to schools that are armed camps where students carry knives and police cannot keep order—there are no locks on the lockers. It is a stunning accomplishment. A new visitor to the school can easily conclude that perhaps lockers are unused because, as happens in some troubled schools, students have been locked in them. But then the students tumble out of the classrooms, casually open the lockers, and trade books no longer needed for the next class. "No, the lockers aren't locked. We try to show each other respect," explains a student. Some students in the school could open anything, says Mr. Washington. Locks made no sense. An honor system did. As Geraldine Kozberg says of the Boston schools: "The streets our kids come from are tougher than we are."[4] Region 7 Middle School established an environment that breaks dramatically with those streets.

Their job was easier than many other schools' because parents sign up their children for the middle school. As one teacher says: "Any parent that would wait in line at the Region 7 office and race to get an application in the mail is a special parent. Very few are not supportive of the school, because they are here voluntarily. That makes the school special." Also, students can withdraw from the school. Each year, several "superflies," as the guidance counselor calls them, spend an unhappy first week or two of school trying to get attention for "macho" behavior. When they learn that the school has no basketball team, is serious about academics, and discourages toughness ("leave it home," says Mr. Washington—"there's plenty of time, no one is here to get married or have babies; let go of it, no one needs to have a reputation here"), they transfer back to their regularly assigned school. The school loses eight to ten students per year that way. Self-selection by parents and students eliminates the chance of a sizable subculture of students who stand in opposition to the school's norms and expectations.

The size of the school is also an asset. While everyone would like the school to be larger so that its program could be richer and more students might benefit from it, the size of the school allows for an intimate environment in which every student is known. As one paraprofessional says: "We know their moods. We know when someone is having a bad day and how to approach the situation. This is a family setting, I guess." Or as Mr. Washington says: "We know who we have to hug every so often and who we should never touch." On a somewhat more negative but equally honest note, teachers point out that the building is so small that there is no place to hide.

Being a school with integration as a guiding sense of purpose has also helped the school. It stands for something, explicitly and sometimes defiantly. The joint sense of purpose brings school staff and parents together. Students hear the same messages at home as at school. Their school experience gains the coherence that so many undefined schools cannot offer. The school stands for a concrete social value, and they can stand with it.

Standards of consideration and human decency are upheld for teachers as well as students. The teachers who started the school with Miss Fisher were all volunteers. They believed deeply in its purpose and values, set the tone of the school with Miss Fisher, and introduced each new teacher to the school's norms. One teacher says that the openness with which students can discuss teachers' behavior with Mr. Washington motivates them to uphold the school's values. In addition, Mr. Washington, while praising any sign of extra energy and sacrifice, will also refuse to support a teacher who is insolent to a student: "One teacher complained that a student was disrespectful to her. It turned out that she had told the student he had Down's Syndrome. He looked it up in the dictionary and was hurt. I did not talk to him about the incident. Instead, I asked her what she did to get his respect." (There is an interesting sidelight here: he looked it up in the dictionary.) Students say they obey the rules "because of our parents, because of Mr. Washington, and because we know they're right." They say obeying rules is "a habit." It ensures them a safe school with trust, and they will do almost anything not to lose that. "They don't want a scary school," says the guidance counselor.

Students ask a visitor what the worst thing she has seen in other schools is.

> She tells them about a junior high school in Indianapolis where there are guards in the halls with handcuffs attached to their belts and a teacher in the cafeteria who threatens students with a paddle to get them quiet: "I've got this new paddle and I'm just aching to use it on someone." The next day, students are discussing why they obey rules: "Because we don't want to be like the school in Indianapolis," one says.

The rules are printed in a handbook and reviewed in assembly. Everyone knows them: "No fighting, cursing, stealing, talking back to teachers, going to other students' lockers"; "no gum chewing . . . some let us break this one"; "discuss your problems before they get serious"; "be responsible for yourself"; "help other people."

> Five students approach Mr. Washington in the halls with a problem: "Mr. Washington, we are a committee." Everything in his schedule stops to resolve their crisis. They go to his office. There has been a fight between two girls. Three boys have accompanied them to testify for Priscilla, a tall girl who looks very unhappy. "Who is the spokesman?" Mr. Washington asks. A boy starts recounting the story with great seriousness. Edie, a tiny girl half Priscilla's height, called Priscilla "Godzilla." Priscilla was angry. One of the boys told Edie not to call names. Edie pushed Priscilla. The boys and Priscilla told her to stop. Edie called Priscilla all kinds of names. She used "the 'F' word" and "the 'SH' word" and said things about Priscilla's mother. Edie sits on a chair swinging her legs, showing no emotion. Mr. Washington asks if anyone has anything to add. Another boy starts recounting the story. Mr. Washington asks him to think about the question. Is he adding anything? No. Mr. Washington thanks them for being Priscilla's friend and for not getting involved by calling names. They leave. Mr. Washington asks Priscilla if she has anything she wants to say. She just wants to point out that she did not hit back or call any names back. Mr. Washington asks Edie if she wants to add anything in her defense. She shakes her head and swings her legs. Mr. Washington compliments Priscilla for coming to him with the problem and for realizing that Edie wasn't really talking about her mother. Priscilla leaves.

> Mr. Washington talks about how important people's names are to them. It hurts people to be teased about their names. "You have made a real problem for yourself today. It's a bad day." He asks Edie what her problem is now, according to Detroit's behavior code. Edie starts to cry softly. Her legs are now still. "Exclusion," she says, as she cries. Mr. Washington tells her she could have solved the problem better. "Couldn't you have done better with your job today?" Edie nods. She is weeping. Mr. Washington says they will look forward to her return to school. He knows she will have better days. He dismisses her to wait in the central office while he does the paper work for sending her home.

A DORT reading resource teacher who works in several schools comments about this incident: it would be so minor in another school that it would not make it to the front office. It would be luxurious to consider this a crisis.

This incident reveals several aspects of the school's norms. The rules are clear and they are uniformly enforced. Students do not hesitate to cooperate with rule enforcement; they initiate it. Personal choice and responsibility are emphasized. Internal locus of control is reinforced, as is group support for school norms. Acts have consequences and students must pay for their acts. Edie has had a bad day in which she has made bad choices. This tiny, angelic-looking girl has emptied herself of every four-letter word she knows. She is not bad; her choices are. When she returns, she can make different choices. Looking at her misery, one wishes for a reprieve. "It isn't sad," says the principal. "It would be sad if no one cared. To bend the rules would undermine the school and betray her."

- Students are expected to involve themselves in the total school program and avail themselves of all services provided.
- Students are expected to respect the rights and responsibilities of other students and staff members as they perform their duties.
- Students are expected to ask for assistance when needed.
- Students are expected to seek satisfactory answers to their questions and adequate assistance in pursuing their special interests and aspirational goals.
- Students are expected to seek help in solving personal problems.
- Students are expected to develop and utilize their talents. [Excerpted from "Student Handbook," Region 7 Middle School.]

Mr. Washington is a tall, commanding figure. When he stands in the upstairs corridor, students say he can see everyone and everything. He is soft-spoken and very firm. He is the school disciplinarian. When three teachers are absent on one day (a quarter of the staff) and there is only one substitute, some students give the PE substitute trouble. Mr. Washington talks to them about cooperation. It is a low-voiced but intense lecture: "All that is asked of you in this situation is cooperation. I expect it of you, and I know it is easy." It is. He conveys to students his rationale for discipline: they need to learn to live in society with one another by adjusting their behavior so that they do not take away one another's rights. "You must respect one another. That is the source of all rules." He is always in the halls, heading off trouble: "John, is there a problem?" he asks of a boy who is becoming a bit high-handed with another student. "No." There will not be a problem. The students respect and admire Mr. Washington. An athlete, he can teach them tennis, swimming, and football. He makes the school safe, fair, and enjoyable. Their parents back him to the hilt. "Mr. Washington is proud of us," students say, and they know they are right.

The positive climate of the school is enhanced by the presence of fifth-graders. Miss Fisher argued that fifth-graders give stability to the school. Given the fluctuations in maturity during pre- and early adolescence, she argued, having fifth-graders gives a greater range from immaturity to maturity for students to identify with. They do not have to grow up so quickly. Mr. Washington adds several points. With four grades instead of three, one-quarter of the students changes yearly instead of one-third, making the school more stable. Also, norms are set and students identify with them before they are full-fledged adolescents who need to hold themselves aloof from adults. In addition, "it takes four years to raise their skill level." The school needs the extra year to teach skills and bring up students' performance. Having fifth-graders makes the tone more academic because the teachers are more successful in meeting the school's instructional goals.

Finally, school climate is set by teachers who are dedicated to working with these students. One teacher whose background is in secondary education says she does not want to teach in a high school. She finds it depressing. There is too much cutting; no one cares: "In the middle school, you get kids who don't want to learn and you can do something with them. They get something from you." Students know the teachers care about them. "They write 'Welcome back' on the blackboard Monday morning." "Teachers take time to help. They teach. In fifth hour, if you don't know something, teachers help you." "In other schools teachers just want to get their paychecks and go home. Here, teachers want to teach." There are clear payoffs for all the hard work, for teachers and students alike. High test scores (after fifth grade, the highest in the region) and numerous prizes reinforce the implicit bargain that schools make: if students will buy into the value system of the school, the school will make them academically successful. Region 7 Middle School makes good on the bargain.

Parent choice, school size, rational rules, high standards for teacher and student behavior, a principal who is an admirable role model and disciplinarian, younger students in the school, low student turnover, teacher dedication, academic payoffs, a central purpose that the school stands for—all play their role in setting the tone of Region 7 Middle School. The "inner-city middle-school syndrome" which, according to the guidance counselor, consists in part of "superflies, supermachos, superpretties, superlovers," is foreign to the school. " 'Sorry,' we say, 'you are here to learn.' " They learn in an atmosphere totally alien to the school one girl came from, which she characterizes in two words: "locks, guards." They learn, as another girl says, because "here we respect ourselves as individuals." It is an environment crafted to their needs in which they are valued and which they in turn value.

The social environment of Region 7 Middle School is like "the transforming experiment" that, according to Urie Bronfenbrenner, Soviet psychologists speak of—an experiment "that radically restructures the environment, producing a new configuration that activates previously unrealized behavioral potential of the subject." Bronfenbrenner describes a "transforming" ecological experiment, "The Robbers' Cave Experiment," in which M. Sherif and his colleagues "were able, within the space of a few weeks, to produce radical changes in the behavior of a group of middle-class, eleven-year-old boys involved in an experimental camp. By altering the structure of activities and social organization, they first evoked high levels of aggression bordering on sadism, and then transformed the same boys into friendly, cooperative, altruistic citizens. This outcome was achieved through setting an objective best epitomized by the classic statement of Vince Lombardi, coach of the world-champion Green Bay Packers: 'Winning isn't everything; it's the *only* thing.' Hatred was [then] transformed into harmony by what Sherif et al. called 'pursuit of a superordinate goal.' For example, the water supply to the camp was turned off and a call went out for volunteers to find an alleged leak in the mile-long water line."[5]

Region 7 Middle School is the equivalent of a "transforming experiment." The "structures of activities and social organization" have been altered to serve a specific population of students, young adolescents from various neighborhoods in Detroit, so as to elicit cooperative, productive, harmonious behavior. The school's highest value is cooperation. It pursues a "superordinate goal," integration. The school epitomizes the nobility and fragility of a larger "transforming experiment"—the American commitment to universal public education.

Meeting the Nonnegotiables

Region 7 Middle School meets the nonnegotiable threshold criteria with ease. Students in fifth grade score third in the region on the CAT reading test, at the national mean of 5.7. After that, they score first in the region. In eighth grade, where the national mean is 8.7 and the regional mean 7.7, their composite score is 9.2. The results are similar in math. Students in fifth grade score second in the region; thereafter, they are first. In the Michigan Education Assessment Program, students score above average in reading but below the state average in math. (The school's math teachers are pressing for homogeneous grouping in math to serve mathematically gifted students more effectively.)

The school's success does not go unnoticed by private schools in nearby affluent suburbs like Grosse Pointe. Many of the school's Black students are recruited into private schools after graduation on partial or full scholarships. Seventy percent of the White students return to private schools. Many other students are recruited into Detroit's two specialized public high schools, Renaissance High School, a college preparatory school that accepts only honor students, and the Selective Class Technical High School. This remarkable academic success is a mixed blessing for the school. Of the 2,450 students in one of the district high schools, 1,200 are freshmen; only 250 graduate. The school never gets most of the finest students that Region 7 Middle School produces, making the middle school that much more politically vulnerable in the region.

Average daily attendance (1980–81) is 98 percent, much higher than the city's average of 74.1 percent, the region's average of 87.3 percent, the region's middle schools' average of 87.2 percent, and even the region's elementary schools' average of 90.8 percent. School attendance is particularly high on Fridays, a quiet tribute to the success of SWIST. There were fewer than five incidents of vandalism in 1979–80, an extremely low figure in the city. Out-of-school suspensions, or "exclusions" in Detroit's lexicon, numbered 26 in 1979–80, again, a low figure in Detroit. In four years, there have been 2 suspensions (meaning that students may not return to the school) and no expulsions (meaning that students are removed from the system). From September through January 1981 there were 33 exclusions because of insubordination, classroom disruptions, fights, cursing, and similar offenses, including 4 repeaters, in contrast to exclusions that numbered in the hundreds in other Detroit middle schools. The school uses exclusion to force the parents to come in. Truancy rates are very low. The principal and the guidance counselor go to homes—"Mama, get your child out of bed"—or telephone—"Get out of bed and come to school. You can't learn as well at home."

Parent satisfaction can be documented by the continuing support parents give the school during political battles and the waiting list of families wanting their children to attend. Parents say there are two changes in the nature of the waiting list. First, it has gotten smaller as the school has suffered continuing loss of program. Second, some parents are now sending their children to the school to avoid busing. "They come here so as not to go to another school," said one parent, "instead of coming here for an interracial experience." Parents give testimonials to the school:

> My child would have been a dropout. In elementary school, his teacher said to me: "That child isn't going to give you anything but heartaches." He had perfect attendance here. He didn't want to miss a day. Summer vacation was too long and boring. Now he's majoring in communications at the University of Texas. He got here and all of a sudden, someone cared for him. I had been getting notes about Roger every other day, with threats about exclusion. Here, the first note said: "It's just a joy to have him in the classroom."

> My kids say it was the best school they were in. It was a new experience, an outlet for them. Every teacher was interested in children. In other schools,

there's rigid discipline. Children can't express themselves. Here, if they see something wrong, they speak up. Someone always has time for you. There aren't too many students, so there's time. No one says, "This one is dumb, this one is smart." And there's a variety of things to do and choose. It's not boring because of the rotation of teachers. Five parents have taken their kids out of school. They say it's too hard and they can't keep up. That's a copout. They just need to get involved and help.

Parents are aware that teachers make real sacrifices to remain in the school. Half the staff have taught more than ten years, one-third five to nine years. Two-thirds have been in the school for most or all of its life. They are highly credentialed. All have course work beyond the B.A. One-third have M.A.'s, one-quarter have course work beyond the M.A. One has a doctorate. Their allegiance to the school is powerful. The guidance counselor did not take a job at the high school four miles from his house. He commutes twenty miles to the middle school because "it is like a family, and kids' needs are greater here." Several teachers come from suburbs of entitlement and privilege to Region 7. They feel they have something to offer the students. Parents agree: "The teachers give a lot of time. When someone devotes that much time, you feel you have to care about your child."

A home-school coordinator, part of a citywide project, calls 15 parents daily, goes into the home, makes personal contacts, help parents teach reading and handwriting, and asks them to go to meetings to show they care. Paraprofessionals called 79 parents to come to school to get the letters students had written home from Proud Lake. "Parents were so thankful. They thought it was great. The school does that extra bit for parents." One parent exclaims: "This school is such an improvement over other schools. Why should there even be a question over what will happen to it?"

Region 7 Middle School is small. It does not have an extensive reputation. It is the sister school of a better-known magnet middle school in another region, the Ludington School, a modern facility in a middle-class neighborhood with strong administrative backing from the regional superintendent and school board. Some of the original staff from Region 7 Middle School are now at Ludington, whose teachers have received in-service training from Region 7 Middle School staff. Even in Region 7, however, despite the regional superintendent's hostility toward the school, a high-level administrator in the regional office affirms the fine, if quiet, reputation of the school and its excellence: "It is an exemplary school. If I were superintendent, that would be my school."

Self-Evaluation

The staff of Region 7 Middle School evaluates itself frequently. They are very articulate about the school's shortcomings. Some worry about the academically gifted in the school; there is not much to "try the soul" of a gifted student in the school. Students are challenged more deeply in the area of social behavior than academics. Camping "tried the soul," as do some of the contests. Everyday classes do not. Mr. Washington worries about "fast-tracking" students in math, which math teachers want. The staff members have "good arguments," according to several teachers, about homogeneous grouping, giftedness, and special education. Some teachers are also unhappy with the school's dependence on test scores as indicators of effectiveness. They set their own criteria of mastery, in both academics and behavior among students and between students and adults.

At end of 1980–81, teachers rewrote part of the school's philosophy, looking at the school "ten years later." They want cross-age tutoring and more out-of-school activities and services. A teacher was assigned to be in charge of special activities. After the reassignment of St. David's to another middle school, teacher morale was very low. They lacked the psychic energy to think creatively about the school. By year's end, reaffirming and rewriting portions of the philosophy, they recommitted themselves to the school's ideals.

Mr. Washington is the school's harshest critic: "It's a good school, but not the best. It's partially successful." He wants 90 percent of students performing at grade level. He wants more learning beyond the building. Some of the teachers, he says, "come from regimented schools. They weren't trained in alternative education. It's a problem for some of them. They don't know what kids can do." He wants teachers visiting alternative schools elsewhere "so they can be amazed by what kids can do. Ask of kids, and they'll give."

Mr. Washington is too impatient with the school to say that it exemplifies what is best in American education: "It's not excellent. There are too many things that have to be done." But he knows they are on the right track, unlike most other schools in the city: "In Detroit, no one really knows what kids can do. They have low expectations about everyone succeeding and inadequate definitions of success." Also, "they haven't sold kids on the value of education. They haven't made schooling relevant to them. Kids are exposed to gangs, drugs, pregnancy. They need to be taken out to *see* the skills it takes to work and to pass competitive exams. Schools need to break away from control and lesson plans, get out of the classroom and out of the building."

Leadership

Region 7 Middle School is an innovative school responding to the needs of young adolescents in a whirlwind of political hostility, budget cuts, and a loss of societal commitment to the school's central purpose, racial integration. The hassles are never-ending. Teachers learn that 1,000 teachers in the system will get pink slips before the end of the school year. Despite deep cuts, there may not be money to keep schools open. The system is recentralizing after decentralizing. There is only one substitute for three absent teachers. Two groups need the auditorium at the same time because there is no other place for students to meet in groups. Though the school is dependent on candy sale income for out-of-school activities, the staff must buy candy from an expensive source—one person who has exclusive rights as sole supplier of candy for Detroit schools' candy sales. The budget was cut more than 34 percent for texts and supplies in all schools between 1979–80 and 1980–81. It was cut again at Region 7 Middle School by 20 percent in 1981–82. The budget is set by staff downtown in the central city offices, based on enrollment. The catch is that the enrollment figure is also set downtown. The 1981–82 budget is based on 409 students, but the school has more students. There is no adjustment upward when new students are accepted. Adjustment is always downward. It takes over a year to get a dryer vented in the home economics room. The fire marshal fines Mr. Washington because the "art gallery" of student art in the main entrance is a fire hazard. Students want to paint the dingy walls of the building, but the Board of Education says they may not do so because of liability and union contracts. "We'll get around to you," they say. They have not gotten to the building in over thirteen years.

The school has an annual Get Acquainted Dance at the beginning of each school year. Eighth-graders chaperone fifth-graders throughout the class day, going to classes together and then meeting for cookies and punch at the dance. The fire marshal shows up annually because there are "too many people in the gymnasium." This very same room is the cafeteria that holds all these students legally, daily. It is legal when the tables are open and the room is a cafeteria. It is illegal when there are no tables and the room is a gymnasium or social hall. "I must fine you," says the marshal. "I know you have to and I understand it," Mr. Washington responds ("and I paid the $50 from my pocket and it's worth it").

People are divided into three groups: those who make things happen, those who watch things happen, and those who wonder what happened.

One person with a belief is equal to a force of ninety-nine who have only interests.

O Lord, help me to reform the world—beginning with me. [Quotations in principal's office, Region 7 Middle School.]

An industrial arts teacher is grossly incompetent. Mr. Washington wants to fire him because he is dangerous. He fears there will be a serious accident. Because of the union contract, the teacher cannot be fired. Mr. Washington eliminates industrial arts as a course, offering it only during Independent Study Time, to get rid of the teacher. A year later, when he wants to hire a new industrial arts teacher, the man he tried to fire is back in the pool; he is the only person available.

We will persist. And we will not deny this opportunity or responsibility to provide access to a humane and just education for all the leftout kids in the leftout schools. To do so would be to break with the most fundamental ideals of the American heritage. [Geraldine Kozberg, "Leftout Kids in a Leftout School."]

Permission must be obtained from the regional and downtown offices for every special activity, even if it is an annual event: camping, skiing, tennis, trips to judges' chambers, to local hospitals, to Chrysler and Chevrolet plants. . . Through it all, like so many other excellent principals, Mr. Washington fights for his school and gets to paperwork only after students' needs. The most outstanding aspect of his leadership style is his utter seriousness. Mr. Washington does not do things because they make him look good or are popular. He does them because they are right. His passionate sense of social justice is thoroughly practical: he wants the youngsters in his school to have every opportunity to live out the American dream. Each decision he makes—whether to force the issue about camping at Proud Lake, to spend money on trophies, to lead parents in marching on the school board, to defy the fire marshal, to praise or censure a teacher or a child—is based on what appears to be his unending reservoir of hope and indignation.

Like other successful principals, Mr. Washington is politically suave when he can be but a rebel when conscience demands. He is no one's pal but everyone's associate, including the students who revere, fear, and admire him. Everyone knows where he stands on breaking out of the strictures of a dessicated curriculum, constant vigilance about integration, absolute respect for children and adults alike, and careful reinforcement of children's curiosity and responsibility. At the same time that he can articulate the vision of the school, he is a practical manager of human energies. No one receives greater praise than a teacher who does something special, beyond contractual duties, to enlarge the world of the students. At the same time,

Mr. Washington knows his teachers well enough to limit the numbers of pressures they themselves add to those already heaped upon them.

Mr. Washington inherited a school whose strengths he fights to keep and whose weaknesses he seeks to overcome. Off-the-record comments from a high-level school administrator and a teacher in another region indicate that the prognosis for Region 7 Middle School is not good: "Region 7 Middle School is in trouble because the superintendent doesn't understand and is threatened. The community fought hard for the principal, who had an excellent reputation in his previous school. The superintendent doesn't like that," one says. "The picture looks bad," says the other. "A school like Region 7 Middle School needs 1,000 percent approval from top administration. It doesn't have it. The school is threatening. It's a question of personalities, status worries, and politics." Parents and teachers say the school is politically unviable because it succeeds.

Whatever its eventual outcome, Region 7 Middle School answers several important questions. Are successful schools replicable? While the middle school has its own tempestuous history, parents, administrators, teachers, and students see nothing unique about the school. The key, they say, is not in being a magnet school. If the school were not voluntary, the job would be harder. Parents and staff say that the school would then respond to that new set of demands. This is the right school for this mandate and this constituency. The key is attitude. Mr. Washington says: "We believe we *can*. A school can have this building and this budget but still succeed. It's all attitude. I don't care about politics. I care about here. We can and will do well. The rest makes my job harder, that's all. But it makes me stronger."

Conclusion

Does effectiveness mean the same thing across all populations of students? People at Region 7 Middle School restate the question: What is required of schools in different social contexts for effectiveness? It is the restatement of the question that gives the school its instructional and political power. Region 7 Middle School is not "oriented to some generally accepted concept of what a school is (a school is a school)."[6] It is a school that breaks out of the mold. The goals, organization, scheduling, curriculum, and norms of the school have been deliberately selected because of the nature of the young adolescent age group and the lives of the students outside of school. It is an effective school because it does *not* do slavishly what other schools do, even other effective schools. Effective schools that are responsive to early adolescent development, then, are mavericks. This quality can put them in jeopardy. As a result, some may ultimately be unsuccessful—that is, political acceptance is not assured. They may lack the staying power that more conventional schools are automatically granted.

Do successful schools for young adolescents practice well what is best in American education or move dramatically away toward new definitions of schooling? There is no way that Region 7 Middle School can respond to its multiple mandates and be "a school that is a school that is a school." It is a magnet school established to promote school desegregation; it is a school created to serve a diverse but predominantly economically deprived clientele; it is an alternative school whose essence is attentiveness to the developmental needs of a diverse group of pre- and young adolescents. A school that takes these three mandates seriously must redefine mainstream schooling for young adolescents in America. Lack of administrative and financial support have damaged and curtailed, but not quelled, the quiet revolution of Region 7 Middle School.

Finally, does it all come down to the principal? Is the key to successful schools a strong leader with vision, clarity of purpose, well-defined priorities, firm and fair discipline, administrative savvy, community status, and boundless energy? The principal is *a* key; but school success cannot be achieved by one person, nor is one person irrevocably essential to a school's success. Dorothy Fisher, the driving and defining force behind Region 7 Middle School, seemed irreplaceable but was successfully replaced. Whether Region 7 Middle School can withstand two such losses in its particular set of circumstances is doubtful. Essential, however, is not the principal, but the productive marriage of principal and external circumstances. That luck plays a role is irrefutable. That principals wring from circumstances every bit of benefit for their schools is also true. Both Edward R. Murrow and Shakespeare are correct about fortune: "Goodnight and good luck" and "The fault, dear Brutus, is not in our stars, but in ourselves."

A school can be successful on a shoestring budget if it and its community have deep convictions about the purposes of schooling that infuse every aspect of the school day. In a time of cost-cutting and sparse budgets, other schools will need to learn, as Region 7 Middle School has, that achieving quality in education without money is more difficult, but possible. The story of Region 7 Middle School is, ironically, an optimistic story. Despite seemingly insurmountable political and financial barriers, adults are carving out an environment in which young adolescents learn, thrive, and exemplify what is best in American values.[7]

Notes

1.   Dorothy Fisher, "It Can Be Done: The Five-Year Story of an Integrat-

ed, Innovative, Alternative Middle School" (Detroit, Mich.: mimeo-graphed, 1976).

2. Ibid.

3. Charity James, *Beyond Customs: An Educator's Journey* (New York: Schocken, 1974):46.

4. Geraldine Kozberg, "Left Out Kids in a Left Out School," *Harvard Graduate School of Education Association Bulletin* 25 (Fall 1980): 26.

5. Urie Bronfenbrenner, "Toward an Experimental Ecology of Human Development," *American Psychologist* (July 1977):528–29.

6. John I. Goodlad and Frances M. Klein and Associates, *Behind the Classroom Door* (Belmont, Cal.: Wadsworth, 1970):79.

7. After a concerted effort of parents, students, and staff, Detroit's Central Board of Education approved a name change for Region 7 Middle School. As of September 8, 1981, the school's name is the Dorothy L. Fisher Magnet Middle School.

5

"Noe Place like Noe"

Samuel V. Noe Middle School
Louisville, Kentucky

If I were at Noe, I wouldn't be rioting. Teachers really care about kids at Noe.

—*Student after high-school race riot*

Noe Middle School should not work. The teachers and principal of Noe were assigned by order of the 6th Circuit Federal Court. The school district was gerrymandered so radically to meet racial balance guidelines that Noe has no neighborhood. The school's catchment area is the second lowest in income in the school system, 26th out of 27. It has the second highest number of students receiving free lunches. The student body is heterogeneous in the extreme. Students from the entire school system who are of middle-school age, scheduled to be bused, and also academically gifted, are sent to Noe for one mandatory year of busing. A large number of hearing-impaired and orthopedically handicapped students from nearby Indiana and other Kentucky school districts are sent to Noe for its special education services. The school board started an alternative program for students who have been suspended from other schools in the district to give them one last chance before court-ordered institutionalization. Noe is one of four schools selected to receive these students, some of whom have threatened principals with guns. The transience of the students in and out of the school district leads to traumatic reassignment of teachers. The hiring and firing of teachers are regulated by their militant union contract.

The school is large. It has over 1,000 students in an open-plan, two-story building, in a city that is hostile to schools without walls. It is hard to imagine who thought of putting over 1,000 sixth-, seventh-, and eighth-graders in a wide open building. It is even harder to imagine adding a large number of handicapped students, students assigned to a special program because of their demonstrated hostility to other schools, 100 academically gifted students who are required to take one class daily at a nearby high school, and a group of 20 students specializing in the performing arts who spend only half a day at Noe and the rest at the Youth Performing Arts Schools next door. To ask teachers and administrative staff, who are in the building because of court-ordered assignment, to take on the task of making this into a school, is to invite chaos. Nor is everything going well outside the school:

> Friday, February 13, 1981, the sewers explode near the Ralston Purina plant, leaving a crater twenty feet deep and twelve feet wide. Roads are destroyed, cutting a large housing project off from the rest of the city. The National Guard is called in to block off 2nd Street. It may cave in. No one can get into the Noe Middle School parking lot without a special pass. The school has no water for washing dishes or taking showers. Everyone is on evacuation alert. If a hard rain comes, they will alter their bus routes and attend another school from 1:30–8:00 p.m. Several students say they are having trouble sleeping because of nightmares. A student is asked if there is anything she is afraid of at school: "I'm afraid about the sewer exploding again and 2nd Street falling in."

There is nothing untoward to fear inside Noe Middle School. It is a school that works.

Meeting the Nonnegotiables

Approximately 40 percent of the students come from single-parent families; close to 20 percent live with a parent and stepparent. Many live in families where both parents work by necessity, not choice. One-fifth of the parents have no schooling beyond eighth grade and another one-quarter have only some high-school education. Approximately 5 percent graduated from college. Parents are predominantly blue-collar workers. The annual income of 35 percent of the parents is under $5,000; 35 percent earn between $5,000 and $16,000; 20 percent earn between $16,000 and $20,000; 10 percent earn over $20,000.

Noe Middle School meets all the threshold criteria this study has used as minimal indicators of school effectiveness. Achievement test scores are at the district mean. Students' scores on the California Test of Basic Skills show a positive discrepancy between predicted and actual scores. In 1974 the students' scores fell in the first through third stanines. They now average in the fifth stanine, with a narrowing range of disparity in performance. Because of its consistent annual gain in performance, the school is able to use scores to fight off back-to-basics proponents.

Welcome to the Noe Middle School. Noe Middle School, which opened its doors in October 1974, was named in honor of Samuel V. Noe, who served as superintendent of the Louisville Public Schools in 1960–69. Featuring an emphasis on flexibility through open educational areas and individualized scheduling, our school, which contains 145,000 square feet, was constructed at a total cost of $4,413,695. [Noe Middle School student information folder]

In 1974, the school's first year of operation, the daily absentee list was two pages long, single-spaced. Average daily attendance has risen from below 80 percent to 92–93 percent. The elementary and senior high schools next door to Noe have average daily attendance rates between 80 and 85 percent. Because teachers work independently on teams, there is a great deal of peer pressure against staff absenteeism. Teachers will come in even if sick to avoid collegial censure. They are more likely to be out for a workshop than a cold.

There are fewer than five incidents of vandalism annually, a figure much lower than in similar and neighboring schools. There are no rumbles or riots. The Noe Middle School is in an area that was planned as an educational park, next to the Youth Performing Arts School and close to the University of Louisville. The elementary and senior high schools in the park each had two incidents during 1979–80 when police were called in. Noe shows no sign of vandalism. The building is neat, relatively clean, and in good repair. There are no graffiti in the halls and very few in the bathrooms. When a teacher became upset about graffiti in one of the girls' rooms, the students went in and washed the walls. Ten students were suspended from school in 1979–80, the lowest number of suspensions in all district (Jefferson County) middle schools on a per-pupil basis.

It is difficult to gauge the extent of parental satisfaction, but there are signs of considerable support. Ninety percent of parents whose children are required to be bused for one year, in order to be in the Advanced Program for the academically gifted, elect to have their children stay at Noe for the two following years. They could enroll them in neighborhood schools where they would still be in an Advanced Program class. Every year, as these parents choose Noe, administrators of the system's Advanced Program are puzzled. According to several of the parents, while they were initially terrified of the neighborhood ("Lee and 2nd Street is the kiss of death") and irate over lengthy bus trips, they now appreciate the school's safety. Also, the school does not isolate their children in a completely tracked program. Most important, their children are performing well and have the advantage of the rich curricular and extracurricular programs offered all the students in the school. They add that their children would protest if they were transferred. They are looking forward to annual events in seventh and eighth grades like camping and social studies simulations. They do not want to miss them.

Another sign of parental satisfaction comes from the district PTA head who, while very hostile to the school's principal because there is no PTA at Noe, points out that "there is a great deal of smiling." Also, students say the school has a good reputation. They have friends who have tried to get in. "People talk good about it"; "visitors come all the time"; "there's no school I'd rather be in." Parents are satisfied because their children are happy. One mother summarizes her feelings: "My son comes home in a good mood."

The staff at Noe are not at all satisfied with the present level of parent involvement in the school. Parents serve on the School Advisory Council, a volunteer group that is very active at Noe and replaces the traditional PTA. Many parents feel free to walk in and out of the building all day. Teachers make frequent contact, especially calling about absences. "They don't let absenteeism get out of hand," one parent says. "Teachers call when they get concerned. In some schools you see more students leaving than coming in." But too many parents take no part in the school and, teachers fear, are more interested in the school as a baby-sitting agency than as a place for learning. Many staff members, including the principal, feel that parents care most that the school is safe, scores are improving, and their children seem happy.

Noe has a growing reputation for excellence. It has a superb band whose television appearances help Noe's good name. Its teams do well in interscholastic athletics. Its special education program is considered one of the best in the district. A school board member says that Noe is reputed to be one of the best schools in Jefferson County. The principal, he says, is held in high regard by the board members and other principals, who see him as an excellent instructional leader and an outstanding manager. The building is familiar to outsiders because it is used constantly for nonschool functions, both during the school day and as a community school before and after school hours. The board member says the school is a focal point for experimentation in the system.

Sometimes schools can point to one accomplishment or event that marked a turning point in the school's history. Noe can point to the satisfaction of one parent, which went far in establishing its reputation in Louisville as a good school. This parent, a school board member with a conservative voting record, had wanted assigned seats in the cafeteria, among other changes, to tighten up the school. Instead, her daughter was assigned to the school's first multiaged team, went on their first outdoor camping trip, and was in their first teacher-based guidance class (the administration is made up of risk-takers). Because of the mother's influence, the school will have a two-story music building. She now gives Noe the positive recognition it earned after four years of public inattention.

The head of the Student-Parent Aid and Resource Center (SPARC), a resource and advocacy center for parents supported by the American Friends Service Committee, wishes there were more schools like Noe. Students feel welcome and important, she says. They sense this is their school. Their paintings and crafts are up everywhere: "Just look at what's on the walls." Noe sees it as a plus that the school is so culturally, economically, and academically diverse, she says. The staff is able to adapt to this school population. They resist sorting and categorizing into tracks. The school is also atypical in its openness to parents. And, she says, the "unified enthusiasm" of the staff makes a big impression at public meetings, where a teacher, counselor, and administrator always speak for the school collectively.

No one outside Noe has given much thought to why it is an effective school. One board member, when asked why Noe is able to meet the threshold criteria, says that he honestly does not know. He feels it has something to do with the design of the building, perhaps being in the educational park complex, and the idiosyncratic personalities of the principal and staff. It is an answer that discourages the staff. They feel that while they are accepted as individuals, their school is not accepted as an institution.

School Organization

In most schools for young adolescents, whether middle schools, intermediate schools, junior high schools, or grades 7–12 senior highs, students are organized by grade level and teachers are organized by departments. Students appear for forty-five or fifty minutes in a teacher's classroom. Then a bell rings, and they all pour out into the corridors for a mad five minutes of sharing confidences, hair combing, slamming of locker doors, and racing to the next class. A bell rings to start another, and wholly unrelated, class. Each student's personality contributes whatever continuity there is to his or her school day. The teachers' disciplines give their day some semblance of continuity. Yet their days are even more fragmented and socially isolated than the students'. They wrest whatever meaning they can from their dedication to their area of specialty and, if their students are lucky, to them. The larger the school, the more hierarchical and centralized its bureaucracy, but the weaker the controls on teacher and student behavior.

The genius of Noe Middle School lies in its organizational structure, which is simple in concept and complex in realization. Noe Middle School is highly decentralized. It is the equivalent of seven semiautonomous schools. Teachers and students are organized in interdisciplinary teams. There are seven academic teams; four are multiaged and three have single grades. An eighth team, consisting of Unified Arts teachers (home economics, industrial arts, music, physical education, art, media, band, orchestra, Spanish, and independent study), serves the other seven teams. Each of the seven has four or five regularly certified teachers and two or three special education teachers. The school day is divided into two blocks of time, team time and unified arts. Team time includes reading, mathematics, language arts, science, social studies, teacher-based guidance, and Spanish (required by the county for Advanced Program students).

The administration consists of a principal, assistant principal, instructional coordinator, two guidance counselors, and a practical arts coordinator in charge of career awareness, field trips, speakers, and other school services. Known as the Supportive Service Team (SST), the administration tells each team when its planning, lunch, and unified arts time are. The teams schedule the rest of their day. They make all decisions about grouping their 150 students for skills, departmentalization, interdisciplinary units, establishing skill subteams, allocation of time, intramurals, teacher-based guidance, and, beyond thirteen schoolwide rules, team rules. Some teams ask the SST for schedule ideas; others say, "We thought you'd like to know our schedule." At Noe, teaching performance is not a function of personal qualities alone. It results from the joint efforts and sanctions of highly motivated and competitive groups. When teachers are asked what one aspect of the school represents Noe, they discuss the team structure.

While students are at lunch and in unified arts, the teachers have planning time, which they allocate once weekly to a joint team meeting. At one such team meeting, seven teachers are choosing themes for practical arts or career awareness, which is part of the guidance program for which each teacher has responsibility. There is lengthy discussion about whether to have two three-week clusters or one six-week cluster. The team leader gives powerful leadership to the group while repeating, "whatever you want to do. . ." A member of SST has come to share information about a student who has returned to his mother after having been in a halfway house. He reinforces good ideas that come up about the career clusters. The team decides to have one six-week cluster in the winter to increase depth. Then, when they offer another practical arts cluster in the spring, students will be able to elect both the topic and the length of time devoted to it. There is strong emphasis on making the choice of topics and the student groupings as diverse as possible to capture student interest and allow for positive peer influence.

> The best thing about teaching in this school is the team. I was in a junior high school, and I was completely isolated. We couldn't even talk about our students in the teachers' lounge because we didn't have the same students. The attitude there was, "we want to survive." [Noe Middle School teacher]

There are two aspects of this team meeting that stun people who have taught in other secondary schools. First, teachers are being acknowledged as professional adults who have the capacity to make decisions about curriculum, allocation of time, grouping of students, and student choice. One teacher comments: "We are given professional courtesies. We are professional people." Second, teachers are not alone. They discuss ideas together, reach group consensus, and have the support of the team for the humdrum and the adventuresome in the school day. Teaching is not a lonely profession at Noe.

At another team meeting, a guidance counselor reports that one of the team's students is being removed from school. After many other incidents, he was physically menacing to a teacher. There is no sense of relief at the removal of the student, who has been a constant source of disruption. Instead, the teachers are depressed by the news of what they see as their failure. The guidance counselor is available to them during the discussion. At Noe, teachers as well as students are acknowledged as having feelings.

> People work and behave better when they are well looked after and feel that those in charge understand and respond to their personal needs. [Michael Rutter et al., *Fifteen Thousand Hours.*]

The group turns to a request from the principal to help him make a decision. He asks them to recommend next year's allocation of teachers to teams. They are now a six-person team. There will be room for discretion in the assignment of an additional teacher. The principal is there to slip in his ideas about having either a Time-Out (in-school suspension) teacher or a drama teacher added to the staff. He also wants to institute a recess period for students. Teachers will deliberate at future team meetings and give him the team's recommendations. A student-teacher from the University of Louisville says whe was initially appalled, then terrified, by the amount of freedom teachers have at Noe. Now she loves it and worries about adjusting to another school. She says she will miss the constant exchange of ideas and careful planning for the team's mix of students. She is ambivalent about the pressure she feels when the whole team is working together on a unit. Perhaps she will not miss that.

Each team has its own distinct personality. One team is known for its excellent reading and intramural programs. Another is known for its social studies simulations. One stresses individualized work at "learning stations," another has more whole-class instruction. One graded team takes a traditional approach to basics, maintains a firm discipline system, constantly questions the academic purposes of its instructional practices, and functions in a thoroughly organized manner. Another graded team is more relaxed, stresses innovative teaching techniques, and values full-team interdisciplinary units more than departmental classes. A multiaged team has managed to pull itself together despite its having started three weeks into the school year. An underestimation of the number of students by the school board led to the emergency assignment of seven teachers at Noe. The overload of students and introduction of seven new teachers to the school's organizational structure caused considerable stress. By mid-year, the team was referred to as a "together" team by SST members, teachers, and students. This team is a happy blend of traditional and nontraditional teachers. They spend a great deal of time planning to maintain a constant mix of solo and team teaching.

While the school has a symbol, the cougar, each team has its own logo, symbolic of the strong identification both teachers and students feel with their teams. Students in multiaged teams are more likely to tell a visitor what team they are on than what grade they are in. The teachers' slogan for the year, "aggressive excellence," implies the competitive pressure to be the best team in the school. Rather than one collective identity at Noe, there are seven team identities.

The team structure is seen by school staff as the school's most important response not only to teacher anomie but to the nature of young adolescents. Charity James observes that "most open-space schools seem to add to a contagious sense of powerlessness."[1] At Noe, each student is primarily a member of a 150-person school. The teams are the equivalent of what Charity James calls "focus groups," in which "teachers can work together to look at each child individually."[2] In multiaged teams, students are in the same "focus group" for three years. They are known as individuals, not as sixth-, seventh-, or eighth-graders. There is no rigidly preconceived idea of what seventh grade or a seventh-grader is. Students in the three graded teams identify with a team for a year at a time, but they also anticipate the next graded team. They see themselves as being in a three-year sequence with the same group of students, if not teachers. They can also anticipate who their teachers will be.

Noe Middle School could be a formidable building for a young adolescent to negotiate. It takes new teachers and substitutes days to find their way—weeks, some say. Its 145,000 square feet are divided into two stories, but the library has five levels, the stairway to the gym is hard to find, the band is in a completely separate building, the divisions of space between the teams are not immediately apparent, and team space is allocated differently on the two floors.

A newcomer needs a map and a dictionary. Students have named the teams. The first multiaged team was called "MAT" (Multiaged Team). Now there are, in addition, MAST (Multiaged Super Team), MASS (Multiaged Super Stars), and MAP (Multiaged Plus). The graded teams are called 6:1, 7:1, and 8:1. Signs with these numbers and initials, plus logos, give some indication of where one is standing, if they can be found among all the student-made materials displayed on ceilings, room dividers, blackboards, and lockers. The walls of the enclosed science classrooms in each team area offer some respite from the initial impression of architectural chaos; they do not, however, help newcomers find their bearings.

Sixth-graders and other new students say they are not disturbed by the building. They learn quickly how to find their team area and the cafeteria. After that they learn that the Unified Arts rooms are placed on the outside walls of the second floor. They have no need to learn where all the other teams are. They feel very secure in their own teams. The decisions that have been made about organizational structure give the students a place they know to be theirs and where they are known. Rather than the nature of the school being determined by its size and population, size and population are cut down to a scale determined by individual needs.

The decentralized school organization is not without its problems. It is possible for a team to become isolated. To offset isolation, departmental meetings, committee assignments, and a strong emphasis on out-of-school social activities help bring teachers together. Ideas are shared by means of a staff newsletter and the curriculum center, a room that is set aside for lesson preparation and files of successful units that teachers recommend to their colleagues.

The emerging common sense of effective schools that is arising from the American research enterprise can take on a profoundly conservative cast. Let us look at the conclusions we have touted. They concern structure, they concern order, they concern predictability, and probably the absence of conflict. I think it is vitally important to avoid being captured by either conservative or liberal in this task before us. We are all looking for a common sense of education; much of that sense may lie in identifying the necessary conditions for students to learn: e.g., structure, order, and predictability. These should be broad grounds that we have discovered in which the further debate over particulars need not be ideological. [Michael Timpane, "Harvard Graduate School of Education Association Bulletin."]

There is also considerable risk in the freedom the teams enjoy. When a team of teachers does not work well together, as has happened once at Noe, the repercussions for the school are larger than when there are a few inept teachers in contained classrooms. A team's failure is felt not only in 150 students' attitudes toward the team, but beyond the team in unified arts, the cafeteria, and extracurricular activities. It is also more difficult for teams than it would be for departments to absorb newly assigned teachers. These are not insurmountable problems at Noe. The constant availability of support from team colleagues and SST members keeps problems at a minimum.

One structural problem, however, has resisted improvement. Teachers in the Unified Arts team do not have a common planning period, nor do they meet with the same group of students all year. Students elect the various Unified Arts courses for six- or seven-week sessions, depending on their team. The unified arts teachers are scheduled in accordance with the schedules of the teams. Students pour in and out of their classes the way they do in departmentalized secondary schools, a period at a time and 150 in a day.

A team meeting of Unified Arts teachers has a tone unfamiliar to other team meetings at Noe. The teachers complain bitterly about students. One teacher feels no compunction about saying sarcastically that he has "read all those goddamn counseling books where everyone's a good kid." He calls 99 percent of the students on a multiaged team "brickheads." The teachers are angry that at the beginning of a new session, students who have elected to repeat their courses have locked out others who have never been able to take them. When pressed by a guidance counselor to come up with a solution, they express a strong preference for removing all choice from the students to simplify scheduling procedures.

Like teachers in most secondary schools, while they have areas of considerable expertise, Unified Arts teachers feel abused by students who are relatively unknown to them. In turn, the teachers are abusive about the students, if not to them. They feel powerless as hordes of new students descend on them, and thus they attempt to remove power from the students. Except insofar as they are attracted to individual personalities, students have no particular allegiance to most of these teachers and vice versa. Lapses in common decency are mutual and circular. To attend a meeting of these teachers is to be transported to an average meeting in an average secondary school. The team is of interest because of the light it sheds on the interrelationship between school organization and teacher behavior. In its lapses, the brilliance of the school's achievement becomes most apparent.

Noe Middle School is highly structured, orderly, and predictable in its approach to skills development. It does not, however, have a "conservative cast." There are many routes to school effectiveness. The organizational structure of Noe is one route. It is important because it helps transform staff and students into a good-natured, industrious, and creative community.

Leadership

In presenting themselves to outsiders, schools select from among many the few aspects of school life they wish to share. While the choices do not necessarily reflect the actual life of the school, they say something not only about the image the school wishes to project but also the balance of values. School people often talk most about instruction, student behavior, or administrative constraints. At Noe, adults tend to talk to outsiders about adults. The administrators talk about successful teachers, especially team leaders. The teachers talk about Terry Brooks.

Terry Brooks is a brilliant principal. His leadership is so creative that school board members consider him unique. The board learns little from Noe as an example for other schools because Noe's successes are all ascribed to this remarkable person. Teachers like to take some credit for the school's effectiveness. At the same time, they see Brooks as the person who makes it possible by giving "the structure for freedom." If Brooks left, they say it would be hard for someone new to come in and try to change the school: "The staff would mutiny if we were told to go back to a departmental structure or if we were given many don'ts," one teacher says. "In the best of circumstances, with the best of people, a new principal would have a hard time," says another.

Terry Brooks's principalship at Noe Middle School began in 1975, the school's second year. Under a court order issued July 19, 1975, faculties were split and principals transferred. There was little time to write a busing plan before the opening of school, let alone to unite divisive, sometimes antagonistic faculties. Not only were schools desegregated, but the city and county systems merged. Two systems had to work together despite mutual distrust. While transferred principals had some choice about how their faculties were broken up, computers did most of the job.

Terry Brooks was the principal of a suburban middle school. Twenty Black teachers and administrative staff members from Manley Junior High School, a Black city school, joined 20 staff members as well as Brooks who were transferred to Noe from suburban schools, adhering to a ratio of 80 Whites to 20 Blacks. During 1980–81, the faculty consisted of 41 regular program teachers. Federal Title I funds and state special education funds contributed 2 reading teachers and 5 reading aides. There were also 14 special education teachers, 4 special education aides, and a media specialist. Because Noe was assigned over 900 students, it qualified for both a curriculum coordinator and an assistant principal. It was also assigned two guidance counselors. When the disruptive "alternative program" students were assigned to the school, Noe was given a special teacher for their class. Brooks mainstreamed the students and reassigned the teacher to the in-school suspension "Time-Out" room. An itinerant band teacher was assigned to the school for three periods daily. A cafeteria guard was assigned by the court as part of the desegregation order. (The guard, while unnecessary for maintaining order, has made it possible for teams of teachers to socialize and continue their planning during lunch.)

While it is difficult now to imagine the process, given the principal's current role in the school, Brooks and members of the Supportive Service Team say he "played the heavy" the first few years. He relinquished the assistant principal's position as an indirect means of dismissing him. The position was later reestablished and filled successfully. He wrote deficiency evaluations for 12 percent of the staff, including all but two members of the math department. It was, he says, "nasty stuff." The school experienced a 75 percent turnover of teachers as Brooks sought a staff that agreed with "Noe's middle-school philosophy." Then, having set up the school's structure, at first comprised of only graded teams, he let the school evolve.

The school was left alone during Louisville's desegregation riots. Parents were relieved that there were no fights at the school. The central office and school board were busy dealing with major conflagrations. The neglect of Noe was a blessing. Since no one outside the school was thinking about educational philosophy, Noe had breathing space and time to establish a track record.

Transferring from Noe can be easily accomplished without blame or rancor because of "incompatible philosophies." Teachers who are not working out are offered this option. The hiring process is more complicated. The Jefferson County Teachers Association (JCTA) has secured teachers the right to select the school they teach in, based on seniority. Because Noe's reputation as an "open" school is widely known, however, many teachers choose not to teach there, just as many would prefer not to teach in this inner-city school in an area with a high crime rate. As the school's reputation has become more established ("the word is out," Brooks says), there have been fewer and fewer inappropriate applicants.

There are no more deficiency evaluations. Most problems that persist have to do with classroom management, not proficiency. The staff is mostly young, with a variety of personalities, interests, and teaching styles that keeps both instruction and social intercourse lively. Their "aggressive excellence" sets the dominant tone of the school under the apparently—and only apparently—easygoing leadership style of their principal. Terry Brooks exercises one area of absolute control: he appoints the team leaders. It is an essential aspect of his leadership. He picks people whose philosophy of schooling for young adolescents is close to his, preferably identical. He meets with the team leaders often both in school and socially. They receive perks that convey any additional status they may require, like joining out-of-town visitors for dinner at lovely restaurants. They are a good-humored, committed, and thoughtful group. They work hard and play hard.

Brooks's leadership style does not fit into any preconceived category. The school seems to conform closely to the hierarchical authority structure of bureaucratic organizations, with a Supportive Service Team that monitors behavior and middle management or team leaders who interpret and implement policy. It also seems to be loosely coupled, as some organizational theorists say schools must be, with teams implementing policy in diverse ways and little direct communication between teachers and principal about policy.[3] Yet again, the leadership style resembles aspects of the sect that Firestone discusses as one type of school. In the sect, goals are "the central, integrating mechanism." Leadership "is not based on position but on the individual's charismatic and exceptional gifts." Control is achieved through "strong, personal commitments of members to [the school's] beliefs. . . . The sect withdraws from the world in order to maintain the purity of its doctrine."[4]

Though too broadly drawn, this description is as true of Noe as is a description of a bureaucratic or loosely coupled organization. Terry Brooks is a charismatic leader. Teachers say: "He is a master of good strokes"; "he praises staff as well as students;" "he makes us part of a family"; he is "visible," "motivating," "uplifting"; "he is an exceptionally gifted leader." Like the sect, Noe's staff has withdrawn from the world, in spirit if not in fact. There is an element of rebellion in the school's individualistic pursuit of excellence, as there is in most successful schools. The principal ignores certain district meetings and does not quite get to certain paperwork, especially when they pertain to issues like a proposed demerit system for teachers. Teachers refer to themselves as "being in the free state of Noe." One comments, in reference to students' independence of thought in a social studies discussion: "Maybe there's hope for the sixties." They are rebels with a cause, infused with the energy of proving their way the only way. They are special. The school's T-shirt proclaims: "Noe place like Noe."

Values are transmitted from Brooks to the staff through many means. The most apparent is through the team leaders and personal visits to team meetings. There are constant communications in mailboxes. Dramatics are also important. Everyone got the message when Brooks burned a basal reader in front of the language arts department in order to communicate his desire for a diversified reading program. One time, and only once, his values were transmitted through "blatant subversive activity—I disconnected the bell system." Money is used as an incentive for experimentation. For instance, Brooks offers discretionary money to a team that comes up with a good interdisciplinary unit, and grant money for the Artists-in-the-Schools program is awarded to a particularly high-achieving team.

Values are also transmitted through in-service training. Because there is no middle-school certification in Kentucky, teachers are prepared in elementary or secondary programs. Terry Brooks is a past president of the Kentucky Middle School Association. Through in-service work, he stresses aspects of his philosophy of schooling for young adolescents, especially direct and active student participation in learning, a strong teacher-based guidance program in which each student has an adult to talk to, interdisciplinary team instruction, and general emphasis on the students' social or affective needs. In-service opportunities also include "esoteric enrichment," as one teacher calls it, which are "issues seminars" on topics like parents in education or futurism. Sometimes a workshop is developed because of a need or interest within a team, like the one a science teacher presented on critical thinking skills. There are also voluntary workshops on subjects like stress or reading in the content areas.

If the shoe fits, you're not allowing for growth. [Sign in teacher's curriculum center, Noe Middle School.]

Teachers appreciate the opportunity for self-governance and the help they receive from the SST in support of their independence. They are, for this reason as well as general philosophical agreement, disposed to follow Brooks's lead. As one teacher puts it: "We run our little school. We have *voice.* We all hear horrendous stories about what is imposed on teachers in other schools, down to control over supplies like ditto paper. We have strong input. Terry hears us and we hear him." As a result, only a small number of teachers at Noe belongs to JCTA, the teachers' union, and some of their colleagues think badly of those who have joined. While they agree that a strike was needed to improve salaries, they see the union as a detriment to good school governance. "Trust is built into a school like this. Job actions break trust," one says. They understand why teachers in other schools need to belong to the union. "You have to remember this school is different. Our support system is *here.* "

Values are transmitted to the teachers through constant direct contact between Brooks and all teachers. He stops in to visit every team daily, commenting especially when he is "pleased not to see 55-minute teacher-directed lessons." Teachers are also, according to the assistant principal, "bombarded with educational stimuli." Reprints of articles are circulated. A faculty instructional newsletter, which teachers write and Brooks edits, attests to the strong instructional emphasis in the school. Articles on Piaget, praise, confidence and self-esteem, corporal punishment ("institutionalized child abuse"), winter perk-ups, and the relationships between students' attractiveness and grades, are typical of the offerings. Playful rewards that the teachers deeply appreciate are offered for one-time tasks, like a bulletin board contest on career education. The reward may be two free planning periods or a Coke.

This high-intensity, low-pressure leadership style evokes work performances that amaze outsiders. A substitute observes that teachers either work hard or they do not last, professionally or personally. She is impressed by how late teachers stay to meet and plan strategies or discuss individual students: "This is the most professional school I've been in." She thinks it was the best school in the system because of its results: "Everyone learns. Kids who don't learn elsewhere do here." A teacher responds to a question about what the administration expects of her: "Everything over and above the call of duty—as much as possible." Another says that it is "hard to get all your work done. You need weekends, vacations. It's very involving. Working here is not a six-hour-a-day job. You can't teach here if you're not willing to put in extra time." When asked why she is willing to, she gives the answer most frequently given to this and similar questions: "We are given freedom; therefore, we're willing to give our all here."

In summarizing literature on effort in the work place, Michael Rutter and his colleagues say: "People tend to be more or less productive according to the prevailing group norm for productivity. . . . Provided people see their superiors as supportive, and provided they accept the work situation, the setting of specific, difficult but attainable goals tends to lead to better work performance." They draw the lesson for school behavior and scholastic success of students: "The message of confidence that the pupils can be trusted to act with maturity and responsibility is likely to encourage pupils to fulfill those expectations."[5] The same message can be drawn, and should be drawn first, for teachers. At Noe it is.

Were Terry Brooks's skills in leadership confined to administering Noe Middle School, it would not be so successful a school. There appears to be unanimous agreement among teachers and administrators at Noe that his greatest skill is seen outside the school, where he is a consummate politician. Brooks pays careful attention to serving on committees and building relationships with civic organizations, who hold banquets and meetings in the school building. On one day alone, a conference of civic leaders is held in the school, with students at the door to greet them and hand them complimentary "Noe place like Noe" T-shirts; the kitchen staff prepares a lovely luncheon for them, to which some students and faculty are invited; staff members play their usual game of basketball after school; they entertain a visitor at dinner; six of them go to a hearing on Kentucky's Educational

Improvement Act in the evening that only Brooks must attend. It is a 16-hour day.

Brooks is an articulate advocate for Noe. He knows how to handle visitors. He pulls in community leaders, parents, and board members with ease to talk to them. He shares carefully selected sore points in the school, creating an atmosphere of openness and honesty. He sets visitors loose to wander in the school, but he knows within minutes that a crayon has landed on one of their heads in a team area on the second floor. He feeds lines about the school to visitors and then praises them for their perceptiveness. He turns the caring and feeding of visitors into an art.

Purposes, Goals, and Definitions

Noe is a big school. To establish the goals and climate that account for the school's effectiveness, a great deal of the school's resources, especially time and attention, must be devoted to the adults in the school. While they derive personal satisfaction from this attentiveness and while that satisfaction is not incidental to the school's achievements, the central purpose of the school is directed to helping young adolescents become responsible and self-directed young adults. This sense of purpose drives the staff to stay one more hour for planning or take one more risk with students, for whom, as one teacher says, "this may be the high point of their lives, given where they live, the schools they came from, and where they go to." The adults are not merely intrigued by school organization or leadership per se. They are obsessed with them because "our structure and curriculum give us the freedom to be caring." If adults talk a great deal about adults at Noe, it is to create the conditions in which they are the freest to care about students.

At Noe, teachers are very articulate about the school's annual goals. They have spent part of the summer working on them and spend team meetings refining them. In discussing current objectives, like increasing interdisciplinary units, enhancing pleasurable reading, assessing school climate, or establishing a parent education program, they refer to "my interpretation of the school's rationale" to bolster their positions. They stress maintaining and enhancing the school's flexibility to be as student-centered as possible. They see themselves as successful because students come to school, stay in class, and "go across the street" (to the high school).

Staff members are insistent that Noe is not a secondary school. It is decidedly elementary, most feel, with its emphasis on a family team for each student. The team is larger than a contained elementary-school classroom and the curriculum is broader; but the students are treated more as they would be in elementary school, as is subject matter. Several teachers say the school is neither elementary nor secondary. Elementary-school teachers are parent surrogates, they argue, and high-school teachers are advisors—"we serve in both roles." Students in elementary school stay with one teacher. In high school they "travel on the hour. Here, they are in teams with a group of teachers. They can like and communicate with one, but they have contact with six. They have a home area. They aren't just numbers." "Kids take priority over curriculum," one teacher summarizes. Brooks says he has made a concerted effort to set the elementary school as the frame of reference, to achieve a middle school with a staff two-thirds of whom have secondary training. According to the teachers, he has succeeded. Everyone talks about the purposes of middle-grade schooling at Noe because everyone makes decisions about the school's growth and accomplishments. There is, as a result, a coherence of definition and purpose that this large, potentially resistant population of students thrives in.

School Climate

The humane environment that encourages teachers' growth at Noe Middle School is translated by the teachers, as well as the administration, into a humane environment that encourages students' growth. The school feels cold when one first enters. It has the institutional feeling of any large school building with metal lockers and impersonal halls. Then one opens the door to a team area and it is filled with energy, movement, productivity, doing. There is a lot of informal relating among students and between students and teachers. Visible from one vantage point are students working on written projects, putting the last touches on posters, watching a film, and working independently from reading kits. A few wander about aimlessly or are distracted by noise nearby. Most know what they are doing, can say why it is important, and go back to their work immediately after being interrupted.

It is noisy, but most people, teachers and students, seem undisturbed or unaware. One teacher uses the analogy of a restaurant: You sit down at your table and focus on the few people you are dining with. Even hearing-impaired students, whose hearing aids amplify background noise and who are often visually distractable, block out the noise around them and watch their teacher signing without disturbance. In *Classrooms and Corridors,* Metz observes that "the most basic problem of order in school is the result of placing large numbers of active young people in very small spaces." In the ensuing tension between order and freedom, she continues, "the choice in this dilemma seems to be most frequently weighted toward considerations of maintaining the maximum order possible rather than giving the maximum freedom possible."[6]

At Noe, one has the sense that there are very few students in the school.

The maintenance of order appears to be effortless for most students and teachers, nor is any special emphasis placed on awarding freedom, which is, instead, a natural part of school life. This feat is accomplished in various ways. Students have two immediate frames of reference from the moment they walk in the school: their team and, within it, their homeroom. In multiaged teams each year, only one-third of the students are new. The other two-thirds help to socialize them into their very small and exclusive school. Procedurally, there is never a time when all students are on break at the same time. It is as if the school had 150 students. Also, because of the team structure, teachers do not deal with discipline alone: "A student misbehaving just does not stand a chance," one teacher says. "The team members are all there."

> It is 9:50 a.m. in a multiaged team. Some students are working on maps of the Roman Empire. An overhead projector shines a map on a screen. Students are working at desks and carrels, or on the floor. A language arts class is doing bookwork. A teacher walks around, helping individual students. Suddenly, a fight breaks out between two students in another team that has a substitute because of teacher workshops. Teachers from the first team are on the scene within seconds, handling the incident swiftly and quietly. Students from two teams are aware of what is happening. No one moves, although the fight creates a stir. Within two minutes, a teacher is sitting with the two antagonists and asking them if they are calm enough so that he can talk with them, and everyone else is back at work. Over 300 students could have joined the fracas. No one did. Later, in this same team, when the students go to lunch, girls leave their pocketbooks out on their desks. Theft is an unusual occurrence, they say. Everyone can see everything. Everyone in the area knows everyone.

In part because they are not isolated, in part because they like middle-school students, teachers set a tone in their teams that is generally relaxed and good-natured. The superintendent chooses the Noe building for meetings "because he knows the fire alarm won't be pulled," one administrator says. If the fire alarm does not ring when civic leaders from Louisville meet at Noe, it is not because the school has had a lucky day. What appears to be luck, Brooks says, happens because of the day-to-day atmosphere of the school. The exchange between staff and students is positive and friendly. Parents point out that the staff are "truly concerned." "They treat your child one-on-one. They want to help, not reprimand." "They let them be kids and let them breathe and be themselves." One mother of an eighth-grader says: "I hate that it's his last year. He'll miss the closeness next year. They don't take the time with kids in other schools. The relationship is unique."

One student, who has been sent to sit alone because of disruptive behavior during an intramural all-star basketball game, derides the school to a visitor: "The teachers run all over you. You can't even whisper. You have no say in anything." As the conversation goes on—and it evokes anxiety in teachers because this boy is one of the school's worst behavior problems —he says that "this is a good school, better than the one I came from where everyone fights. Not here, because here you get in big trouble. There they just suspend you." "Then what is 'big trouble'?" he is asked. "Here, your mom must come. There you can fool your parents. Here, teachers don't let you break rules. They're very strict." "Are they caring?" he is asked. "Of course." "It doesn't sound like it." "If they didn't care," he answers, "they'd let us do anything we want. They're strict because they care." The teachers need not have worried.

The students banter with Brooks or ask him for help with their work. There is a lot of touching between members of the SST and students. Students say they can talk to team leaders about a problem, go to their advisors, talk to the guidance counselors, Mr. Brooks, or the assistant principal. Each has his or her favorite person to go to.

> It is early in the morning on a busy day at Noe. If a list were kept of the day's special activities, it would rival the length of the absence list. Two girls walk through the corridor towards the front door. "They're not keeping me in this school. It's a dull place," one says. "There's nothing going on." They walk into the office instead of out the door and ask for the assistant principal. One of the girls tells him she's "splitting, leaving, won't stay." It takes a while, but he learns from her that it is her fourteenth birthday and that a teacher has assigned her detention. She will miss the school bus and, therefore, her cake and candles.

> The assistant principal says he knows it is hard to be in school at all on a birthday, let alone to stay for detention. But, he points out, she can get home on a public transportation bus in time for her party. "No, you drive me home," she demands. He says he is staying to play basketball, but will take her home after 5:00. He says he has a clipboard—shouldn't she get fourteen whacks for her birthday? Isn't that traditional? She starts smiling and protesting. Then he asks her what her options are. She says she'd rather stay Monday. He thinks that is reasonable and says he will talk to the teacher about it, reminding her that she must stay today if the teacher says she must. If so, he'll make sure she gets home for cake and candles. He will lend her the carfare which, he realizes, she does not have.

This is a small story. Noe does not have big stories. In another school, the student might have walked straight out the door. Instead, she had someone to turn to. Perhaps the teacher did not know she was backing a student against the wall because it was her birthday. The assistant principal, by his availability and manner, gave the girl a way out. She did not have to walk out and become a statistic. The teacher will be able to understand because Terry Brooks gives teachers options, including not teaching on their birthdays. And if she does not understand, there will be bus money for a student who would rather be a truant than say she does not have the fare. It is a small incident because the school has time for small incidents before they become large.

Some teachers in other schools give up because of physical assault. They know how to deal with kids here. In the reading lab with the big boys, the teachers know how to explain discipline without provoking them. They kids aren't backed into a corner. [Parent, Noe Middle School.]

The rules that bind students in common standards of behavior do not come about by chance at Noe. The process of including students in the behavioral expectations of the school is deliberate, careful, and eminently reasonable. The school has thirteen rules that everyone is asked to follow, like respecting and obeying adults, coming to school on time and with required class materials, not smoking, fighting, or wearing hats, combs, or "rakes." These thirteen rules were formulated and agreed upon by all teachers in the school when Brooks became principal and are modified annually. They uphold them all and expect students to. Beyond the thirteen, rules are established by individual teams at the start of each school year. Students play an active role in setting these rules. As a result of this process, gum-chewing is allowed in some teams but not others. During lunch, some of the students may be allowed to leave the cafeteria to go outside, while others may not. Students do not protest the difference: they have formulated this rule for their team, and students relate most strongly to their team.

We Depend on You

We at Noe Middle School strongly believe that a positive learning atmosphere depends upon your help and cooperation. In order that Noe can be a good place to learn and live for everyone, we are asking that you follow these rules:

1. I will respect and obey the authority of all adults in this building.
2. I will respect school property and the property of others.
3. I will speak in a quiet and polite voice.
4. I will not fight or horseplay at school.
5. I will walk in the building.
6. I will not smoke on school property.
7. I will behave in an orderly and mannerly fashion in the cafeteria.
8. I will eat food and drinks in the cafeteria only.
9. I will have a signed pass to be out of class.
10. I will not wear a hat, rake, comb, etc. while in the building.
11. I will leave my "toys" (radios, tape players, ball, etc.) at home.
12. I will come to school and class on time.

13. I will bring pencil, paper, and other required materials to class each day.
[Noe Middle School student information folder]

After the rules have been decided upon—a process that can take several days—parents, homeroom teachers, and students sign a statement of agreement about the team's rules. It is a pact. "What is the purpose of discipline?" students are asked by a visitor. "To make us behave well anywhere we go"; "to make us respect one another more," others say. They do not necessarily like the rules. One boy says that not fighting is dumb: "It's too hard not to fight back." Others agree. But they know what the rules are, they know the problems they will have if they break them, and, for the most part, they feel a sense of participation in the rule setting that makes them try harder to live within them than if they were seen as the arbitrary rules of adults.

Besides rules and punishments, there are positive rewards. A schoolwide monthly competition for keeping the cafeteria clean results in a special showing of a movie to the winning team. Some teams have a reward system in which students earn "Cougar points" as a result of successful behavior. When the requisite number of points has been accumulated, the team gets to go swimming, skating, to the movies, or some other popular activity.

Because teachers schedule students and handle discipline within the team, the guidance counselors are freed to counsel. They offer students behavioral contracts that are signed by the student, teacher, guidance counselor, and parent. Students can ask to be "put on contract." The student and teacher both have to want to sign. If advisable or necessary, it is possible to waive the parents' signature and keep the contract in-house only. As many as forty students may be "on contract" at a particular time.

A good instructional program reduces discipline problems. Students and parents cite the excitement of trips to the Louisville Orchestra, to the space museum in Huntsville, Alabama, or camping. One parent says students get to experience what they learn, not just to learn through books—like camping to study outdoor life or the fifties simulation to study history. Students stay involved in school and out of trouble. Students like activities they could not get in other schools, like learning to use computers at the University of Louisville: "It's not paper and pencil all the time," one student says. They like team and schoolwide parties, dances, movies, baseball games. Some say they especially like advisor-advisee, which is the teacher-based guidance program. While they disagree about whether the school was strict, depending on what schools they had come from, they all agree that they are kept very busy with hard work (one student cites ten projects in one month) and warm, relaxed, special activities. "It's not a dead school. It's active, alive," a seventh-grader says. "We behave because it's not boring," another says.

"The attendance rate is high and people behave because this school is active," a friend of hers says. "You have everything to learn and nothing to lose."

It is also argued by some students, parents, and teachers that multiaged grouping reduces behavior problems among students who might feel uncomfortable in a single-age group. Apt younger students not in the Advanced Program can accelerate without standing out. Less apt eighth-graders can work together with sixth- and seventh-graders rather than being labeled as remedial. Students whose physical development is either rapid or slow are more likely to fit in with the diverse growth the three-grade span offers. For those who feel that they are too pushed as sixth-graders in multiaged teams or that eighth grade is too easy, there is the alternative of being in graded teams. Students who have transferred from schools with grades seven through twelve are especially appreciative of being in just one grade. For those whose comfort depends on one or the other, the choice is there.

Unlike many middle schools that see themselves as adhering to a "middle-school philosophy," Noe Middle School has an active interscholastics program in basketball and track. Terry Brooks stands behind this policy. Some students are good in math and some in sports, he says. Louisville's civic clubs do not offer athletics to youth on Saturdays; interscholastic athletics are therefore all the more important. Attendance is raised and behavior problems are lessened because of the program, he adds. Individual teams set their policy about intramurals, which play an important role in the team spirit of some groups. But interscholastics, with a drill corps of 80 and 30 cheerleaders, has its place.

Brooks argues that the band is also very important in the lives of some students. There are 70 sixth-graders with no previous experience in one band, 90 in the advanced band, and 200 in the total program. The auditorium is packed for concerts. The production in 1979–80 of *The Wizard of Oz* involved 500 students. All these activities bind students to the life of a school that offers diverse ways in which to achieve recognition from peers and adults. The fact that Noe is a community school may also make some students feel a greater sense of ownership. The gym opens at 6:15 a.m. and closes at 10:00 p.m. The high school across the street has had to install solid steel doors because of vandalism. There is no problem at Noe, whose vandalism rate is the second lowest of all middle schools in the system.

A final observation about school climate at Noe needs to be made. Teachers are often asked what their expectations for their students are and whether they are the same for all students. The wisdom of the research literature is that high expectations equally held are important factors in achieving and accounting for school effectiveness. Teachers know that researchers think that "high" and "the same" are the right answers and usually respond accordingly. Not at Noe. The teachers and principal at Noe are honest about not holding very high expectations of their students' academic achievement when they compare them with students in other Louisville schools. They see the ability of their students as the same or lower than other schools' students. They do not think even one-third of them will complete college. When asked what level of achievement can be expected of their students, most answer that they will achieve at or slightly below the national norm.

These answers do not represent a ceiling of expectations that the teachers or principal impose on students. They represent a realistic appraisal of their day-to-day experiences. Their perception of students' abilities does not lead, however, to predictable behavior. For instance, a surprising number of teachers at Noe believe that they should be held accountable for students' achievement in evaluation procedures, an unpopular stance in most schools. Their morale is extremely high. They see Noe as one of the best schools in Louisville. Teachers hold in highest contempt a school board member quoted (actually, misquoted) in the local press as having said that poor children could not learn. The fact that these teachers never question that every one of their students can learn is reflected in the derisiveness of their manner as they tell this story.

Teachers' expecations for student social behavior is well defined by written agreement with each student. Their expectations for academic behavior is for progress as continuous as possible at varying rates of sophistication. Observers of schools are accustomed to hearing teachers mouth lofty platitudes about their expectations for students that are not observed in classroom practice. At Noe, teachers speak conservatively about their expectations but act in accordance with lofty goals. Group support and esprit de corps fuel their sense of mission. For many, as for their students, this will be the best place they will be all day. The academic emphasis at Noe is derived not only from perceptions of students' abilities, but also from perceptions of their needs and an unrelenting sense of mission. Teaching is a calling at Noe. Realisitic espectations, just as in hospitals and churches, yield to an ardent sense of vocation.

Public Policy Issues

A significant contribution to the well-being of Noe Middle School students and staff is its racial climate. Students say Blacks and Whites get along very well. "Desegregation worked here," one says. They compare the tension and outbursts of hostility in other schools to the friendships at Noe. An eighth-grader observes that "teachers are color blind. They set a good example." One student says: "We're all equal here. There's no need to feel like a big shot." Several years ago, while the city was in the grips of race riots, Noe went about its business peaceably. In one Louisville school, to this day, the principal gets on the p.a. system to prepare the school for the worst: "Remember, today could be our day." In that school there is also a countdown over the p.a. for the last thirty seconds of every switch in classes.

It is the last afternoon of "Fifties Week" for the eighth-grade team at Noe. Students have been working hard for four and a half days on this social studies simulation. Among many other activities they have put on a dramatization of the desegregation of schools in Little Rock, Arkansas, with Blacks verbally assaulted and the National Guard called in by Eisenhower. Now they get to have their malt shop and sock hop. They are dressed like high-school students in the fifties, their outfits influenced by their research and the Fonz.

There is a dance contest with some terrific jitterbugging by a White girl and a Black boy. They win the contest and are proclaimed "the queen and king of Fifties Week." Elated, they hug each other, do a demonstration dance for the assembled admirers, and hug each other again.

At the same time, in a coincidence of time and place that fiction would not risk, a Black boy at the high school across the street puts his hand on a White girl's behind. The school blows. Several students are taken to the emergency room of a nearby hospital with knife slashes on their faces. A few are Noe graduates.

The next day the mother of a sometimes truant boy at the high school reports that her son, who had wielded a knife, has said to her: "If I were at Noe, I wouldn't be rioting. Teachers really care about kids at Noe."

Noe has an advantage that the high school will not have for several years. The students at Noe have been in desegregated schools for almost all of their schooling. That this is a considerable advantage, no one at Noe disputes. But there is a lesson to be learned that will serve the high school as it becomes equally advantaged. School structure affects school climate. As Janet Schofield reports in her research, positive interaction increases between Black and White seventh-grade students as they spend time together in close contact. Eighth-grade students who have not been together in school previously or who are being pushed into a heavily White, high-status, accelerated track and a heavily Black, low-status track, do not have improved relations. In addition, while there is some carryover of positive intergroup relations among the seventh- and eighth-grade students who have been in close, positive contact, when they return to their unequal status conditions, there is a predictable decrease: "The results demonstrate that students' interracial behavior is quite responsive to the structural characteristics of their school environment," Schofield concludes.[7] The study is suggestive of what may happen to Noe students when they cross the street.

In Noe's many accomplishments it is easy to overlook a more subtle revolution in students' attitudes. First, sex equity is a given, both in the overt messages of curriculum and in the subtle messages adults send to children. It is so ingrained in the life of the school that no one even thinks to mention it. Second, a regional supervisor says that Noe is the only school she has seen where the mainstreaming of handicapped students really works. Parents talk about Handicap Awareness Day, one day a year when students at Noe get to choose a handicap, to be deaf, blind, or confined to a wheelchair, and then cope as best they can. "They are becoming compassionate. They have learned better than we ever have how to let the handicapped be independent and do for themselves." They have also learned to take responsibility for other human beings' welfare, helping them from class to class and looking out for their needs. "I used to point to them on the street," a student says. "Now I understand their feelings. I can talk to them." Another says: "Some don't act handicapped. They play with their wheelchairs. It helps us accept anyone, anywhere, who is handicapped." "This is a remarkable accomplishment," a visitor comments. "Why?" asks a student. "They don't hold us back. They have the same capabilities we have."

Self-Evaluation

Teachers and administrators at Noe engage in constant self-scrutiny through team meetings, SST meetings, and frequent gatherings of team leaders and SST members. They use as their criteria for success mundane indicators like student behavior, test scores, progress in the TRIP program, and attendance rates. More important to them, however, are their successes in interdisciplinary units and in breaking away from lecture-oriented teaching methods.

In addition to this ongoing evaluation, Brooks meets with team leaders and individual teams every June to evaluate the previous year, identify problem areas, and choose school and team goals to work on during the upcoming year. He has also encouraged team members to establish openly their expectations of one another, a process resulting in a statement of fifteen minimal expectations for team members, like: each teacher will be on time for school; each team member will enforce team and school rules consistently, in accordance with team decisions; each team member will maintain order in his or her own class area; each team member will share in the responsibility of maintaining order outside class areas, i.e., before homeroom, assemblies, breaks, dismissal, to and from Unified Arts; each team member will actively support team instructional decisions. The teachers have very high standards for themselves and each other. They give "calamity day" awards to teachers who are falling down on the job. They have been known to give a teacher a miniature ferris wheel as a "my classroom is an amusement park" award. The social outcasts at Noe are the weakest teachers on teams. In other words, evaluation at Noe is more a process of self-scrutiny than of testing students, typical of the school's emphasis on adult behavior as the key to student outcomes.

Curriculum and Instruction

There is a wide diversity of teaching styles at the school, from direct whole-class instruction to individualized instruction. While teachers on teams tend to blend their styles and become more alike, students are usually exposed to a variety of teaching approaches within a single day. A student teacher comments that she need merely look around her in the team area to be exposed to several different instructional methods. Most teachers encourage students to talk to each other about their work, to get up and move around without first getting permission, to select their own seats, and to change them according to the demands of particular activities. Walking through the school, one sees chairs in a row facing a blackboard in one area and ad hoc groupings of furniture in another.

Teachers are cordial and welcoming. They make easy transitions from one activity to the next, many managing individual, group, and whole-class work with the dexterity of a juggler. While most teams have a relaxed atmosphere, the intensity necessary for engaging students' attention is achieved through teacher personality and the inherent interest of the curriculum.

With Noe's extensive commitment to individual progress, in many teams it is difficult to see instruction or hear the transmission of ideas. In heterogeneously grouped classes, with groups of students intent on different activities at the same time, teachers work quietly with students or students work independently on their own individual projects, lessons from teacher-made learning activity packages, or commercial kits. An observer does not hear a compelling exchange of ideas. In this setting, most striking is the diversity of approaches taken simultaneously to work with an academically and developmentally diverse group of students. Teachers are not teaching to a preconceived idea of sixth grade or to the average ability of a group of students. They are coaxing students through a variety of learning activities at a variety of levels, appealing to different interests and learning styles.

The teachers are predominantly an experienced group, 45 percent having taught between five and nine years, 36 percent having taught more than ten years. One-third have been in the school five or more years, one-third one to four years, and one-third are in their first year at the school. Thirty-five percent have their masters degrees, and 25 percent in addition have work beyond the M.A. They are extremely aware of the diversity of early adolescent development, especially the social, cognitive, and physical changes young adolescents experience. They are attempting to share that information with parents through a parent resource center in the school that offers two or three programs a month, during the day and at night, on subjects like parent stress and early adolescent development. The center is building a library collection for parents that includes tutoring aids for different school subjects.

Teachers see their primary responsibility to be teaching academic subjects, their second to be enhancing social skills in meeting these responsibilities. One parent of an Advanced Program student reports that before Noe, her child was wasting his time. The work at Noe is very hard and there is a great deal of it, so her son had to learn to use his time well. He goes to the library two or three nights a week. Another parent says that her child made straight A's before Noe. He transferred and got a C+ in a course. She was upset because he wants to be a veterinarian and needs good grades to get into school. The guidance counselors at Noe calmed her down. Both parents emphasize that teachers tutor students after school on their own time to help them over rough spots. The relaxed atmosphere of the teams is deceptive. There is a lot of hard work, with standards that are evidently very high for these students.

---

1. **Enforce team rules.**
2. **Be firm but fair.**
3. **Know your students.**
4. **Set high standards.**
5. **Plan your work carefully.**

Good luck!

[Poster in curriculum center,
Noe Middle School.]

It is not possible to talk about *the* curriculum at Noe because of the different grade organizations and team decisions made. There are some common elements, however. All students take language arts, reading, social studies, science, and math all year. They take units of unified arts one hour daily for six or twelve weeks, according to their teams, and practical arts (career guidance) and teacher-based guidance all year. Advanced Placement students are required by the Jefferson County School System to take Spanish, for which they go to a neighboring high school. Youth Performing Arts School (YPAS) students take team subjects at Noe for half a day and are at YPAS for two hours. Students may take band, interscholastic sports, cheerleading, and pep squad as extracurricular activities. In 1980–81, all sixth-graders took band for six weeks.

Students who require special scheduling, like YPAS, Advanced Program, and some special education students, are assigned to the three graded teams to ease scheduling problems and to give the multiaged teams as much flexibility as possible.

In the multiaged teams, social studies and science curricula are divided into three separate one-year curricula and then offered in three-year cycles, so that all students, whether sixth-, seventh-, or eighth-graders, are studying the same unit at the same time. Everyone gets to take all the units over a three-year period. Social studies and science classes are heterogeneously grouped. Math and language arts are homogeneously grouped by ability but not age. Title I students who go to the reading lab are pulled out from language arts or social studies, a practice Terry Brooks will be happy to see ended.

The school day at Noe is divided into two major areas: team time and unified arts period. During the five-hour team block, the student will study core . . . and participate in the advisor-advisee, group activity, and practical arts program. During the unified arts period, the student will participate in art, home economics, industrial arts, music, and physical education activities. From 7:30 a.m. when homeroom begins, until 2:00 when the dismissal bell rings, the faculty at Noe is dedicated to making school an exciting, enjoyable, and meaningful educational experience for you! [Noe Middle School student information folder]

Every student receives directed reading instruction for forty minutes every morning and takes math forty or forty-five minutes daily. Some teachers block social studies and science for two hours, according to their personal judgment and the team's agreement. Terry Brooks is the school's curriculum evaluator. Systemwide content specialists no longer monitor the school. The former county system had a strong supervisory system. After merger, Brooks held supervisors at bay and established his teachers' rights to implement curriculum units they developed. It is now beyond the pale for a district supervisor to criticize the school's curriculum. At the same time, teachers from Noe serve on curriculum development committees and attend subject-oriented workshops. They feel they influence curricula in the school system.

While they follow the system's curriculum requirements, teachers use the system's curriculum guides as they need to or want to, in much the same way they use textbooks. They find some of them helpful but do not feel compelled to cover the subject matter. Department chairpersons and the school's instructional coordinator help with curriculum coordination within the school and between middle school and high school, which has to be watched more closely here than in traditional schools.

Developmental Responsiveness

Although most of the school's success is attributed by staff members to the team structure, there is also deliberate attentiveness in the curriculum to the diversity and needs of young adolescents. Students' need to gain a sense of competence and achievement is met by a wide variety of opportunities in skills development and creative expression. The system's new reading program, Total Reading Improvement Program (TRIP), was introduced systemwide at the sixth-grade level in 1980 in response to low test scores. At Noe, all multiaged teams and sixth-graders were in the program from the outset, with the rest of the student body joining in 1981. The teachers are very excited by it because it has helped them identify the specific skills each student needs to work on, eliminate teaching what students already know, and achieve the individual continuous progress for each student that is always their goal. Their positive, open attitude toward a new and demanding system stands in sharp contrast to teachers in some other schools, whose apprehensiveness makes them less enthusiastic. Teachers at Noe see TRIP as one more way to help their students become competent in an essential skill.

One science teacher, having read a great deal about Reuven Feuerstein's work with learning-disabled students in Israel, has begun working with ten learning-disabled students on Instrumental Enrichment, Feuerstein's program that helps students with learning problems reach higher levels of abstract, representational thinking. Students learn to use intrinsic and extrinsic cues (all these terms are used with the students, who work with them in class) to develop strategies for problem solving, at first with dots, angles, and curves, and later with more sophisticated problems. (A student tries to turn his paper filled with dots to solve a geometric problem. "No, you have to turn it with your head," the teacher says.) Brooks would like all students to learn the thinking skills this teacher has introduced into one team's program. The students feel special "in a good way," one of them reports.

The emphasis on basic reading and math skills in no way squeezes out other areas of competence. No tradeoff is made between "back-to-basics" and room for adolescents to develop. On one day, for instance, students in one team are making books for the Young Authors Books Contest, a citywide contest to promote writing. They have written their books and designed the jackets. Now they are learning bookbinding. At the same time, some students in a history class are working on three-dimensional models for a unit entitled Work and Leisure in History. They are going to have their own History Day in preparation for History Day at the University of Louisville. They can enter their reports and models if they like in a competition sponsored by the university. There is a great deal of writing, making, and doing going on during the morning, until the students return to homeroom to settle down. They then go to the gymnasium for their intramurals all-star game, played against Mr. Brooks, teachers, and SST members. This marks the high-spirited culmination of their basketball season. During the year, they will have similar games in football, volleyball, and softball. There must be at least two females on the floor on each team at all times. In the all-star game, the shortest boy on the team is the hero of the game.

The team then returns, triumphantly, to class. No one needs to get them started on their return from the gymnasium. They settle into completing posters for their advisor-advisee unit on drugs until lunch time. During this morning, students have worked on improving their math and reading skills, have been making books and models, have cheered on their team-mates in a 30-minute athletic tournament, and have done art work on posters. Three of the activities have involved competitions that the students love. Each of them has allowed different students to shine. In another team, students are preparing for a Pioneer Life unit. In home economics, girls are making pioneer skirts and boys are making vests. They will also quilt pillows. They leave for a square dance rehearsal. Students say this emphasis on creativity is one of the best things about unified arts. It is made possible because of interdisciplinary teaching.

Students are especially enthusiastic about the band, where success motivates them to attain more success. The band teacher walks from Noe to the band room in the YPAS building. On the way, many students greet him in the halls. He is very popular. As he enters the band room, everyone stands and is silent. Soon, he becomes upset because several students have forgotten to bring their music: "I don't want to think for you. I want to teach you music." He is a perfectionist in getting every instrument tuned to the correct pitch. Then they play. He is not pleased with their work today and lets them know it. They are the only middle school entering a contest at high-school level four. Last year they received a straight "superior" from four judges. The band teacher is a disciplinarian and a perfectionist. His style is a different experience for the students, and they love it. He makes them competent.

A striking aspect of the curriculum at Noe is the diversity it offers students. Already built into the team structure is diversity of people and ages, with teachers able to schedule according to the various needs and interests of the group. ("Counselors counsel. We schedule. We can schedule according to a student's need, not a computer's.") Through their numerous special activities, the teams then build a curriculum to intrigue a diverse age group they see as being jaded or antagonistic by the time they get to Noe. In one week, the school is hopping with Young Authors, Science Fair, meeting with members of Leadership Louisville (a civic organization), rehearsals for Pioneer Life, and the fifties simulation. Students talk about the mock presidential nominating convention they held, a social studies debate on tariffs between the North and the South, newscasts and reports they prepared on the Monroe Doctrine, their camping trip, and the science trip they are planing to the space museum in Huntsville. All students in the school go on a major trip each year (thanks to candy sales). Brooks likes them all to have special things to look forward to. He wants each team to have a large event like Fifties Week. At Noe the excitement occurs within the curriculum. There is no organizational distinction between curriculum and special events.

Fifties Week is one out of many such events. Students prepare long and hard for it. The simulation is a packaged curricular unit from Interact. (Teachers at Noe do not insist on being endlessly creative. They seek and use good packaged materials, like Feuerstein's and Interact's.) It is 1956. Students attend Elmwood High School. A "principal" and a "guidance counselor," both students, are in charge of all the students' schedules for the week. They have turned the multipurpose room into Elmwood High and a neighboring malt shop that sells sundaes and real malts to all the students. (At the end of the week, girls on roller skates deliver sundaes and malts to teachers throughout the building.) Activities during the week include the movie *Rebel without a Cause,* a debate (resolved: the 1950s should make Americans hang their heads in shame because of political apathy, bad taste in dress, etc.), advisor-advisee discussions about changes in values, five mini-courses like Heroes of Rock and Roll, and a dramatic reenactment of Little Rock (the last line is: "Blacks and Whites are learning from each other"). Teachers are careful to point out to the students that the fifties were not all rock and roll and "happy days." They carefully review the incident at Little Rock, stressing that it marked a turning point in the government's willingness to stand behind the Supreme Court's school desegregation order. They review the 1975 court case in Jefferson County and Judge Gordon's ruling to bus for desegregation. During the week, the contrasts between seriousness and fun keep the students going. One day they see a tape by Dick Cavett, *Time Was: 1950s;* the next day they see *Grease.*

A great deal of research goes into these activities, especially the debate, to enact the cultural, political, and historical events. Students are intensely involved. The last day, they thoroughly enjoy themselves. In costume, they show off the dances from the fifties they have learned in a dance mini-course, at their sock hop.

The school's commitment to giving its early adolescent students opportunities for self-exploration and self-definition is expressed in the curriculum through the teacher-based guidance program. In the advisor-advisee session, a minimum of twenty minutes daily, students say they discuss their problems, such as divorce or the death of a new sibling. It is a time when they can express their feelings with no fear of ridicule. They also discuss alcohol abuse, prejudice, school and life survival skills, risk taking, and human sexuality. Students say that in the sex education sessions they learn a great deal from films, question-and-answer sessions, people from clinics, and special readings. During one advisory period, for instance, students see the film, *Then One Year,* which presents straightforward information about the adolescent growth spurt, differences in growth between girls and boys, and the variability in physical growth among boys and girls. The film portrays girls' worries about the size of their breasts and the menstrual cycle and boys' worries about erections and ejaculation. It sends an unequivocal message about masturbation: do not worry. The message of the entire film is that it takes time to get used to so many changes, but that they should not be worrisome. In a discussion afterward, one teacher emphasizes accepting responsibility for sexual behavior. Another invites written questions, to be discussed the next day.

Students report no problems in getting to be with friends. School is informal and active enough that friends can work together in classes, as well as being together at lunch, break time, "actually, as much as you want." While they agree that, aside from the media center, there is no place for privacy, they insist that they do not want privacy; they want to be with their friends. Young adolescents have a strong need to assume increasing amounts of responsibility for themselves and others, albeit for short periods of time and in structured settings where they gain approval from adults. There are several striking examples of such opportunities within Noe.

First, nonhandicapped students have responsibility for helping orthopedically handicapped students maneuver around the school if they need assistance. Second, guidance counselors have started a student liaison program in which teachers meet with students to get their ideas about the advisor-advisee program. Third, if there are more special events going on than a team can take part in, students decide which they will do, just as they choose their unified arts classes. In some teams they help make out the team schedule. Fourth, and most unusual, students help run WNOE, a closed-circuit television news program in which students broadcast world, national, local, and school news every morning.

WNOE is an extracurricular activity that is part of the communications program in unified arts. Every morning, students from homeroom staff news teams make school announcements instead of listening to a disembodied voice on the p.a. Once a week, a $100,000 question is asked. Students do library work and submit the correct answer. A winner's name is drawn in a raffle. The prize is a candy bar. Prizes won by students for athletics, poster contests, band performances, and other events are presented by the principal on camera. Students' parents are often in the studio, watching proudly.

During Fifties Week, the WNOE staff consisted of students taking part in the simulation. The broadcast started with *Rock around the Clock*. The school menu and information about disaster area evacuation plans were announced. Students were told it was Knute Rockne's birthday and were given an update on Atlanta's missing children. The sports announcer read sports news while dressed in fifties garb. Brooks thanked students "for a good day yesterday, especially with all our visitors." He thanked them for the cleanliness in the cafeteria. He reminded them to make sure they listened to all announcements about evacuation and then playfully predicted the next day would be a snow day. A student ended the broadcast reminding viewers that on this day in 1933, Franklin Delano Roosevelt said: "The only thing we have to fear is fear itself."

A short production like this involves 58 students on a rotating basis and a lot of work. Students who work on camera try out for their positions. To qualify to learn to operate the camera, students need only show an interest in learning media techniques and show up. They take a proficiency test later. Just as students love the social studies simulations because "we participate, so we know how it feels," they love participating in WNOE, with its glamour, rewards, and unusual opportunities to learn new skills.

This is the best place some of these kids will be all day. [Noe Middle School teacher]

There are no out-of-school opportunities for community work at Noe, which comes as a surprise given the school's efforts to offer a diverse program that responds to early adolescent needs. Staff members at Noe are not reflective about out-of-school youth participation. It is as if the entire school has made a subconscious decision to ignore the issue. When teachers and administrators begin to explore why this has happened, they have a cogent explanation. Aside from the fact that they work at over 100 percent of capacity now and do not want to give up anything in the existing program, they know intuitively that it is politically wise to keep their students in the school building and create as rich an in-school program as possible. The school lacks a neighborhood base. Some parents would be frightened to have their children leave school "at Lee and 2nd." Pressing parents on this issue after they have calmed down about their children's safety in the school might trouble the political waters again. The school has become an enclave. The outside can come to them, in the form of people using the building as a community school or for meetings; they are not about to impose on the outside. If Brooks were to say "thou shalt" to the staff, they would develop a community service program. He would be adding to stress inside the school and outside. They all feel it is not worth it.

The school's weakest response to the developmental needs of young adolescents is in its physical education program. Students who go to YPAS or Spanish miss PE. Other students have PE for only one session a year, in unified arts. Brooks would like them to have it every day, but there is no support for that in Jefferson County. Intramurals and interscholastics help, but they are pared down because of the system's budget problems. Noe is less damaged than many other schools because the community school program keeps the gym open early mornings and late evenings. It is still not enough. Because of the high intensity of instruction in some teams, Brooks wants a recreation director, recess, and time just to play.

The Community

That Noe Middle School thrives as it does in the context of Louisville's public opinion about schools is to some people nothing short of a miracle. Their attempts to account for its acceptance are also replete with contradictions. Unlike cities such as Detroit and Chicago, parents in Louisville cannot move to the suburbs to put their children in different schools. The county and city systems are merged. "There's only one game in town," a school board member says. To satisfy parents' demand for an academically oriented college preparatory school, the system has opened the Traditional School, which requires two years of Latin in middle school and two in high school, and accepts only students who have no record of any behavioral problem in school. It is, some parents say, "an elite public private school."

For parents who might be attracted to the Traditional School, the Advanced Program at Noe, in conjunction with its other activities, seems satisfactory. They say, however, that Noe is not well known throughout the city, whereas the Traditional School has been highly publicized in the media, not the least example of which was a syndicated column by William Rasberry of the *Washington Post.* In it he castigated the Jefferson County School Board for ignoring the wishes of 4,000 parents whose children were on a waiting list for the Traditional School. Some community leaders and school board members want an entire system of traditional schools, with students who cannot hack the work or the behavior code placed in alternative programs. They have used Rasberry's column to buttress their argument that the board is unresponsive to parental preference.

Noe, however, is in no danger despite community antipathy to open-plan schools, numerous school closings, and a system nearly bankrupt financially. There are forces in Louisville that run counter to the Traditional School movement. Some parents fear schools that skim the most academically apt students off the top and remove them from other schools. Also, they are no longer furious about busing, partly because intolerable conditions like 26-mile bus rides in one direction have been eliminated, partly because some feel desegregation has worked in their schools. Parents who withheld their children from school for fifteen days to protest busing, including the head of the PTA, are opposed to the Traditional School's elitism. Some now find themselves in the ironic position of publicly opposing neighborhood school closings on the grounds that these schools have made progress in the very desegregation plans they opposed several years ago.

Meanwhile, Noe Middle School, which benefited for several years from the inattention caused by chaos elsewhere, continues to twirl off in space, alone. Many in Louisville do not pick up its sound waves. People in the community do not believe in Noe as a concept; they write it off as a unique phenomenon totally dependent on a brilliant administrator. Many admire it while asking for busing to be stopped and Traditional Schools to multiply. A television reporter points out that Kentucky is known for bourbon, the Derby, basketball, and crazy parents attacking troopers. Now, thanks to Ralston-Purina and William Rasberry, it is also known for sewer explosions and 4,000 names on a Traditional School's waiting list.

Brooks has caused the school to turn inward and become a self-sufficient community. In this community, teachers worry about multiaged vs. graded teams and heterogeneous vs. homogeneous grouping. They wish researchers could tell them if all their efforts to individualize, to have interdisciplinary classes, and to have heterogeneous ability grouping make a difference. "If they don't make a difference," Terry Brooks says, "we're all a bunch of fools. A lot of extra effort is based on a wish and a prayer." They think a lot about whether they are rebels staking new claims or are in the grand old tradition of one-room schoolhouses, multiaged and tied to community needs. They do not feel, in any event, that they belong in the 1980s because of the decade's emphasis on convergence. "Noe is a problem child because it is divergent," one of them says. They insist on their uniqueness.

They feel that refusals of other schools to learn from Noe are "concessions to mediocrity." Visiting other schools like Centerville Middle School in Ohio was important to Noe's development. Based on such schools, Noe should be in a White, middle-class neighborhood. It is, according to its models, the wrong building and the wrong program for the wrong community and the wrong students. If it works here, it can work anywhere, teachers say. In the final analysis, the staff feels that if the community paid too much attention to what Noe is doing, it would cause the school serious trouble. At the same time, everyone agrees that the school has made it in the system because of its record of success and because "Terry has done his political homework." None of this makes any sense, says a visitor. Terry Brooks replies: "Don't study it too hard," as he leads his staff in a quiet secession into "the independent state of Noe."

Notes

1. Charity James, *Beyond Customs: An Educator's Journey* (New York: Schocken, 1974):67.
2. Ibid.
3. For discussion see National Institute of Education, "Instructionally Effective Schools: Research Area Plan" (Washington, D.C.: mimeographed, 1980): 10,
4. William A. Firestone, "Images of Schools and Patterns of Change," *American Journal of Education* 88 (August 1980):462–64.
5. Michael Rutter et al., *Fifteen Thousand Hours: Secondary Schools and Their Effects on Children* (Cambridge, Mass.: Harvard University Press, 1979):188.
6. Mary Haywood Metz, *Classrooms and Corridors: The Crisis of Authority in Desegregated Secondary Schools* (Berkeley, Cal.: University of California Press, 1978):148.
7. Janet Ward Schofield, "Complementary and Conflicting Identities: Images of Interaction in an Interracial School," *The Development of Friendship: Description and Intervention,* ed. Steve Asher and John Gottman (Cambridge: Cambridge University Press, forthcoming):284.

6

Inspired Malcontents

The Shoreham–Wading River Middle School
Shoreham, New York

They absolutely know me here.
—A Shoreham–Wading River Middle School seventh-grader

Organization

A sample student schedule at the Shoreham–Wading River Middle School looks pedestrian. An eighth-grader, for instance, has advisory daily, either French or Spanish four times a week, PE twice a week, required arts courses four times a week for ten weeks each, and math, English, science, and social studies daily. Health takes the place of science for one quarter of the school year. Band, orchestra, or chorus electives are offered four times a week before first period. The curriculum for seventh-graders is the same. Sixth-graders have math, science, social studies, and language arts five times a week, and foreign language, arts, and PE three times a week each. Interscholastics, intramurals, and clubs are offered after the eight-period school day, from 2:20 to 5:00.

The organization of the school is not surprising either. The physical plant has four classroom wings that radiate off the media center. Students are divided into four houses, or as the school calls them, to the confusion of visitors, "wings." These organizational wings have two classes each of grades six, seven, and eight, but there is no multiaging in the wings for core subjects. Teachers in grades seven and eight are in teams of two teachers who usually share the classes in the standard combinations of language arts/social studies and science/math. Sixth-grade teachers function in teams of two for some activities and across grades for some, such as math. Students usually stay in the same wing for three years. While unusual for most junior high schools, this organization is becoming common in many middle schools today.[1]

The bland appearance of organizational charts and sample schedules belies the richness of the educational environment at Shoreham–Wading River Middle School. The school is a luminous example of unconditional dedication to the academic, personal, and social growth of its early adolescent students. It reverberates with originality.

Purposes, Goals, and Definitions

The middle school's first principal, Dennis Littky, said in an introduction to the school written for parents: "The approach to education that the middle school takes begins with the fact that it *is* a middle school, and that it has the opportunity to build a curriculum around the specific needs of eleven-, twelve-, and thirteen-year-olds, a group little considered in educational literature. The school is not, therefore, an 'advanced elementary school' or a 'baby high school,' but recognizes that there is a certain kind of education appropriate to students at this stage of their development."

This "certain kind of education" is expressed through every aspect of school life at Shoreham–Wading River. The school is a coherent realization of a philosophy of schooling that begins with a knowledge of early adolescent development and requires that every practice—curricular decisions, instructional techniques, school organization, parent involvement, even (or especially) hiring—be scrutinized in light of that knowledge.

At an evening meeting for the parents of incoming sixth-graders, Cary Bell, the school's third principal, tells parents that curriculum does not come first; understanding the nature of pre- and young adolescents comes first, and everything flows from that understanding. Dr. Bell shows a slide-tape presentation on the Shoreham–Wading River Middle School made several years earlier to highlight the school's curricular responses to early adolescent development. "Our curriculum goals are the same from year to year, but our methods change." The slide-tape discusses teaching basics through experiences, young adolescents' need for the arts, for experiences that make them feel confident about their abilities, for caring adults, and for a variety of teachers and experiences.

The new assistant principal, Bonne Sue Adams, reinforces everything that has been said, giving specific examples of how instructional strategies are based on the staff's conviction that early adolescence is a special time in life and therefore needs a school "that is neither an elementary school moved up nor a high school moved down. We are child-centered because of the special physical, cognitive, and emotional needs of the students," she says, and then moves to a discussion of skills to reassure parents that "we're not in the business of having joyful illiterates here." Nonetheless, the evening ends on the note that this age group has powerful social and emotional needs, so they will be in a school "with caring people who deal with emotions as well as brains, with the child as a growing social person."

Curriculum: Developmental Responsiveness

This school philosophy is expressed through established curricular events that make the day-to-day operations of Shoreham–Wading River Middle School, rather than the mundane or witless offerings of many middle-grade schools, a fertile learning environment for students, staff, and parents. The school effervesces with advising, community service, farming, the arts, Authors' Week, Booktalk—standard components of the curriculum available to all students.

Every school day begins with Advisory, a commitment by the middle school and the school board of 75 minutes (and a double bus run) to a concept central to the school: pre- and young adolescents need to have a trusting relationship with at least one adult in the school where they spend a minimum of six hours a day. The rationale for Advisory is related to family life as well. As it was explained to parents in a "Friday Memo," one of a series of short papers written by school staff to explain the school to parents, policy setters, and visitors: "As adolescence approaches and children's peers become more important to them, it may be increasingly difficult for children to communicate honestly and trustingly with parents and other adults. Even if the family structure is strong, adolescents begin breaking away and looking to test themselves with other teenagers. Children are accessible to each other, but what about other adults?"

The middle school, always setting policy based on its understanding of early adolescent development, argues that its students need consistency and stability in their communication with adults. For this reason, they are opposed to the typical school for young adolescents: "[Most] schools move children quickly through 45-minute periods, not allowing anyone much of a chance to get to know one another. In most schools, nothing is built into the program to allow children to look at the total picture of what is happening to them and to have the guidance and support in doing so. The Shoreham–Wading River Middle School has built its entire program around the concept of an advisory system, one that emphasizes consistency, support, and advocacy for every child." From 7:50 to 8:28 a.m., when some students come to school on an early bus run for band or chorus, every student has a one-on-one talk with his or her advisor at least once monthly. From 8:30 to 8:40, the start of the regular school day, homeroom chores are taken care of in an advisory group whose small size is made possible by using all professional staff as advisors.

Advisory begins in an easygoing manner between one adult and approximately ten students. There is a lot of touching and banter as everyone settles in. The mood is comfortable and low-key. Aside from providing guidance, personal counseling, and a mechanism for taking care of routine chores, Advisory provides a calm beginning to the school day.

From 8:40 to 9:05, the school becomes silent while everyone reads. This is SSR, or Sustained Silent Reading. One teacher comments on the importance of SSRs being part of the 75-minute advisory period: "It's cool to like teachers, because of advisory. It's cool to like authors, because SSR takes place with one's advisor. Reading is made very personal." When the school is deeply absorbed in SSR, students can partake of the peace and quiet they need as much as adults do.

The advisor holds parent-teacher conferences at least twice yearly. Teachers submit grades and narrative comments to the advisor, who is in charge of knowing everything going on academically with his or her advisees and conveying this information to parents. Complaints about students' behavior are referred to advisors, not administrators, unless they are recurrent or dramatic. Advisors are expected to be students' advocates. They also share enjoyable activities with their advisees, like breakfasts at McDonald's, bowling, camping, roller-skating, and picnics, to strengthen their relationship.

During the one-on-one advisory period each month, discussions revolve around schoolwork, plans, feelings, discipline, television programs, or anything else the student and advisor want to share. The important message, whatever the specific content, is that there is an accessible adult who is listening. If there is a crisis, a relationship has already been established so that there is a contact person standing ready. No one can get lost at Shoreham–Wading River Middle School.

As I have observed the 10-to 15-year-olds over the last twenty years, individual contact with nonfamily adults who can develop ties of mentorship, friendship, and simple availability has assumed great importance to me. The teacher-advisee system is one device to achieve that—I'm sure there are many others as well. Teachers usually serve as advisors. I am unimpressed with a counseling arrangement. Teachers I have observed [who] are the best in [the advisory] system are quite often flexible in their shifting of roles and comfortable with acting as a teacher in the classroom and an older friend-uncle-sister-role outside of the class. [Larry Cuban, Stanford University, former superintendent of schools, Arlington, Virginia, letter to author, October 29, 1980.]

When teachers are asked what the most important aspect of their school is, they invariably point to the advisory system. As one teacher says: "If everything else were traditional, we would still have teachers really knowing students and being advocates, helping with everything confronting them as they become adolescents." Teachers say there is an unexpected benefit from the advisory system, since they get feedback about curriculum and instruction during talks with their advisees. "It's a form of evaluation," one says. "I can pursue what's working and drop what isn't because of students' willingness to communicate." Through Advisory, students get to explore their feelings, share themselves with an adult, identify with one person who will be an advocate if necessary, and to identify with a small group of fellow students with whom to start the day, together with an adult, in a genuinely sociable manner.

"Connect" is the key word. I'm a big outlet. You can connect. You can plug into me. [A Shoreham–Wading River Middle School teacher]

Many aspects of the curriculum at Shoreham–Wading River Middle School vie with Advisory for first place when students, staff, and parents are asked to identify one thing that expresses the philosophy of the school. Community service is always high on the list, if not first: "A school serves a community by educating its children. If, in addition, by serving the community in other ways it can educate its children better, then the community is doubly blessed," begins a "Friday Memo" on community service. In 1979–80, 484 out of the 560 students in the school took part in the community service program, which is staffed by a full-time coordinator and three assistants. It grew from a small volunteer effort to a program with a budget of $27,600, which covers adults' salaries but not the four mini-buses that, while shared by other schools for their activity programs, are used almost exclusively by the middle school.

Students cite community service as something deeply important to them. They work with younger children in the district's elementary schools, with preschoolers at Head Start Centers, with the elderly in a nursing home, with retarded children at BOCES (Board of Cooperative Educational Service) centers, and on career apprenticeships. They learn to care for others, outgrow pity and appreciate the insights of the infirm or the handicapped, tap the experiences of people different from themselves, and perform essential duties for which they are held accountable. People truly depend on them. The students perform real work and, as their journals indicate, conclude that they are valuable.

We begin with the assumption that our society provides little opportunity for intergenerational relationships; that preadolescents and old people alike have

needs specific to their situations; and that a curriculum embodying young working with old has much to offer. Students may learn about aging and the aged and about society's failures and responsibilities in relation to the elderly. They may learn skills of working with the old and lonely; and they may develop caring relationships and a sense of personal responsibility and accomplishment. [Winifred E. Pardo, community service coordinator, Shoreham–Wading River Middle School, "Middle School Students Work with the Aged," unpublished paper.]

In preparation for their community service experiences, students receive specialized instruction from people who work at the sites, and from films and local speakers. Those students who work with preschool and kindergarten children use the Exploring Childhood curriculum from the Educational Development Corporation (EDC). On the job, they learn the importance of preparation, pace, and communication skills. To aid them in being reflective about their experiences, they keep journals and have discussion groups after each work session. Sometimes they become activists as a result of their work. Students who served at a nursing home interviewed senior citizens and wrote a book about their experiences. They wrote newspaper articles and appeared on television talk shows to protest the treatment of the elderly in their community. As one teacher concluded: "Two kinds of previously unharvested human resources—old and young—now give to one another."

Ten students and three adults—a drama teacher, a community service assistant, and a visitor—are riding in a van to a BOCES unit for the severely handicapped at St. Charles' Hospital. This is the last visit for the students, who have worked in puppetry with handicapped teenagers two hours weekly for ten weeks.

The students have elected the service unit as part of their social studies class. Many parents were wary about this particular experience because of its potential for being too disturbing. Some saw it as a waste of time. Thirteen students signed up; three dropped out after the first session because it was depressing.

In the van, an apprehensive visitor asks students if there is anything one needs to know in preparation for a first visit. "Robert!" several exclaim. Robert is a boy their age who had an extremely high fever three years ago. Now he has no vocabulary and has poor body control. Robert yells. His piercing screams, like a peacock in the wilds, unnerved them in the beginning. They have become able to figure out what Robert is attempting to communicate.

At St. Charles', the middle-school students enter the classroom which has become familiar to them and greet their partners in puppetry. Most have formed relationships with their partners since the first shocking visit.. Some of the BOCES students seem extremely pleased to see them. Some are in wheelchairs. They are the most alert. Others walk vacantly about the room. The middle-school students capture their attention and they begin to work on their puppets. The adults help with the puppets, set up a small theatre for an impromptu puppet show, and provide doughnuts and juice to commemorate this last visit.

The middle-school students are no longer afraid. One girl, a social loner back at school, has won group acknowledgement because of her ability to communicate with her partner. She prattles, while choosing colors for their puppet's dress, about homework and other adult impositions on her life. She is able to carry the conversation along while acknowledging with unpremeditated naturalness any contribution her partner makes.

Some pairs do puppet shows on the "theater stage." The drama teacher helps them through rough spots and keeps the tone upbeat and the pace lively. She congratulates them all after the puppet show. Her verve is essential to setting the tone for the session. Even more important to the middle school students is the surprise appearance of their social studies teacher, his first visit to St. Charles'.

Robert is given a doughnut and suddenly screams. It is a bone-chilling shriek. "I felt the same way when I tasted my first Dunkin' Donut, Robert," the social studies teacher says quietly. His students look at him in awe. He is a natural.

The BOCES teacher, while feeding a doughnut to a paralyzed boy, says she thinks this has been an excellent experience for her students. They are usually segregated and, when not, are made fun of by children their age. They crave attention from age mates. "Most are starved for attention. It gives them a feeling of accomplishment, perhaps some connectedness. Who knows? They can't tell me."

In the van on the way back to the middle school, a discussion starts about the origin of each BOCES student's handicap. Only three or four have been handicapped since birth. The rest have been injured recently, one in a car accident that has left her brain-damaged and partially paralyzed, one because of taking a drug overdose that has "wasted" her permanently, Robert because of a sudden high fever, another because of a cerebral blood clot. These middle-school seventh- and eighth-graders know in the pits of their stomachs what most young adolescents usually cannot grasp: they are not immune. It is that knowledge which is most deeply disturbing to them and to the adults with them, all of whom are parents.

Even during the sharing of fears on the drive home, however, the mood is positive. They have survived this experience, they have done it together, and they have done it well. They feel they have triumphed. In fact, two girls and a boy conclude they have come to like several of the students they met, and this affection is more than reciprocated. One of the girls with cerebral palsy has a crush on her partner. The teasing begins.

The students notice that their visitor is writing notes in a steno pad. Why and what, they want to know. The problem is, the visitor explains, that it is very difficult to capture the nature of this experience. What adjectives or adverbs or nouns can possibly describe the people they have just worked with? From the back of the van, words come hurtling toward the steno pad: drooling, screaming, braces, aggravation, grabbing, unfocused eyes, stuttering, paralysis, twitching, crooked teeth, preoccupied, searching eyes, hard to understand, eager to laugh—and the one word that has become a signal for them and binds them all: Robert.

In its commitment to community service, Shoreham–Wading River Middle School is responding to what they and many social observers have concluded about the role of youth in American society. As Charity James, a British educator, observed after visiting American schools: "Of all the recommendations I would make as a result of my year's observation, the most urgent is that Americans make a concentrated effort to find ways in which the energy of the young can be made welcome."[2] In reference to school climate and achievement for "really difficult problem students," Duckworth has observed that "one has the notion that a group-based, service-oriented activity outside of school would be far more viable in terms of channeling work energy and legitimating the purpose of work to these students than much that can be offered in school."[3] Garbarino, conducting research about the socialization of youth to adulthood, remarks that "the key is how well adolescents are involved in a network of *genuinely* important productive analogs to actual adult functions. When the social logic of adolescence as entree to adulthood is clear, the transitional institutions and rituals have self-evident meaning. Where the connection is tenuous, obscure, or lacking, then those same transitional institutions and rituals lose their meaning and may be the object of hostility. The application of this idea to schools and schooling is clear."[4]

These observations are not new. What is different is that Shoreham–Wading River Middle School acts on them. The school recognizes young adolescents' need to engage in activities that demand responsible behavior from them, to test their competence in a variety of arenas, and to make meaningful contributions to their communities. The school also recognizes its community's need for these contributions. Surrounded by their peers and supported by adults, students at the middle school serve their community and, in so doing, gain a more profound sense of who they are and what it means to be human.

The schedule for the community service program is posted on a large chart in the community service office. In the first three months of 1980–81, 44 students were engaged in career apprenticeships in aviation, solar energy, the arts, veterinary medicine, law, and politics; 70 students worked with library story hours, at nursery and preschools, and with handicapped young children; and 12 students every five weeks visited parts of the community in a health van, distributing information about preventive health care. In the same three-month period, students were also taking large measures of responsibility for school-sponsored events like a variety show, a photography exhibit, an exchange program with a Japanese school run for the children of Japanese businessmen in New York, Mount Sinai Harbor trips, a trip to New York City and Fire Island, orchestra concerts at an elementary school, a presentation of a large student-made multimedia show called "American Voices," a Thanksgiving food drive for migrant farm workers, a "Reading is Fundamental" book fair, and a visit to the school by Brookhaven Lab Nursery School students.

Some opportunities for students to shoulder responsibility do not show up on the service charts. The most exceptional of these is the farm. The farm was designed and built by eighth-grade science classes, with its genesis in a unit on environments. Students who had worked on plans for a farm as part of the unit decided they wanted to build the farm they had designed. It required checking zoning laws, learning about caring for animals, conducting cost analyses on boarding animals, building to scale a model with complete cost and time schedules for construction, and making a presentation to the Board of Education to ask for permission and matching funds to clear land and start building. After prodigious work and with permission granted, the science classes became involved in building the farm on a site 150 × 80 feet, under the direction of the shop teacher. They also cleared a garden plot 30 × 100 feet and developed a small orchard of 12 dwarf apple, peach, and pear trees. Two years later, in 1976, students added a bicentennial barn, 25 × 30 feet, based on colonial barn plans, for sheep, goats, rabbits, and hay storage.

A description of the opening ceremony for the farm appears in a 1977 "Friday Memo": "The school band played, a member of the Board of Education stood proudly with a gold shovel, and the dedication to the farm began. With marching music in the background, twenty-five eighth-graders were announced, each carrying a chicken into its new home. Four students made speeches and then, as the band began the finale, a tractor with flags streaming came up the drive into the center of the study body with the farm's first goat, Annabel. The farm was here to stay."

There are now ducks, chickens, rabbits, turkeys, quail, goats, and sheep. Every week two students take responsibility for the upkeep of the farm. They and others tend to early chores from 7:40 to 8:30 and continue to care for the animals during lunch, after school, and on weekends. Units on shearing, carding, dyeing, and weaving wool are worked into art classes. Science classes learn about breeding. When babies are about to be born, students take their sleeping bags to the barn and camp out during the vigil. Students lead young children on tours through the garden and farm. Volunteers learn procedures for animal care and take more than eighty "practicals" (exams) on them. Older students help younger students learn the "practicals," as do adult volunteers.

Opel the goat has taught our students to care, feed, and respect her. She has motivated students to read and write about goats and to take on daily responsibilities. In the spring, she is planning to teach the students about birth and caring for her young. ["Friday Memo" no. 2–77, 1977.]

The school year starts with about 125 farm volunteers, who continue to work through the fall, until a harvest breakfast. In winter, about 30 diehards persist in working outdoors, the number swelling to close to the original roster in the spring. Students learn about organic gardening and self-sufficiency. Three and a half miles from the nuclear power plant that gives the school district its munificent tax base, students are reminded by the inexorable demands of the farm and garden that they are living on a fragile planet. School life is not insular for these students who live in a White, middle-class, exurban community. Instead, they gain direct access to the natural life cycle of plants and animals. They study and live side-by-side with birth, growth, and death.

There is a group of students who spend every free moment outside with the animals. Others are repelled by their nakedness and odors. For over one-fifth of the students, the farm is an important part of school life. The students become competent tending to animals who are utterly dependent on them. They make a difference to the well-being of other living creatures. The farm affords these students a way to express themselves and a unique insight into the interrelatedness of people, land, and animals.

Some students, when asked what Shoreham–Wading River Middle School stands for, say, "the arts." Parents say some people in the community refer to it as "the art school." Through an arts program that pervades the life of the school and surrounding townships, students at the middle school are given rich and multiple opportunities for self-expression and service. Students at the middle school are scheduled for "arts" three times a week in sixth grade; four, in seventh and eighth.[5] They take general Music, media, home economics, theater, ceramics, woodcrafts, woodwork, studio art, and visual art. The school also has an "open arts" policy: students may go to any of these arts classes during lunch and early in the morning to pursue their classwork or to try out new skills. The beauty of their products is acknowledged within the school by a showcase filled with their work and by the door to the principal's office, which is framed with vivid panels of stained glass. Outside the school, stores in neighboring townships display the students' crafts, and cultural organizations commission them to design publicity posters.

The school's two-day arts festival in June is a highlight of the year. Enamels, prints, pottery, woodwork, and other crafts are displayed outside. Food is served, and students, parents, staff, and neighbors gather to admire the products of a year's spectacular creativity, accompanied by the music of student ensembles. Community residents and teachers are invited to display their work side-by-side with the students'.

An art teacher taught stained glass techniques to students from an alternative English class who are reading one to two years below grade level, to give them a new area for achievement and self-expression. They in turn taught classes on stained glass to adults from the community. This activity, like many others, is an outgrowth of the philosophy of the arts faculty, whose overriding goal is that students be successful in the arts, and, through success, choose to return again and again. They do.

General Music is a required class in New York. It is usually a dismal pencil-and-paper class rejected by teachers as well as students. At Shoreham –Wading River Middle School, General Music has become electronic and computer music. Students haunt junk yards and learn to make instruments from their finds, especially from the hubcaps of demolished cars. The music teacher, who refers to General Music as "the travesty of music education," teaches electronic, improvisational, and experimental music, and some rock and jazz, stressing the fundamentals of rhythm, harmony, and melody: "If I taught art, would they just *look* at art? If you want to teach music, have them write and do music." Students "compose, play, and listen." They set their own poetry and the works of modern writers to music. Some evenings, they go to clubs where their teacher performs: "My preparation comes from playing in clubs. College did a horrible job of preparing me." The music teacher has found his niche: "This is home. I would never leave Middle School. It's a real turn-on for me."

I swear to you I believe in hubcaps. It's not a gimmick. This is all for real. Kids know when something is a gimmick. [A Shoreham–Wading River Middle School music teacher]

Instrumental music is taught in the sleepy hours of early morning by a different music teacher, who taught at Mark Twain Junior High School, a magnet school in New York City for gifted and talented students. "This is a better school," he says—"They care more. In the advisory system one person is responsible for establishing close contact with a student, for liaison with teachers and parents—for being a representative of that child. In music, also, we fit the program to the child, not vice versa." There are over 200 students, more than one-third of the study body, in the instrumental music program. Students set their own goals, from taking individual lessons to performing in group competitions. The students have won regional band contests and an exchange trip with British band students. They keep journals during competitions, analyzing their own feelings and other bands' performances: "The intonation was poor in the third clarinet." Through jazz band (a highly select group of 20–25 students who meet one night weekly), through large musical productions that use original Broadway production scores, through beginning, intermediate, and advanced bands, special brass, woodwind, dixieland, and mixed ensembles, and through individual and small group lessons, students are urged to become proficient with an instrument and to develop discerning taste. The instrumental music teacher believes in offering an enticing variety to lure students toward musical proficiency: "As a teacher of mine used to say, kids are like spaghetti. If you push it, it bunches up. If you walk around the table and pull [he walks around a desk and slowly pulls the air], it comes over *so* easily."

In the media class, students choose a project from among four types: animated films, such as object animation, content or flat animation, drawing animation, and pixilation; slide show productions synchronized with sound (the school has a sound mixer); video projects; and photography projects, using 35 mm cameras and developing equipment for mobiles or vignettes. The planning stage of each of these projects is given the greatest emphasis in the course, along with work habits and effort. Students produce zany animations inspired by Monty Python, painstaking animations of eggs cracking, and wistful beach scenes (students may take cameras home to shoot the scenes). With only 10–15 students at a time–"a luxury and a strength," the teacher says–students are given the attention they need to gain confidence in what for most is a new art form.

New York State's art curriculum deals only with graphic arts. State evaluators criticize the lack of a survey art course that follows the curriculum. The state does not recognize electronic music, home economics, woodwork, and media as "art." Because the school has been granted experimental status—middle schools are "experimental" in New York—the superintendent can back the arts teachers when they submit a statement of their philosophy in answer to a negative evaluation.

More examples of students' expressiveness abound. In woodwork class, they build lovely wooden boxes to make autobiographical statements. One girl's box contains, in careful arrangement, bubblegum, a comb, tapes, a small stuffed animal, and pictures of rock stars. In woodshop, where students make larger and heavier items than in woodwork, fourteen students at a time work on a playground they are building for the school. The literary magazine, *Contemplations,* won a prize at Columbia University in 1980 for its literary and graphic excellence. The 1981 issue published contributions from sixty-six writers. The art teacher stayed home with the art staff for two days to work on the superb graphics for final copy. They compete against high-school students as well as middle-schoolers, and win. The school is serious about the arts and has the funds to support the small classes, equipment, and supplies that a superior arts program requires, and the staff that such support attracts.

Authors' Week is yet another special activity built into the school's curriculum that entices students to consider themselves in relation to the rich variety of making and doing in people's lives. Based on student interest, availability, and diversity, authors are invited to Shoreham–Wading River Middle School to discuss their craft. Students sign up to meet with individual authors. They must have read at least one book by the author. A host class guides each author through the day. Students prepare questions for their sessions with the authors, each of whom receives a student-made gift at the end of the visit. Students learn that writing is a discipline. Writers get to meet their readers. In some cases, they review their manuscripts in progress to try out new ideas with the students. Sometimes an author stays several days to work with a group of students on his or her manuscript.

The brochure for Authors' Week of 1981 cites Carlyle: "We have not READ an author until we have seen his object, whatever it may be, as HE saw it." In 1981, students met authors and editors like Paula Danziger, Arnold Adoff, Richard Peck, Avi, Paula Fox, M.E. Kerr, James Lincoln Collier, Edward Packard, and others whom they selected on the basis of their reading. They got to meet the people behind the books they read and to see their works as the authors saw them. At the end of the week, 80 percent of eighth-graders said, in response to a questionnaire, that they liked to write. This figure has gone up consistently for four years because of Authors' Week. The result of another question pleased the teachers. When asked four years ago who their favorite writer was, "Judy Blume won hands down." In 1981, no one said Judy Blume "because they have been given the opportunity to become aware of too many other authors." Two teachers keep track of students' answers annually and report their findings at one of the weekly Monday morning staff breakfasts.

The success of Authors' Week is made possible because it is not an isolated special event. Books are important at Shoreham–Wading River Middle School. Sustained Silent Reading and *Contemplations* express the school's commitment to reading and creative writing. So does Booktalk. When a new social studies teacher was hired, a colleague welcomed him with the challenge: "What will be your contribution to our school life?" He responded with Booktalk. Students sign up to read books and then meet every three weeks to discuss them in groups of about eight students and one adult. Booktalk started in the eighth grade and has evolved into a school-wide replacement for monthly book reports. In All-School Booktalk, which is multiaged, there are sixty groups of students meeting during any one of the four academic periods with an adult—principal, teacher, secretary, janitor—who has also signed up to read that book. SSR, Authors' Week, and Booktalk all make reading social and creative as well as solitary, through the close association of students and adults in what the school calls "celebrations of reading."

Everyone takes part in Booktalk. My daughter has discussed books with the custodian. I think that's pretty terrific when I think about it. I do have to think about it. [A Shoreham–Wading River Middle School parent]

Sometimes, as with the farm, one teacher's assignment becomes a curricular "happening," as the school gets caught up in the ferment of one class's activity. "American Voices," a multimedia show produced by one English class, was such an event. As an English class was deciding which out of the many possible quotations from citizens throughout American history to read onto tapes for "American Voices," teachers and students from other classes started lobbying for their favorite notables and quotations. Debate increased, so the teacher invited other staff members to nominate their five favorite candidates for inclusion and to make brief statements of support. The entire school got involved in the whirl of researching, orating, and voting on behalf of their "voices."

The multimedia show has been taken on the road to Sidwell Friends School in Washington, D.C., and to Laredo Middle School, as part of the two schools' exchange program, and to a New York State social studies conference, each time by a different group of twelve students. They go in their "American Voices" T-shirts and with their ever-present journals.

The Shoreham–Wading River Middle School is built on the premise that the preadolescent child needs a stimulating, stable, humane, and supportive environment. We feel that the only true way for a child to get prepared for the future is to learn to deal successfully with the present. . . . Students will be exposed to different people, different environments, and different materials, in an attempt to give personal meaning to the curriculum which will lead towards an increased pride in their work. The emphasis is for each child to be successful in some areas of school life through which a positive self image can be built. [The Shoreham–Wading River Middle School philosophy statement]

Curriculum at Shoreham–Wading River Middle School is an expression of the school's commitment to creating a learning environment responsive to the needs of young adolescents. Through the arts, whether in classes specifically called "arts" or in academic subject areas, young adolescents make meaningful contributions to their school and out-of-school communities; they interact naturally and constantly with peers and adults; they explore and define their feelings in relation to their own making and doing and the creativity of others; they have a multitude of opportunities to gain a sense of competence in a broad variety of skills; they are physically as well as intellectually active; the diversity of activities seems boundless; and the unmitigated emphasis on self-expression and inventiveness takes place within a structured environment deliberately determined by adults who are concerned about young adolescents' need for limits.

When Goodlad and Klein observed elementary schools, they were struck by the constriction of instructional practices: "We saw few teacher-made devices, little construction employing saw and hammer, few field trips or preparations for them, little exploration of the outdoors or of fantasy. Are we losing our touch with the world of real things? Our ability to create, to make things with our hands? Are these matters being taken care of outside the school? Is school to be concerned only with the academic?"[6] After just one or two days at Shoreham–Wading River Middle School, a visitor finds these questions surprisingly irrelevant. The school has moved far away from a pigeonholing of subject matter; a division of human endeavor into "academic" and "extracurricular;" a radical disjunction between thought and action; and an artificial disengagement of school from community.

Shoreham–Wading River Middle School is a different order of school from those observed by Goodlad and Klein. It is centered on "the world of real things," or "fabrication," to use Duckworth's term. Duckworth, discussing the connotations of the various meanings of work in schools, observes that "life in a school organized around student work-as-jobs is likely to be quite different from life in a school organized around student work-as-fabrication: in the former case, issues of subordination predominate; in the latter case, issues of accomplishment predominate."[7] The distinction between jobs and fabrication is one that Hannah Arendt makes, counterposing to labor the image of *homo faber,* "man the maker." Duckworth argues that in schools based on student fabrication, "work takes on the sense of culture, understood in its broadest sense, with connotations of growth, achievement, and in a certain way, self-actualization, where the self is not understood as something over against society but rather a facet of society."[8] Schoolwork at Shoreham–Wading River Middle School is, to a remarkable extent, fabrication. It is the work of *homo faber* in as many of his incarnations as an unprovincial, inventive staff can sustain.

The diversity of experiences available to students at the middle school is so great that some parents and teachers worry about the pressure it puts on students. In one week of early April, 1981, the school was in the throes of Authors' Week; students taking French had just returned from a week in Quebec; thirteen students were at Laredo Middle School as part of the

Colorado exchange; other students were working feverishly on the last stage of *Contemplations;* an eighth-grade team was planning a trip to Great Adventure and historical sites in Philadelphia; twelve students were going off to present "American Voices" to a New York State social studies conference; and students in one team were selling pizza to raise $2,000 for a social studies trip up the Hudson River on Pete Seeger's environmental sloop. In two days of that week, visitors to the school included many authors, people observing Authors' Week, two teachers from other Long Island schools, and Colorado exchange students.

Diversity is also offered through an athletic program that involves 80 percent of the students, a school store that students built and manage (students handle the money—it grosses $10,000 annually—do the necessary merchandising, and wait on customers during lunch), and special days like "gum day" or "junk day" when "you can just mess around, and with teachers, too," according to the students. During lunch, students stress the different places they can go to: gym, outside, arts rooms, the library, the farm, and the blue room, a former garage that is now a lounge with games, electronic and percussion instruments, and a blasting record player.

When students discuss Shoreham–Wading River Middle School, they say that only one need of theirs is not met in school, the need for information about sex: "They completely ignore sex education," one student says; "the superintendent won't get into it." They learn about first aid, alcohol, tobacco, and other standard items in health, and about fetal development in science. A seventh-grade boy complains: "They teach us after." "After what?" he is asked. "They teach us, you know, about it after. They don't teach us about. . ." He turns red and lapses into silence, sorry he has started at all. "Do you mean they don't teach you about contraception?" he is asked by a visitor. "That's right. They show us films in science that start after, with the fetus. That's too late." A seventh-grade girl adds: "It's too late by seventh grade, anyway." Several students say they read books in the library that "teach us before," and can point exactly to where they are on the shelves (as can the librarian). They love the library and are happy to read about "before" there. They discuss "it" in Advisory and on trips with faculty members. In a predominantly Catholic community, the superintendent has decided that, given all the other risks schools take, sex education should be left to home and church. Some students and teachers disagree.

Instructional Practices

Teachers at the middle school place a great deal of emphasis on academic content, more than one might expect in a maverick middle school that emphasizes personal and social growth and development. While it seems incongruous to say that the staff believes students develop through academics just as they do through the arts, service, and athletics, it needs saying. In some schools, this perspective has been lost in debates between "back to basics" and experiential learning. In many, it has been lost because of an inattentiveness to standards pertaining to intellect. Academic emphasis has not been lost at Shoreham–Wading River Middle School, perhaps because of the nature of the school's clientele. Students enter the middle school scoring above the national norm on standardized achievement tests. Many come from highly cultured backgrounds. Like any good school, the middle school meets its students where they are and takes them on from there. Their starting point is very advanced in comparison with inner-city students, on the average. In a good school, everyone "levels up," as Rutter says. In the middle school, they "level up" from an advanced base.

The academic emphasis in the school is also a product of the quality of its staff. Dennis Littky, who as first principal was able to hire his own staff, selected people who felt comfortable with teaching young adolescents, who were knowledgeable in their academic fields, broad in their interests, and very expressive. Then "he let us teach our own obsessions." This seasoned staff continues to teach with an obsessive intensity.

We think about everything we do. That's our program. Some teachers are very academic so the students get a well-rounded program. We have bright people here. You're not going to get your baseline education. [A Shoreham–Wading River Middle School teacher]

Some teachers follow the New York State curriculum closely. Others devise their own curricula while meeting the general expectations of the state. As one teacher says: "There is a lot of autonomy. The state curriculum mandates American Studies in eighth grade. You can drive a truck through that." The foreign-language teachers adhere to the state curriculum to ensure articulation with the high school, but the program is "very middle school," as a district principal says.

In a seventh-grade, second-year French class, conducted entirely in French, students practice ordering food at a butcher shop, a bakery, and a dairy. They add francs and centimes and count change. Around the room are French paperbacks like *Ça ne va pas, Charlie Brown,* and *Babar en Amérique,* maps of France that students have drawn, their compositions on French-speaking African countries, and their personal photographs with answers to questions introducing themselves (some have added their own comments). There is also a sign reminding students that "homework more than one day late is UNSATISFACTORY." It is in English, lest first-year students misunderstand the teacher's expectations.

The students turn from ordering food to writing compositions on "Ma Famille" or a member of the family. They are learning composition skills as they would in any English classroom, because the middle school believes in "English in every classroom." They prepare an outline, write at least five sentences about their topic, put them in logical sequence, have a classmate look them over and make suggestions for improvement, and then show them to the teacher. Later, they will present the short composition orally to the class, without notes and, the teacher hopes, without memorization. The teacher moves about among the thirteen students in the classroom, helping them and keeping them on task ("are you using your time well?" she asks two boys who are clowning around, leaning over them quickly and looking at their work). Toward the end of the class period the teacher works with the entire class again, preparing them for the vocabulary in their homework assignment. She reads, then has volunteers read after her. It is a beautifully paced lesson in a French-speaking environment.

Next year, the students will be in a real French environment, Quebec, learning a language through survival. Students are given identity cards that identify them as Americans learning French and requesting that only French be spoken to them. They then attack "survival activities" like going up to a stranger to ask for directions, ordering food in a restaurant, changing money, working out the logistics of train schedules, and playing soccer with local students. They go on two trips, the first for five days early in the year so they can identify areas needing improvement, and the second in the spring to motivate that improvement, to see the difference in their skills, and to practice them further. They keep journals, which they write in every evening; they debrief; and then they go out each evening to attend something in French, like a film, a hockey game, or a cultural event, in order to have fun in a foreign language.

Instructional style at Shoreham–Wading River Middle School is as diverse as its teachers. In one classroom, a math and social studies teacher (who teams with a language arts and science teacher) is drilling about twenty students on converting fractions to percentages by means of a lively game. The technique is simple and successful: if you miss an answer or fail to answer in three seconds, you stand; if you miss again, you stand on your chair; a third time and you stand on the table. The pace is rapid-fire, and the tone is humorous. The students are tense and delighted. Then the teacher adds decimals to the game, in preparation for a test they are about to take. There is no attempt to trick them in the test or to have them do poorly. When they say they have had enough drill, the test begins. He asks whether they would rather write their answers as percentages or decimals. They vote and split down the middle. He decides that either one is okay. Giving the test is a political act for this teacher because it prepares students for the Standard Achievement Tests. Scores need to be kept up so that parental support remains high, he says. Not all teachers agree. Several ignore the tests as much as possible.

The period is over but the students have become interested in conversions, so math class continues. It is a double period, and therefore there is no need to truncate the lesson prematurely. When they have finished, they move to a section of the room with two double-decker lofts, mattresses, grubby coverings on old, run-down furniture, and dog-eared paperbacks. The students sprawl on the mattresses and couches, taking part in a fast-paced review that touches on the importance of food surpluses in establishing civilizations, a comparison of Mayan Indians with Egyptians, the concomitant appearances of pyramids in two parts of the world, and the inaccuracy of the viewpoint that Mesopatamia was the "cradle of civilization." Sitting under posters of American Indians, they begin a unit on the Iroquois Indians, comparing their creation stories with the Old Testament's and relating their form of government to contemporary American government. It is a dynamic discussion triggered by a social studies textbook but governed by the strength of the teacher's personality. The students are with him every second. At one point in the review, students discuss New Mexican pueblo adobes. Several of them look at their classmates sitting close to one another on a double-decker structure and discussing the first apartment buildings in America. They note the humor.

In another classroom, the day begins with an advisory session of eight students. After SSR, the teacher talks with several students about their choices of books for Booktalk. Others are reading on a fine sofa and wicker chair in a corner of the room. A green ribbon for the children of Atlanta is pinned on a burlap bulletin board. The room has the air of a modern, well-kept study, replete with plants and posters of paintings by Edward Hopper and Georgia O'Keeffe. The room has class. It is a haven in the midst of all the tumbling, cluttered, busy environments of the school.

You hire professionals and trust them to teach what they are most qualified to. They get their rewards from teaching kids what they do best. [Shoreham–Wading River Middle School assistant principal]

The advisory discussion shifts to the subject of their eighth-grade beach trip. Will it be a roller-skating trip, instead? Which do they want? One girl sits to the side, putting rouge on. A boy is still reading his book from SSR as students enter the room for second period. "Every day the room looks different," one of them exclaims. "And do you know what's funny?" says the teacher about the new seating plan. "I never change the furniture in my house." Twenty eighth-graders spend a few moments deciding whom they are sitting near and begin to work individually on Booktalk choices. Meanwhile, the teacher invites them to come in early the next day to get better grades on a spelling test she is returning. They discuss the emblem of the T-shirt for their media production and then review vocabulary words from *Never Cry Wolf,* a book by Farley E. Mowat that they are all reading. They work together on a worksheet the teacher passes out to them.

Then the teacher begins a discussion about the chapters they have read for that day's class, getting them to see the humor of Mowat's position in the Arctic as he realizes that he who went as a biologist to observe wolves in their natural habitat is now being observed by them. She takes books from a display to read to them the arguments of authors who disagree with Mowat's contention that wolves do not prey on healthy caribou. The students want to know who is right. One suggests that they write to the authors to ask them to resolve the conflict. There is easy interchange that is more akin to an informal discussion than a model lesson with a clear beginning, transition, and conclusion.

No example of the students' work is on display in the room. The students appear to feel the sense of belonging that guests experience in an exclusive but utterly familiar club. The teacher shows students a replica of a wolf's paw print. Its size stuns them. She then poses questions to guide their reading of the next four chapters. Her tone is soft and enthusiastic. She shows them a picture of a caribou's skull. "What does it remind you of?" After a pause, a student answers, in what is a high point of cultivated classroom discourse: "Georgia O'Keeffe." The room that appeared to be solely an expression of one person's taste has also been subtly arranged to stimulate her students' ability to observe the connectedness between life and art. The students spread out on the floor and the couches to read for 15 minutes. They are very relaxed and smile as they begin to appreciate the quiet fun of Mowat's book. This has been an "English" class.

Teachers at the middle school spend a lot of time deliberating about curricular and instructional decisions, based on the nature of pre- and early adolescent development. Decisions that were made originally by Littky on the basis of early adolescent development now appear to them to be reaffirmed by the work of Herman Epstein.[9] They have received in-service coursework from Epstein, a biophysicist from Brandeis University, David Elkind from Tufts University, and Pat Arlin of the University of British Columbia. They are starting to test students to see on what Piagetian level of cognition they are functioning. The process they are engaged in, and about which some are very excited, is called "cognitive level matching" (CLM). According to Epstein, the brain does not grow in weight and arborization constantly, but in spurts that are predictable by age in 85 percent of the population. One of the periods in which the brain-to-body ratio increases is from 10 to 12. Then there is a plateau until the next, and last, brain growth spurt, which comes between 14 and 16. The increased complexity of neural networks makes possible greater complexity of thought. Epstein proposes matching the expectations of teachers and the complexity of the curriculum to the child's level of cognitive development, or cognitive level matching.

Brain growth theory is interpreted differently by teachers in the school. For some, the message is that middle-school students are in a plateau stage and thus should not be frustrated by abstract curricula inapproporiate to their cognitive maturity. "Don't analyze too much," one teacher says. "They aren't cognitively ready." To another teacher, the question is: "To what degree does intervention foster movement from one cognitive level to the next?" He is excited by the process of reviewing the curriculum to begin answering this question, so as to teach "to the leading edge of the child's cognitive development." *Leading edge* is a term used by several teachers in the school, who are optimistic that the percentage of students moving from one level of cognition to the next will increase. "Epstein is not saying to be passive," one teacher insists. Another, fearful of the ramifications of a curriculum based on a hypothetical plateau in over 80 percent of seventh- and eighth-graders, calls it "the dead-brain theory."

Epstein's work is highly controversial among many investigators, including neurophysiologists, who say that it has never been replicated and is based on a misunderstanding of brain growth and its measurement. It is less controversial among middle-school educators. What is exciting to teachers at the middle school is that "we are thinking about how kids learn." Such comments come as a surprise. What, one questions, were teachers thinking about before? "We have been thinking a lot about *what* kids learn, not *why* they learn," one teacher answers. Attention to CLM is confirming for the middle school what they have been doing all along, especially an emphasis on diverse experiences for a diverse age group. They are drawing from Epstein the message they wish to hear, some stressing "the leading edge" and others "the plateau." The school is ten years old, and a new theory, albeit untested (but now a bandwagon that attracts such hyperbolic one-liners as the assertion that it might "provide a basis for a theory of education for the first time in 3,000 years"[10]), is invigorating teachers who demand a philosophic base for what they do.

School Climate

Cognitive Level Matching, the Bay Area Writing Program, to which the district has made a large in-service commitment, and other new techniques keep the teachers alert to the nature of their task. The reputation of the school is also important in keeping the school excellent: "Kids come expecting wonderful things to happen. Teachers can't let them down," the assistant principal says. Finances help as well. The school seeks and receives grants for new programs, and the district supports self-renewal. The nature of the school day also motivates teachers. One teacher, who had taught in six different states, says that previously she had moved to new jobs because the differences kept her alert. "I've been here for seven years and I'm still doing something different. Sometimes it's frantic, and I have to seek the threads of continuity. And I go home much more tired than in the other schools. Teaching from a textbook is easier than this more integrated approach. But this is more exciting. I don't get bored."

Small class size, an adequate budget, unlimited use of mini-buses, excellent professional colleagues, enlightened administrators, strong parent support—this is a great district. Where else would all this happen? The district invests in teachers. The Bay Area Writing Program, Cognitive Level Matching, and collegial support for these changes—these are the riches I draw upon and contribute to. [A Shoreham–Wading River Middle School teacher]

Staff members are involved in most aspects of decision making through faculty meetings, Staff Council (composed of two teachers from each wing), a weekly Monday morning breakfast, and a weekly internal newsletter. The climate is conducive to active participation. The teachers are paid a high compliment by the principal of a district elementary school, who says: "I would raid this staff if I were starting a new school." The middle school's principal, Cary Bell, who was appointed along with Bonne Sue Adams, the new assistant principal, in 1980, says that the school's strengths are derived in large measure from Dennis Littky's having hired his own staff from scratch. The school was new, and teachers were hired specifically to work with the age group and with this particular school's program. Some moved from different regions of the country when they were recruited by Littky, because the school's philosophy was so attractive to them. As time went on, those who did not adapt left or were fired. The teachers who have remained want to be there.

The middle-school teachers are not universally appreciated in the district. One administrator says: "They're all hammers and no nails. They are creative change agents with a strong sense of territoriality who were young, radical innovators. Littky wanted teachers who don't go home at 3:00. He got them." Another administrator is less charitable: "They're too damned powerful in their diversity—too spoiled." Although he is credited by parents with having created an exceptional school program, the staff is Dennis Littky's greatest legacy.

Students are drawn into the culture of the school with ease. The school's reputation precedes their arrival. They anticipate doing well and having a wonderful time. One student says: "They want your opinions. And you can express youself in lots of ways. You can make what you feel in art. You can talk alone with teachers." "It's hard not to learn," a seventh-grader says. "The teachers are strict and expect a lot." One student called the school "regimented," a judgment apprehensive parents would be delighted to hear.

It is hard for some parents to see the controls in the school. No bells ring, the p.a. system is dismantled, and there is no written behavior code. One teacher, whose son attends a nearby junior high school, is convinced that controls at the middle school stem from constant communication with adults, especially in Advisory: "I ask my son, 'Did anyone speak to you today?' Here we do. We run with them during lunch, we talk with them in Advisory, we discuss books with them. They are always in conversational situations with adults—they're not lost."

A former school board member thinks that the board's decision not to have a school lunchroom helped its tone immeasurably: "Other schools said the cafeteria was their major problem. It's too much of a hassle. And we didn't want expensive space used for a cafeteria, with a mass of kids throwing food." Students eat in their wings or, in warm weather, at picnic tables outside. They go to the arts rooms, the library, the farm, the gym, the blue room, find their advisors, or just "hang around" the wing, according to their personal desires. Lunch becomes yet another time when their personal preferences count. "It's hard not to like a school that is so unlike school," an eighth-grader says.

The Shoreham–Wading River Middle School district is a generally homogeneous community that supports order in the schools and backs teachers' disciplinary measures. The community serves up to the school a group of students who, for the most part, acknowledge the importance of getting an education and have been taught to respect adults. The school does not have to socialize its students into a more vigorous set of behavioral standards. When there are value differences, they tend to be in the opposite direction. Teachers work hard to get students to loosen up, to express themselves in a variety of mediums, and just to be children for a while. Several teachers see themselves as actively opposing the possessiveness of middle-class children who have not learned to share their worldly goods or to take care of one another: "In Ocean Hill-Brownsville, everyone was poor and everyone shared. Here it's a major accomplishment to get kids to share a yogurt when someone has forgotten his lunch." The locks are coming off the lockers, slowly, to emphasize trust and caring.

Students know what the school's rules are, even without a written behavior code. "What is not allowed?" they are asked. "Drugs, cigarettes, alcohol, running in the hall, egging teachers on, cursing, cutting, disrespect for teachers." When asked how they know, some say: "You just know." They find the question absurd, as if they were born knowing the rules. "Are the rules imprinted in your genes?" The question makes them laugh and then think. After some discussion, they decide that they learn rules in Advisory and "from experience." They say they learn good character "from home, from the examples teachers set, and from their praise." They also feel that there is as much peer pressure to conform to rules as to dress. Behavior is important to them.

There is no subgroup of students hostile to the school that creates a countervailing culture, according to adults in the school. Students say there is such a group, "the heads," but can identify no more than "a couple in each wing," which is the same estimate adults give. "They have problems," a student said. "They take drugs. But they don't push them. One of them sold aspirins as if they were hard drugs. That's our only drug problem."

The layout of the building in three manageable classroom wings, the constant but informal presence of adults moving about as students do, the small size of groups that move at one time in the corridors outside the wings, the lack of a cafeteria—all contribute to an atmosphere that is never tense but also never quite orderly. As the principal says: "This is not a school that can be calm. It is epitomized by high energy." The energy spills out into the corridors and beyond, to the garden, farm, and playing fields. It is creative energy.

When students and staff are asked what one word symbolizes the school, they tend to identify an activity, like community service, the farm, or Advisory. Some teachers say the symbol is communication. One says: "It's a network of people supporting one another." Another says: "It's like a bridge game. Two partners are trying to get the best possible hand, the best match." Students tend to give three answers. First, some stress the financial base of the school. "What symbolizes the school? Money," one says. Another says: "Lavishness." Second, many students say that the school is symbolized by the arts, especially the arts festival, music, and *Contemplations.* Most agree with the students who say simply: "Opportunities."

Community

The school's history is a turbulent one. Neither Shoreham nor Wading River, the two Long Island towns the school now serves, had middle or junior high schools. Shoreham had two elementary schools and Wading River had one. Students were bused to Port Jefferson for junior and senior high school, along with students from several other towns that were elementary districts only. As enrollment increased, Port Jefferson phased out some of these districts, warning Shoreham and Wading River that their students would be phased out one year at a time. Meanwhile, the state pressured four districts to centralize their school systems. Shoreham and Wading River, thinking this proposed centralized district would be too large, fought hard for the closer control of a small district. Even though the state offered building aid if they centralized, a four-district merger measure was defeated by Shoreham and Wading River. The two towns then merged their school systems and, in the end, received state aid.

During the period before the merger took effect, the Shoreham School Board began planning a middle school. They rejected what a former board member called "the egg-crate school plans" of the architect they hired as they became increasingly influenced by a district principal who convinced them that they could be experimental. He started educating the board about the possibilities for a middle school as opposed to a junior high. He got them to read authors like Charles Silberman and to visit middle schools around the country. The board brought in consultants on open schools and had a Community Day, during which the consultant worked with parents and other decision makers. As they became interested in more experimental uses of space and time, they achieved consensus about building a modern school with three open-plan classroom wings.

Meanwhile, the new middle school started, crammed in a wing of Miller Avenue Elementary School in Shoreham for an extra year because of the change in architectural plans. Tension built in a community nervous about the direction the board was taking. That was 1972, Dennis Littky's first year. Littky, a professor at the State University of New York at Stony Brook with a doctorate in child psychology, was trying to accomplish change in schools via teacher education. He was, at the time, supervising teachers in the Shoreham School. Twenty-seven years old, with limited experience in school administration, bearded and casually garbed, Littky was the unlikely candidate the board hired on the recommendation of the district principal. "The board had taken a stand that they should provide as many options as possible to create a variety of educational environments in which children might succeed," a current board member remembers. "Littky fit the bill as someone who believed in doing that. The board took a chance that he would know how."

With merger in 1973, the middle-school staff grew from thirteen to over thirty teachers in less than two years. The sixth grade stayed at Miller Avenue under the direction of Jane Wittlock, Littky's assistant principal, while grades seven through nine moved into the new but unfinished building. The next year forty tenth-graders were added, waiting for the new high school to be completed. Although in the middle-school building, the ninth- and tenth-graders were administered by the high school.

Meanwhile, two communities with divergent educational philosophies that were having difficulty melding in one school board were passing judgment on the school. It all looked like chaos to the community: program changes and organizational shifts, students jammed in one open-space area of Miller Avenue and then in two different school buildings, a program that included alien components like Advisory, teams, and interdisciplinary units, and no easily identifiable curriculum. Many stormy board meetings were held about the school's lack of discipline, anarchic conditions, teachers' casual dress, and a perceived slighting of academics. Littky was often vilified. One by one, board members were voted out of office.

No single event legitimized the school and gained its acceptance in the community. An extremely vigorous group of parents fought hard for it: "I feel I own several bricks in this school," one says. A new superintendent was hired from outside the community after the merger. He calmed parents down while supporting Littky. Some say the school sold itself. Year by year, more parents came around as their children loved the school and did well. Some parents were shaken by the Vietnam War: "We knew we didn't have all the answers and were willing to listen." The first fine arts festival, with its beautiful art and music, brought the community out in force. Some think that was a turning point, Littky's dream made tangible for the community to experience. The school board president says the festival "gave visible indications to the community of the talent kids have if they're allowed to show it."

Leadership

Littky was "myopic" about the school, according to one principal. "It was all he cared about." When the school "took its traditional rebellious stands, he won, sometimes at great cost to himself—but he won." At the same time, he and the staff ran workshops for parents on subjects like pre- and early adolescent development, social studies simulation games, and standardized testing. He changed the "hippie" image of the school by keeping it neat and clean while refusing to compromise on program. He showed parents who worked at the Brookhaven labs that their children were excelling in math and science, as they wished. Others were delighted by the field trips and a school that showed "movies of the week" at consecutive lunchtimes during long winter months. He fought off parents and the superintendent who wanted a "conservative wing" of the school, with required Latin, but he also acceded to putting some walls up to improve acoustics.

Littky's forte was public relations, according to a former school board member. Littky used the "Friday Memos" to educate the community: "The

. . . flexibility of the school's structure has helped to take it out of the realm of politics," he reported in a 1977 memo. "It is not a school that is particularly for educational 'liberals' or particularly for educational 'conservatives.' The staff believes that a school can, for example, have a fully developed curriculum in the arts as well as a fully developed program of academic skills, that students can both take part in frequent field trips and score high on standardized achievement tests." The memos described intramurals, the farm, community service, advisory, SSR, Booktalks, foreign-language instruction, junk yard music, the school store, Authors' Week, the greenhouse. . .

In one of his most inspired moves, Littky divided the school district into sixteen zones. He established a Parent Liaison Committee with one chairperson for each zone in order that every neighborhood would have a parent representative. This communications network became his mouthpiece and his ears. Meeting one time monthly, the parents were oriented to how and why the school functioned as it did. Each representative spent half a day in school, observing and learning. At meetings, they came with comments and questions from their zones, concerns people would not communicate directly to the school but were willing to discuss with a neighbor. Representatives called to remind families in their zones about important meetings and budget votes. The chairperson from each zone was given a looseleaf notebook with curricular goals from every class, a district calendar, a suggested script for his or her first phone calls in the zone, community information for new families, a handbook about school policies, the middle school's philosophy statement, the year's list of advisories, sample schedules, and curricular overviews by teams. The Parent Liaison Committee still functions as a successful communication link that scotches rumors, advocates for the school at board meetings and for parents at school meetings, and advises the administration about issues of current concern in the school.

Open houses, parent tours, questionnaires at parent-teacher conferences through which parents could express their feelings about the school, invitations to parents to go on field trips, the parent council—all helped convince the parents that the red-bearded rebel knew what he was doing. Classes for parents about pre- and early adolescent development helped parents understand the school and gave them a forum for sharing what they thought were isolated child-rearing experiences. Parents read Fritz Redl and Charity James on the needs of young adolescents and school philosophy. They read John Dewey to connect philosophy with specific school practices. Littky was granted tenure with only one negative board vote.

I was a teacher in an inner-city school. I chose to live here because of the philosophy of schooling in the district. I went to hear Dr. Littky and was stunned and ashamed about my years of teaching. I was impressed by what he said, that children can think, not just feel, and that what's going on in their heads is valuable. They aren't just empty pitchers for us to pour information into. In my career, everything was teacher directed. [A Shoreham–Wading River Middle School parent]

A teacher says that the community may now be unhappy with individual personalities of teachers, but not with the school's program: "That fight Dennis won. Kids even came to school when they were sick; they learned, they got into good colleges. We have nurtured their gifts. The parents realize this. We've got a winner." That it is a winner has been acknowledged in a 1981 *Newsday* article which some feared might be an exposé. The reporter planned to visit the school for a few hours but stayed for three days, producing a laudatory cover story. The community service program has been chosen as an exemplary youth participation program by the National Commission on Resources for Youth. Administrators and teachers make presentations at national meetings of professional organizations. The community service program, the Quebec trip, and Authors' Week have been featured in educational publications. Students' art work is on display at exhibits on Long Island. *Contemplations* is one of the few literary magazines to receive the highest rating at Columbia University. The band receives a rating of "excellent" at the regional competition. The school has so many visitors that they have been limited to Visitors' Day, scheduled one time a month, so as not to be disruptive.

This constant recognition has secured the school's position among most parents and board members, but it also has the potential to boomerang. As the school is cited more frequently as a model, there is a ripple of jealousy in the district, according to a board member. The rivalry could become dangerous for the school, especially since some principals feel its national reputation was gained at the expense of other schools that were passed over because, as one principal said, "Littky was a favorite and got what he wanted."

Littky left when he was ready to move on, living in a cabin by himself in the woods of New Hampshire, starting a small newspaper to build local pride, and only after several years deciding to take on the next administrative challenge with a traditional New Hampshire high school. ("We're waiting to see if he can work miracles again," a staff member says, sure that he can.) One district principal says that Littky "left at the right time. He dealt successfully with the community's antagonisms, left a good program and a superb staff with community support and staying power." He was "the right person at the right time, a generator of ideas, whipping people into a state of excitement."

After he left, Jane Wittlock, who had worked hand-in-hand with Littky, first as a lead teacher and then as assistant principal, became principal for two years. In a quiet way that complemented Littky's flamboyance, Wittlock accomplished much. When the search for Littky's successor began, the majority of the staff was eager for her to assume the principalship. The staff was deeply concerned to have someone who was in tune with the philosophy of the school, would maintain its momentum, and emphatically not introduce major change. Some say that as a result she was a "caretaker principal." An elementary-school principal says: "She dealt with an implosion after Dennis left. There was too much free-floating energy." Although there is deep disagreement about this assessment, there is consensus that the transition from Littky, while accomplished, was difficult.

The new principal, Cary Bell, benefits from the backlash against Littky: "There are members of the community who are pleased that I wear suits and shoes at meetings," and is hurt by it: "They want me to shape the school up, on their terms." Some of the original teachers find the transition disappointing: "The spirit is gone. You could feel the intensity when you walked in. We all had to pump out 130 percent. It was a high. I couldn't stop talking about the place. Dennis sustained me. We were reflections of his thoughts." Others see positive benefits from the change: "Dennis was top drawer. His perception of a school was what I always dreamed it could be. He was concerned with providing successful experiences for staff as well as students. But things may change for the better. We are evaluating some sacred cows, thinking about programs. The spirit isn't gone. It's here, in the teachers." Another teacher adds: "It does not all hinge on the principal. Dennis built a unique staff based on a solid philosophy: the philosophy reigns because of the staff."

Others say the staff reigns because of Littky: "Dennis was most brilliant in his ability to let his staff take on as much responsibility for the school as possible. It's this attribute that has helped make the school so strong," according to Wittlock. The entire Community Service Program was developed and administered by one staff person, who prepared the budget, wrote the goals and objectives, hired the staff, and created the schedule. "Dennis never interfered. He just gave support." At the end of the first year, when the seventh and eighth grades moved into the new building, Littky asked Wittlock to stay behind in Miller Avenue Elementary School with the expanding sixth grade. "I hired six teachers, two aides, and secretaries, held staff meetings, conducted parent nights, and wrote all the teacher evaluations for the next two years. Dennis rarely came to see what I was up to. When I look back on it, it was really incredible. He just handed over one-third of the school and let me run it. He was smart enough to know he couldn't do it alone." Everyone can remember many instances when

Littky "let us take risks and responsibilities." Wittlock agrees: "I think that is why the teachers feel they have such a stake in the school."

Some feel resentful when Littky gets all the acclaim: "Because someone allows something to happen isn't everything. He absorbed ideas of the staff, and they became his. He was very important because people felt pressure to grow and change, while being cared for. People would say: 'If we're giving so much to kids, who's giving to us?' We got as much as possible. We even got five personal counseling sessions a year, if we wanted them. But is a program a program if it's tied to one person? We didn't change or collapse when Dennis left." One teacher summarizes: "People thought we would die on the vine without Dennis, but we were strong enough that we were more than just Dennis Littky."

Dennis Littky taught me about myself and kids. I became an outstanding teacher because of him. He encouraged me every day and gave me strength to go on. Sometimes I'd say: "Time out!" There was too much of the flash and the shine. But all the motives were for kids. He believed in being humane to kids. He taught us how to implement his philosophy. He made us solid about who we are. [A Shoreham–Wading River Middle School teacher]

Meeting the Nonnegotiables

Shoreham–Wading River Middle School meets threshold criteria for school effectiveness with such ease that no one thinks to mention absence, suspension, or victimization rates. They are extremely low. There are no graffiti in the school. The farm and garden have never been vandalized by students. Standard achievement test scores are well above average and meet parental expectations. Among educators, the school has what may well be the widest reputation for excellence of any public middle school in the country, although, given the narrow range of discourse about intermediate schooling, that reputation is not well known.

Parent satisfaction grows yearly. In the spring of 1977, two investigators from Teachers College of Columbia University surveyed parents of the Shoreham–Wading River Central School District. Their report documents a median income of $23,448, with 94 percent of students coming from two-parent families and 41 percent of women working outside the home. Half of the respondents had lived in the district fewer than five years, so they had not taken part in the early school battles. Three-quarters of the parents were happy or very happy about education in the Shoreham–Wading River schools and 80 percent were satisfied or very satisfied with their children's progress. Seventy-four percent of the parents were happy or very happy with the middle school, only five percent lower than the rate of satisfaction for elementary schools and 12 percent higher than the rate for the very academically oriented high school. Eighty-two percent agreed that "the most important thing a student can get out of school is a good background in basic subjects," and also agreed that "it is important that students learn about the arts and humanities in school." Parents were most concerned about, and most satisfied with, reading and math.

Discipline was of greatest concern to parents of high-school students. The evaluators noted: "Surprisingly, discipline was not as important at the middle-school level as had been expected. This age group is traditionally thought to be a source of serious discipline problems, but survey results in Shoreham–Wading River do not confirm this expectation."

Some parents say the middle school is great if you have bright children. Mine are average. My child is writing a book on her own time. My children learn here that "I can." They don't learn that "I can't." [A Shoreham–Wading River Middle School parent]

Some persistent parental complaints reflect the joy that students experience in the school: "One of my problems is getting my child to come home," a mother said. Others complain that school plays too large a part in their children's lives because "there are too many good choices." They cannot find times for family activities, even on Saturdays. One parent says her children wanted vacations from school "just to space out for a while" after the intensity of school activities. A working mother says her children "never have to come home to an empty house; they are always at school." A mother who is on the community service staff says: "I went to work here because my daughter was here all the time."

Public Policy Issues

The major conflicts that have created immobilizing stress in some school districts are absent in the Shoreham–Wading River Central School District. The population is almost entirely White in the district and surrounding townships. There has been, as a result, no conflict over or accommodation to school desegregation. Because of the district's tax base, its citizens have not had to tax themselves heavily to support the schools or make choices among equally attractive programs based on finances. The Long Island Lighting Company (LILCO) is building a $2.2 billion nuclear plant. As its annual tax assessment rises, more money is made available to district schools.

Sex discrimination is not an issue; Title IX was accepted gladly by the community and is monitored by an ongoing districtwide committee. The high school has an awareness day about sex roles that the middle school is planning to emulate in Awareness Week. Special education students have been identified under P.L. 94–142 only relatively recently. The middle school has 36 identified special education students, 32 of whom are mainstreamed into the regular classroom. The district hired a pupil personnel director for the first time in 1980–81. There has been conflict between parents who want the district to provide funds for special education services outside the district and parents who want the children to be served within the district. "Everyone is learning," says a middle-school special education teacher.

Even unionization has not created undue stress in the district. All but three teachers in the district belong to the New York State United Teachers Association, which is affiliated with the AFT. The relationship between the union and the board is amicable, according to the copresident of the association, a teacher at the middle school: "We consider ourselves a professional organization. Grievances are worked out in a positive climate. The board and the administration appreciate our contribution. It is, of course, made easy because of LILCO. We aren't quibbling about salaries and class size. Money makes a difference. All of us know we have it better than anyone else."

Self-Evaluation

While relatively untouched by the major social debates that swirl about and within public schooling, Shoreham–Wading River Middle School is not pacific. It is composed of a group of highly individualistic teachers. One of them says: "We are products of the 1960s." They are not an affable group, nor are they easily led; but they are very open to change, self-critical to a fault, and thoughtful about issues of substance related to fitting practice to purpose. They are never satisfied with the school or their own performance. At the core, they are a group of inspired malcontents. Their worries are manifold and important. Several teachers would like for their colleagues to develop crisp curricular goals and to agree on a common set of expectations for each grade level. Such a change would be anathema to others, who, as one says, are "engaged in purposeful activities, not mindless idiocy." They want to be left alone to be the individual crafters of curriculum and instruction that has made them the key to the school's survival.

One teacher is concerned, as are many others, that "we are dynamic people vying for 300 percent of students' time. They are overwhelmed with offerings—at least 70–75 percent are. Others are not that involved. We need to pay attention to that 75 percent [sic] who are not participating, not involved." The error is indicative of the intensified self-scrutiny in the school. The problem of students' missing classes, or "pullouts," is persistent. All the trips and exchanges frustrate the teachers, who want their students in class. Each principal has said, in effect: "Trust what is happening to them when they are out of your classroom"—but the issue remains unresolved.

Programs for gifted students are also worrisome. Littky refused to have homogeneous grouping for the academically gifted, except, under parental pressure, in math, a policy that is still enforced. Some teachers worry that the school does more for students with special artistic and athletic gifts than with academic gifts. Teachers debate about "whether whizzes should advance more or explore other areas." While the school has a half-time teacher for the gifted, most staff members feel the program is, in the words of one teacher, "a mess, with some kids coming in early, some having a special class at lunch, some being pulled out of class two times a week. It's a hodge-podge."

I don't care for all the favorable publicity we get. We should work on being as good as our notices are. [A Shoreham–Wading River Middle School teacher]

Jane Wittlock, who is now a teacher in the school, struggles with a question that characterizes the thoughtfulness of the staff. She wonders whether girls and boys should be separate for part of the day at this age. Separating the sexes makes sense to her, given the nature of the age group. She searches research reports and other schools' practices for some insights. Cary Bell, her successor, wonders about "creating and maintaining." The meaning of the farm is different now from what it was at its inception, he points out. The creation process has now become a maintenance process. How many things can the students maintain and still create anew? What will be given up? Does the staff expect infinite growth? If the farm has different meaning now, what is it? What takes the place of that creative process? The reflective staff will grapple with these questions and debate them hotly at times. They will not take kindly to decisions by fiat. They will thrive under leadership that energizes them to decide.

Conclusion

A parent says: "We're doing best what's easiest here." The message that observers might draw from Shoreham–Wading River Middle School is that a school needs a brilliantly creative principal who can choose his own staff to teach in a new building, under experimental status, in a White, middle-class community with a rich tax base. Many visitors from other schools draw that conclusion and leave impoverished. Others agree with the staff that components of the school program are easily transportable. Experiential learning ("It doesn't take fancy buses"), the advisory system, an open library and arts system, Booktalk, teaming, an entrepreneurial staff that writes grant proposals or helps students build a store—"these need consenting adults, not money," as one teacher says.

I'm going to be here beyond any one administrator's duration. I'm possessive of the school, as are most of the people who were here from the beginning. About everything that happens, I say: "This is my school and it reflects upon me." [A Shoreham–Wading River Middle School teacher]

Beyond recommending components of the school's program, members of the school staff feel they have learned lessons to contribute to the educational community. A teacher, formerly from a ghetto school, says that money was not the key: "If LILCO goes and the community can't assume the tax burden, we'll go back to classes of 40 instead of 22. I've done it both ways. If we lose our equipment, fine. I was a scrounge before, and I can be again. It shouldn't change what goes on in the school. It may make it better, because we'll have to plan and create. Teachers make the school, not money." Several other teachers who served under three principals at the school also see themselves as the key: "Principals come and go. Teachers make the school, and we'll still be here years from now." Another teacher disagrees: "You need a stable administration that can survive politically, whether by saying to use basal readers or by multiaging three grades in one class. I've had it both ways. The key is basing programs on kids' needs. That's the lesson to be drawn from our experience. You need a politically adept leader to make that possible."

Shoreham–Wading River Middle School is a highly visible school in a judgmental community that is increasingly but by no means completely supportive. Parental uproar or loss of administrative support is always a possibility—and the teachers love a good fight, as do the parents. The school can be seriously harassed. To date, it has held sway, but "there is always someone who wants to knock the middle school down a peg, to get it to shape up, to have someone go in and turn it around or clean things up," as one district administrator says. There is more external pressure and resentment than meets the eye. One administrator says he "didn't realize a school like this could exist with all the pressures from the outside." Then he adds: "It's a credit to the staff."

For several years, everything extraordinary about the school was credited to one person, the principal. This school, like so many others, taught some observers that the principal is *the* key. Since then the school has changed, as any living organism does. Its philosophy, the resulting program, the staff that creates and implements it, and the parents who support it, have remained dedicated and expert. Littky could not have succeeded without an ardent group of parents who fought numerous battles, the freedom to use his talents to select a staff equal to his challenge, and a superintendent who backed him because of his own vision for the school. The experimental status of the school gave Littky flexibility in assigning elementary and secondary teachers according to their talents rather than their certification; it gave him the freedom to develop some of the art classes. This was advantageous, not crucial. He would have succeeded without the tax base, with any group of young adolescent students, and in any building.

If, in the evolution of a school the principal is *the* key, it is because of decisions made that are institutionalized beyond the stewardship of one person. Littky gave teachers the encouragement and autonomy to lead their own programs. He established networks of relationships, via teams, wings, staff breakfasts, meetings, the "Friday Memo," and the interdisciplinary stimulation of programs like community service, the farm, and the arts, that continuously renew teachers' creativity. Littky's legacy is an informed group of parents who orient new parents in the community to their educational philosophy; a group of teachers who invigorate new colleagues with their evangelical zeal; and a driving energy that defines as the school's major responsibility the personal growth and development of its students in as many facets of human experience as possible.

Notes

1. This description pertains to 1980–81. The middle school continues to experiment with different organizations of the school day and the wings.

2. Charity James, *Beyond Customs: An Educator's Journey* (New York: Schocken, 1974):22.

3. Kenneth E. Duckworth, "Schools as Student Work Organizations: Report of the First Year of Research" (Eugene, Oregon: Center for Educational Policy and Management, mimeographed, November 30, 1979), p. 113.

4. James Garbarino, "The Role of Schools in Socialization to Adulthood," *Educational Forum* (January 1978):172.

5. See n. 1.

6. John I. Goodlad and M. Frances Klein and Associates, *Behind the Classroom Door* (Belmont, Cal.: Wadsworth, 1970):81.

7. Duckworth, p. 64.

8.   Ibid., p. 57.
9.   See e.g. Herman T. Epstein and Conrad F. Toepfer, "A Microscience Basis for Reorganizing Middle Grades Education," *Educational Leadership* 35 (May 1978):656–60.
10. Attributed to "the researchers," in Jerome Cramer, "The Latest Research on Brain Growth Might Spark More Learning in Your Schools," *American School Board Journal* 168 (August 1981):17.

PART III
Recurrent Themes in Successful Middle-Grade Schools

7

The Challenge of the Schools

Successful schools for young adolescents pose a challenge. If they did not exist, we could be more accepting of the status quo, if not more gratified by our results. The presence of these schools creates personal disequilibrium that leads either to denial or learning. On the one hand, we can stress the idiosyncratic set of circumstances and personalities that makes each of the successful schools a unique institution. On the other hand, we can look for the themes that thread their way through each of the school's stories and their common, replicable elements. These schools are different because they are the same. It is this paradox that demands exploration.

The most striking feature of the four schools is their willingness and ability to adapt all school practices to the individual differences in intellectual, biological, and social maturation of their students. The schools take seriously what is known about early adolescent development, especially its inter- and intraindividual variability. This seriousness is reflected in decisions they make about all aspects of school life. The schools do not achieve their results by chance. Region 7 Middle School, for instance, fights to keep its schedule of mini-courses on Friday so that every student can exercise responsible choice, be with friends, and pursue personal interests. Noe Middle School and Western Middle School expend a large amount of energy on a complex school organization so that small groups of students are known by small groups of teachers who can vary the tone and pace of the school day based on their needs. Shoreham–Wading River Middle School constructs its school day around an advisory structure so that every student has daily contact with an adult who has time to listen, explain, comfort, and prod. These school policies represent thoughtfulness about a population of school-age children whose developmental needs are compelling.

One hears rhetoric in schools about educating the whole child, a poorly defined intention difficult to observe in practice. For the most part, schools act on achievement goals, under which are subsumed concerns for personal growth and development. The primary task is academic. Other tasks are of

167

interest insofar as they contribute to or impede the school's academic purposes. This is true even in schools that have added courses in sex education, child care, death and dying, and other nontraditional areas that bespeak an interest in the social development of adolescents. The courses are add-ons to a previously defined curriculum whose goals remain fundamentally unchanged.

The four schools set out from the beginning (with the exception of Noe, where redefinition occurred in its second year) *to be positive environments for early adolescent personal and social development, not only because such environments contribute to academic achievement, but because they are intrinsically valued, stemming from a belief in positive school climate as a goal, not a process toward a goal.*

A central weakness in most schools for young adolescents is a widespread failure to reconsider each school practice in terms of developmental needs in order either to incorporate responsibility for meeting them into the schools' academic and social goals or to keep them from being barriers to attaining those goals. The four schools begin with an understanding of early adolescent development that is not tangential to but rather helps form the schools' central set of purposes. Decisions about governance, curriculum, and school organization, while different in each school, flow from this sensitivity to the age group. Given massive individual differences in development during early adolescence, it is doubtful that a school for the age group could be successful without this sensitivity. This study cannot conclude that developmental responsiveness is a key factor in school success at the intermediate level because developmental responsiveness was an entry criterion in school selection. The study does find that staff, administration, and parents of the four schools claim developmental responsiveness to be central to their success. The study finds that developmental responsiveness does not preclude academic success. The study also finds that developmental responsiveness is appropriate in a broad range of communities with a broad range of clientele.

As Sherlock Holmes properly reminded Henry Baskerville, the prior question is, "Does the beast exist?" The null hypothesis asserts that there are no exemplary schools. If we can discover evidence that there are, we shall leave to future researchers the detailed and important work of discovering why they exist and how (if at all) their success can be copied. [Robert E. Klitgaard and George R. Hall, *A Statistical Search for Unusually Effective Schools.*]

There is no simple cause-and-effect model to account for successful schools for young adolescents. Explanations seem circular. For instance, stable student attendance is a prerequisite for success in learning; success in learning leads to high attendance rates. Dedicated teachers are essential to school performance; good schools attract dedicated teachers. Community support appears to improve school outcomes; student discipline and achievement result in community support for schools. The components of successful schools, like the components of failing schools, are inextricably interrelated. The schools described in this book argue that they cannot establish this complex pattern of positive interrelationships without making a serious commitment to developmental responsiveness. The attainment of each characteristic of successful schools is dependent on recognizing and working with pressing aspects of growth and development during early adolescence.

For instance, adolescents do not accede automatically to the wishes of adults. Order is not maintained and lessons are not learned in the relatively unnegotiated manner of the elementary school. An orderly and serious academic environment cannot be achieved without the cooperation of a group of students whose strivings for autonomy preclude unquestioning obedience. Similarly, the importance of the peer group for personal comfort and standards of behavior can be a powerful impediment to public policy imperatives like racial integration. Early adolescence can also be particularly stressful for handicapped children, because the strength of peer group attachments and adolescents' fear of the "abnormal" are barriers to social mainstreaming. Also, as boys and girls begin to differentiate between what is masculine and feminine in light of their extreme self-consciousness about physical development, meeting the demands of a sex equity policy requires as much of their enlightened understanding as their parents' and other adults'. Being guided in school policy and program by the demands of early adolescent development is imperative. Schools cannot simply continue doing what they did at the elementary level.

It is very disquieting to visit successful schools. One would expect that it is difficult to be a good school and easy to be a bad school; but like superb musicians, the staff in good schools make their craft look easy. One has to struggle to remember vignettes from other schools, where everything seems very difficult:

> A teacher sits in the back of the room, her legs up on her desk, asking students questions from a textbook. The students, bored and listless, sit in straight rows facing no one in the front of the room, answering laconically to a blank blackboard. When the principal enters the classroom, the teacher lowers her legs to the floor. Nothing else changes.

> A teacher drills students for a seemingly endless amount of time on prime numbers. After the lesson, not one of them can say why it is important to learn prime numbers.

A visitor asks a teacher if hers is an eighth-grade class. "It's called eighth grade," she answers archly, "but we know it's really kindergarten, right class?"

In a predominantly Hispanic school, only the one adult hired as a bilingual teacher speaks Spanish.

In a biracial school, the principal and guidance counselor cite test scores with pride. They are asked if the difference between the test scores of Black and White students is narrowing: "Oh, that's an interesting question!" the guidance counselor says in surprise. The principal agrees. It has never been asked by or of them before.

A teacher in a social studies class squelches several imaginative questions, exclaiming: "You're always asking 'what if' questions. Stop asking 'what if!'" When a visitor asks who will become president if the president-elect dies before the electoral college meets, the teacher explodes: "You're as bad as they are! That's another 'what if' question!"

There are things individual public schools cannot control. They have no control over how much education or money the parents of their students have. They have no control over the mix of backgrounds in their school population. They have no control over buildings, school finance, union contracts, insurance laws, and court orders. The people who do have control over these things do not work in individual schools. If the policy decisions they made were altered, perhaps achieving school success would be easier. But altering these decisions is not necessary to change any of these vignettes from unsuccessful schools. Schools have power to rid themselves of incompetence; they can set norms that discourage meanness; they can scrutinize their curricula and instructional practices to minimize aimlessness and mindlessness; they can be thoughtful about larger issues like social justice and school performance.

Visiting successful schools is disquieting because one learns how much control schools can have. Administrators in these schools say they take the control they need to make their schools outstanding academic and social environments. They control their philosophy, goals, norms, expectations, organization, large areas of curricular and instructional practices, their response to the community, to some extent the community's response to them, and the quality of their response to public policy.

While they have no control over their students' previous schooling experiences—in two cases the students have usually attended successful elementary schools, whereas the other two middle schools are havens from bad schools—these schools seem to control even the outcomes that the public wants most from schools: achievement and disciplined behavior. There can be no better news for public schools.

Despite obvious differences, these successful schools share certain characteristics with private schools. There is an element of parental choice in some of them, through actual school selection in Region 7 Middle School, through voluntary busing in Noe, and through the possibility of selecting the type of class one's child will attend in Western Middle School. Each school stands for something and, although young, has a proud history, as many private schools do. Curriculum development is controlled in large measure at the building level. A strong sense of personal efficacy pervades the schools' administrative staffs. The principals manage in varying degrees to select their teachers. Morale is high. There is a feeling of exclusivity in the schools.

They feel they are "different" and they are. It is not possible to meet the threshold criteria, to be responsive to a specific community and to the developmental characteristics of young adolescents, and also be standard. A school can be different by doing better what most people assume schooling is all about, as Western Middle School does; or it can be different by redefining aspects of what people assume school is all about, like Shoreham –Wading River Middle School. Either way, the school becomes a distinctly individual institution.

There will not be a single model for success, nor should we want one. Families, work sites, communities—all forge their own individuality and so must schools. In the 1960s and early 1970s, critics berated schools for being depressingly the same. Now there is strong pressure for them to be distressingly similar, whether from the middle-school movement that espouses a new orthodoxy or from school researchers who want to identify *the* list of components that accounts for effectiveness. The message of these schools is much more complex and also more promising. The historical and demographic context of the individual school counts far too much to allow for orthodoxies or formulas; from diverse contexts, schools can fulfill similar goals.

Purposes, Goals, and Definitions

In most schools for young adolescents, two areas of confusion and ignorance converge: confusion about the purposes of schooling and ignorance about early adolescence as a critical developmental stage in the life span.[1] This unfortunate convergence occurs just at the point in young people's lives when they begin to seek self-definition. It is a dangerous and wasteful situation from which we reap the bitter rewards of apathy, hostility, and rejection. *The four schools have achieved unusual clarity about the purposes of intermediate schooling and the students they teach.*

These schools have reached consensus about primary purpose. In Region 7 Middle School agreement is nearly unanimous that it is teaching academics. In Shoreham–Wading River Middle School, the only school where the majority of teachers do not identify academics as their first responsibility, two-thirds of the teachers say they feel most responsible for the personal growth and development of their students. In all four schools, even when there is strong emphasis on academics as a central goal, the emphasis on enhancing personal growth and development is also strong.

The schools make powerful statements, both in word and in practice, about their purposes. There is little disagreement within them and little discrepancy between what they say they are doing and what they actually do. As a result, everyone can articulate what the schools stand for. School staff, parents, students, and community leaders tend to use the same vocabulary in discussing their school. While this achievement is in part the result of the principals' superb community relations skills, it is also a reflection of clarity of purpose.

Schools may see their educational objectives as applying equally to the fostering of an enthusiasm and interest in learning, of confidence and the ability to take responsibility, of adaptability to cope with life changes, of the development of personal relationships, or of individuality. Schools have a choice in the norms they select. [Michael Rutter et al., *Fifteen Thousand Hours.*]

These are confident schools. Each one stands for something special, whether it is being the best in the county, desegregation, diversity, or the arts. Each has a mission and knows what it is, and in each case it is both academic and social. The schools have become confident in part because each had a special purpose at its inception, even before it had a principal. Unlike most schools, they were established for more than reasons of demographics. In every case, a principal then took hold of the possibility for definition and proclaimed it within the school and throughout the community. Each school became special. People within the schools have reacted by producing beyond anyone's reasonable expectations.

This is one of the lessons of the four schools. Made to feel like chosen people, staff and students have banded together in their specialness and achieved accordingly. The sense of definition that comes from the exclusivity felt by each school is important in keeping staff morale high and retaining parent support. Most important, though, is the sense of purpose it gives the young adolescents. It helps bind them to the school. It is incumbent upon adults to articulate something that a school stands for and that students can be defined by and stand with. These four schools, through a mixture of historical fortuitousness and outstanding leadership, have done so.

The four schools are also unusually well defined as to their place in the continuum of schooling. A quiet revolution is under way in middle-grade schooling. Some schools are pulling out from under the shadow of high school; they have ceased to be junior replicas of senior high schools without the intrinsic motivating factors of colleges and jobs. While in most cases the change from junior high schools to middle schools is in name and grade level only, and middle schools are actually mini–junior high schools, an increasing number of middle schools are becoming more elementary than secondary in philosophy and practice.

The principals and teachers of these four schools insist that theirs are not secondary schools. The schools resist departmentalization and its emphasis on teaching specific content of specific disciplines in specific time slots. They do not see young adolescents as being ready for secondary school nor do they want them to be. Region 7 Middle School resists the pseudomaturity of street-wise children, which staff members see as inimical to their academic and social goals. Western Middle School parents are offended by what they see as premature teenage behavior in other schools. Staff members and parents at Noe emphasize the school's role in helping children become responsible, independent, and self-directed young adults, but they are criticized by the neighboring high school for "coddling," "mothering," and "spoiling" the students. The same is true of Shoreham–Wading River Middle School. Each principal says he or she would prefer hiring teachers with elementary backgrounds to teachers with secondary-school preparation.

We are witnessing a policy shift in schooling for young adolescents that is generally unacknowledged. Part of the public's confusion about the trend toward middle schools is the absence of public discourse about whether middle schools are meant to extend the elementary years upward, thereby prolonging childhood, or are meant to extend the secondary years downward, thereby acknowledging and perhaps encouraging the earlier emergence of adolescent capabilities and behavior. Several staff members in each of the four schools say they are doing both, and that this is exactly what it means to be a middle school. Intermediate schooling for them has a definition of its own that is neither elementary nor secondary. *Most of the principals, three of whom have elementary-school backgrounds, and most of the teachers, identify their schools as more elementary than secondary. Because these are such coherent schools, there is greater consensus about this issue than in most middle schools.*

The Principals

Why do some schools adopt the characteristics that promote academic achievement and social development? Every study of school effectiveness concludes that strong leadership is a key, perhaps *the* key, to excellent schools. It is not clear from the literature what strong leadership entails. *Each of the four schools has or has had a principal with a driving vision who imbues decisions and practices with meaning, placing powerful emphasis on why and how things are done. Decisions are made not just because they are practical, but for reasons of principle.*

The leaders of these schools are ideologues. They have a vision of what school should be for the age group. They have the creativity and courage to ask, as Sarason says we must always ask if we are to understand the significance of existing regularities in schools: "What are the alternative ways one might think about this particular aspect or regularity?"[2] They are able to articulate a different vision of schooling based on their answers to that question. They do for teachers what Perrone says teachers cannot do for themselves: "With few exceptions, teachers are not in settings where they can step back and observe systematically the broad range of ways in which young people respond. Thus, they are unable to articulate a different vision of themselves and young people in a different school environment."[3] The principals in the four successful schools articulate that vision and have the continuing energy to work toward it, objective by objective and year by year. They are not worn out, nor have they retreated into ironic detachment or managerial defensiveness.

On the other hand, they are not wasteful dreamers. They do not expend their energies on the unattainable. There is a hard-rock practicality about them. They do not talk about education in the abstract; they talk about schooling for their students. They are considered masterful politicians by their colleagues. They educate their superiors, the parents in their community, and the teachers. Through their vision and practicality, they articulate for their schools what Burton Clark refers to as the "organizational saga," a collective ideology that defines an organization's identity and purposes.[4] The principals make these schools coherent, binding philosophy to goals, goals to programs, and programs to practices.

What makes a good school—for young adolescents or anyone else? It will vary, of course, given the students to be served. At the same time, I've yet to see a very good school where the kids and teachers didn't like each other and at which there was any sort of fundamental disagreement as to what the purposes of the school were. Both teachers and kids have to be motivated around similar goals, and a sense of purposeful order is obviously necessary. None of this is surprising, though it is wretchedly difficult to accomplish in practice! [Theodore R. Sizer, former headmaster, Phillips Andover Academy, letter to author, November 2, 1980.]

The story of each of these schools covers years—most of the principals say at least three or four—of designing, politicking, making mistakes, regrouping, redefining, and just letting things jell. None of these schools was outstanding at the outset. The principals are stubborn: they perservere.

The principals' authority is derived from their acknowledged competence. They are authoritative, not authoritarian, leaders, although one often senses that a strain of authoritarianism is being kept carefully in tow. The principals' perspective about schooling for young adolescents is effectively articulated and transmitted to the staff; thus, power can safely be entrusted to the teachers. Being a strong principal means knowing when and how to relinquish power. While the particulars of school governance differ from school to school, the schools have in common highly autonomous teachers. They understand how the whole school works, and in most cases they know why. They are decision makers about school climate, organization, curriculum, instruction, and usually, about budgets.

The principals see their major function to be instructional leadership. It is their job to sustain their faculty's commitment. They set standards for performance and establish the norms and taboos for adult-child relationships. They feel competent to advise and evaluate in the classroom. The professional and personal support they give their teachers helps account for the high percentage of teachers who have taught in these schools since their inception. Contrary to expectations developed from observing many other junior high and middle schools, good teachers tend to stay in these schools.

The principals also secure the autonomy of their schools in their districts. In many school systems, districtwide departmental supervisors evaluate teacher performance within given disciplines. An English or science supervisor can therefore have more influence than the principal over curriculum and instruction. In schools where the principal encourages teachers to depart from departmentalized curricula and rewards teachers for interdisciplinary work, subject-oriented supervisors can be a serious barrier. Each of the four schools has established its curricular autonomy, either by gaining experimental school status, by being respected in the central office, or through open battles won by the principal.

The schools are relatively autonomous in terms of governance, as well. The principals have gained the confidence of the central office by running good schools that have high test scores and few parental complaints. Two have fought angrily in public on behalf of their schools. Two never quite get around to obeying certain directives. One way or another, the principals have had the political savvy and the excellent performance to gain a large area of latitude in which to lead their schools.

The hiring and firing of teachers is an interesting case in point. The one impediment to school improvement that principals most consistently cite is the role of unions and other teacher organizations in limiting principals' flexibility to select and dismiss teachers. Only two of the four principals cite this as a problem. Each school has been successful, either with the present or original principal, in acquiring some control over hiring and firing.

In one school, the principal's hovering and negative evaluations of incompetent teachers hastened resignations. Two of the principals have gone to court or mediation to fire teachers. One principal fired all but one member of a department in the opening years of the school. Two principals have eliminated positions to rid the schools of incompetent staff. At the same time, and crucially important to these schools, two of the original principals hired their own staffs from scratch, and the other two brought some of their teachers to the school with them. All had at least a nucleus of teachers with values and attitudes held in common. These teachers socialize new teachers into the values of the school. In addition, these teachers form the core of a social group that ostracizes lazy or inept teachers. The ensuing resignations usually make firing unnecessary.

It is testimony to the quality of leadership in these schools that many of the teachers see unions as unnecessary to their self-protection while strongly supporting them for teachers in other schools. The pettiness and arbitrary insults or tyrannies of day-to-day work conditions that have made so many teachers, who might once have been ambivalent about unionization, become enthusiastic union members, are absent in these schools. When the teachers do express gratefulness to their union, they refer to class size, wages, and benefits, in other words, to policies set beyond the principal's office.

It is also testimony to the principals' political astuteness and commitment that despite unions and district regulations, these principals manage to maintain some control over hiring and firing. The effort it takes can be herculean. The greatest protection these school have is their strong definition; now that their reputations are established, teachers can and do self-select on the basis of their level of comfort with the schools' philosophies and programs. Nonetheless, the greatest barrier to maintaining these successful schools is the principals' inability to determine freely who should and should not be members of their staff.

These principals, however, tend not to cite barriers to success. They feel adequately empowered. If there are obstacles, they feel confident about overcoming them and assume they will be strengthened in the process. Except in Detroit, where Region 7 Middle School has been seriously limited by decisions made at the district level, staff members reflect the confidence of the principals. Although each of the schools has been helped and hurt by fortuitous turns of events and circumstances, their principals reject the suggestion that luck has played a role in their success. They feel strongly that they have shaped circumstances. As one says: "I made my luck." Their strong sense of personal efficacy pervades the schools. Not a single teacher cites federal or state regulations as an impediment to his or her success. With the understandable exception of Region 7 Middle School, no teacher cites district policy as an impediment. It is acceptable in these school to discuss loss of flexibility. It is evidently unacceptable, or perhaps unrealistic, to discuss insurmountable obstacles.

Staying power is always an issue when a school is successful. The quality of an ordinary school is not identified single-mindedly with the principal. If the principal leaves, no one suggests that the school will fold. It is assumed that anyone can run an ordinary school. The excellence of a successful school is perceived as fragile because it is seen as an anomaly, dependent on one person. In addition, while conventional schools are typically granted community support automatically, support for successful schools is neither automatic nor universal. It is usually tied to the principal. As a result, successful schools are in double jeopardy politically when their principals leave.

These driven, possessive, and sometimes defiant principals are critical to the continued excellence and support of their schools; but they alone are not responsible for their schools' success, nor are they indispensible. First, each original principal has or had an assistant principal or a group of administrators who have been essential to the school's performance. Western Middle School had an assistant principal, a curriculm specialist, to whom Mrs. Parrish is deeply indebted. Miss Fisher had Mr. Washington. Terry Brooks has the Supportive Service Team. Dennis Littky had Jane Wittlock, an excellent instructional resource to the teachers. In one system, the principal has had the unswerving support of a powerful superintendent. In two others, the principal cultivated the superintendent's support, which, though erratic, was secure during crises.

One person is not sufficient because the task is too large, too lonely, and sometimes too dangerous. A maverick principal can be like Cordelia's image of King Lear, the "poor perdu" who is the expendable sentinel, stationed at the farthest post to pick up signals and warn others in less endangered positions. All these principals have required the emotional and political support, as well as the good common sense, of at least one close colleague.

The histories of two of the schools are evidence of the resilience of the schools that these maverick principals created. Both Region 7 Middle School and Shoreham–Wading River Middle School were synonymous with their principals, who were irreplaceable—until they left and were replaced. The argument has been made that while their departure was a rupturing experience for each school, it was also healthy. It was personally repugnant to Miss Fisher to continue working in a political climate she detested. A principal with a vision of good schooling in desperate times was required. Shoreham–Wading River Middle School needed some time to evolve and then to begin questing again. Littky might have led the school through this process, but he was not essential to it. While at present it is difficult to imagine Western Middle School without Wilma Parrish or Noe Middle School without Terry Brooks, the other schools tell us that thinking the unthinkable, while painful, is not lethal. *The major contribution of the principals is to make the schools larger than one person.* They institutionalize their vision in program and organizational structure. The principals are good enough leaders to leave a legacy behind: their staff, a powerfully defined school, an educated community, and a tradition of excitement, sensitivity, and striving for excellence.

Nonetheless, there is a lesson to be learned from these four schools about the importance of particularly talented people to successful schools. We tend to bemoan the fact that school success is dependent on talented administrators. The notion that good systems are ineffective without good people seems to defeat educational policy setters, who seek principal-proof school management just as they seek teacher-proof curricula. The two lessons we have learned in organizational theory, educational research, industry, and in schools, are that people perform well when they feel special, and that a charismatic leader binds people to a vision, to each other, and to their task. These principals have learned the first lesson well. They are very entrepreneurial. From motley sources of funding come dinners, trips, extra supplies, and other perks for their outstanding teachers. The parents are confident about the specialness of the schools. Most important, the students know that they are in a very unusual place, and behave accordingly.

The second lesson needs to be learned. When the principals are asked who or what sustains them, they never point outside the school. They have created their own sustenance in their staff and in the vision they have for their students. These are very independent and resourceful people. Not every potentially excellent principal is so stoic. True, attention needs to be paid to the preparation, selection, and dismissal policies of principals, to increase the pool of effective leaders and delete the ineffective. But attentiveness is also required to help provide for talented principals the sustenance they provide so well to others.

School Climate

The climate of a school is made up of a myriad factors, none of which by itself determines the way the school feels, its tone, or its culture. No formula accounts for the means by which these four schools have achieved their warm and productive atmospheres. *The individual decisions made by each school reflect one school's thoughtful response to the developmental needs of the age group and the particular needs of that school's clientele. Underlying their varied responses is a commitment to the intellectual, social, and personal growth of each child. While such a statement is identical to the standard rhetoric of schools, it is as close to fact in these schools as is possible in a less than perfect social institution. Important factors contributing to the schools' climate appear to be the physical setting, the means by which order is achieved, teachers' working conditions, their beliefs and expectations, and the acknowledgment of reciprocity in human relations. Crucially important are the quality of leadership and the clarity of purpose already discussed.*

Physical Setting

The school building has not been shown to account for academic achievement in any study of effective schooling. This is fortunate, since principals have almost no say in the building they are assigned; and communities are stuck for decades with architectural choices made by previous generations. Adolescents, however, are very sensitive to physical environments: witness the attention they pay to territorializing their space at home and the difficulties for children, as they approach and enter adolescence, if there is no private space that can become only theirs.

The students in all four schools comment often on their physical surroundings, both on the tone of the building as a whole and the decor of individual rooms. When asked how the school feels, they invariably include its physical attributes in their answers. Rutter's findings give us a hint of the importance of the physical setting. While they correlated with no other outcomes in his study of effective secondary schools, the care and decoration of the classroom and the school as a whole correlated with pupil behavior.[5] A pleasant, comfortable environment is one way that adults show their concern for children, one that is not lost on young adolescents.

The physical environment contributes to school discipline in two ways. First, students reciprocate the care expressed in the building by making it their building. In each school, when asked whether they make meaningful contributions to their school, students stress their role in cleaning up the outdoors, decorating the classrooms and corridors, building reading lofts and playground equipment, and refraining from writing on walls. Second, the layout of schools like Western Middle and Shoreham–Wading River is helpful in preventing some things from ever becoming issues of discipline and control. When there are architecturally discrete wings, wide corridors, bathrooms located in or near each wing, spacious gymnasia and music rooms whose noise is far from classrooms, large shop areas that minimize safety problems, and classroom areas small enough to maximize small group feeling, many traffic and behavior control issues can be easily avoided.

The buildings enhance, or at least are not barriers to, the schools' goal of creating small, knowable communities of people in familiar, personalized space. With the exception of Region 7 Middle School (which has a warm and productive climate nonetheless), school buildings are large enough and their space is planned in such a way that they are not crowded. It always appears, despite the low absentee rates, that there are fewer students in the schools than their enrollment figures lead one to expect. Hoards of expressive, restless bodies are not cramped in small spaces, setting off periodic explosions. Besides aiding discipline, school architecture contributes to community support. Parents in Shoreham–Wading River say the decision to build more walls decreased their initial anxiety about the school. When the building is an expression of what the community wants, as it is in Alamance County and Shoreham–Wading River, it is a tangible sign of school responsiveness to parents. Not only is an entire area of conflict removed, but an additional unifying symbol is created.

The school building also either contributes to or drains staff morale. When the staff of the middle school moved into their new building in Shoreham, their energies were released further for creating a new program for their students. Were Region 7 Middle School to be given a more adequate building, a large area of expenditure of energy would be eliminated. While these people seem to have boundless energy, of course they do not. No statistical study will show that the building lowers scores at Region 7 Middle School or that scores would be raised if they moved. But in coping with the constraints of a small elementary-school building, energy is diverted that these creative people might use well in other arenas.

Achieving Order

Young adolescents are impulsive, self-absorbed, antagonistic to and dependent on adult authority, alternately energetic and enervated, vociferously independent and slavishly conformist. Many, perhaps most, teachers and administrators despair of socializing this age group that is so seemingly careless, thoughtless, indifferent, impervious, scatalogical, and labile. When teachers complain about young adolescents, the animal imagery is pervasive: "they behave like animals"; "it's a jungle"; "that school is a zoo."

What does socialization mean? For many school people, it means indoctrination. Students are to learn and repeat the idealized values of the previous generation, especially those pertaining to hard work and decorum. What socialization can also mean, beyond making children obedient, is making them human. A socialized young adult's behavior can stem from a profound inner sense of what it means to live as a vulnerable human being in a community of thinking, feeling, mortal people. It is easy to train children to ape adult behavior, although such mimicry is usually short-lived. It is difficult to inspire them to adopt such behavior because of a growing inner awareness of the imperatives of communal life on one planet, in one country, in one school, and in one home.

These successful schools insist on the common humanity of their inhabi-tants. They insist on the school as community—and the students assent. The students' positive responses to being held to such difficult expectations require that we begin to understand the means by which these schools achieve such outstanding success. Most striking is the level of caring in the schools. In the careful assignment of students to teachers and houses, in counseling, on school-sponsored trips, in home visits, in teachers' use of personal time with students for weekend canoeing expeditions, baseball games, and jazz com-bos, hours upon hours are spent in and outside of school on behalf of the personal welfare of the students. This level of caring, which we all need and flourish under, is especially important for a vulnerable age group as they take the shaky first steps toward emotional independence.

The relationships students have with adults are important to the com-parative calm that is characteristic of these schools. *Young adolescents are not ready for the atomistic independence foisted on them in secondary schools, which is one of the causes of the behavior problems endemic to many junior high schools. Behavior problems lead to omnipresent control mech-anisms, resulting in the dissonant combination of an overdose of both unearned independence and overbearing regulations.* Young adolescents are told, incorrectly, that they are adults, and then infantilized when they do not measure up. The four schools grant more independence than elementary schools do, while establishing strong support groups (houses, teams, wings, advisory groups). Gradually, students gain increasing amounts of independ-ence. They remain, however, in a highly personalized environment. The nature of the schools' organizational structure establishes continuity in adult-child relationships and opportunities for the lives of students and adults to cross in mutually meaningful ways. In each school, students express their appreciation for being cared about and known. They are actively aware of being liked, which is notable only because, in most schools, young adolescents are generally disliked.

Every student should have the opportunity to form an intense relationship with at least one adult. It is hard to describe the specific characteristics that would make up such a relationship because it varies with each individual. The characteristics which come to mind include: trust, non-threatening, challeng-ing, intellectual equality, and caring. The adult in this relationship has often

been described as a "significant other." She or he might be a teacher, secretary, janitor, or principal. While a "significant other" is hard to describe, most of us have had such a relationship with an adult while we were adolescents. If we think back to that relationship (or if we were lucky, relationships), it was often one of the most critical relationships of our lives. [Karl Stauber, Needmor Fund, letter to author, November 5, 1980.]

While school size does not help explain the sense of community these schools establish, the size of the students' frame of reference does. In Noe, a school with a student population well over 1,000, students belong to teams of approximately 150. In Shoreham–Wading River Middle School, students belong to small advisory groups within wings of approximately 140 students. The houses at Western Middle School have around 155 students, and within them, students identify with single classes, teams, or blocks. Region 7 Middle School is small enough that students identify with their age mates and the school as a whole. They are also members of sets of between 110 and 140 students. The groups of students are small enough that, as the teachers and paraprofessionals in the schools say, they know the students' moods and do not make the interpersonal mistakes that would be unavoidable in large, more impersonal settings. The students are secure in being known, and staff members are relaxed because of their deep familiarity with the students and their confidence in dealing with them.

Equally important, in dividing the schools into subsets and assigning students to groups, the schools take the initiative in setting the students' social frames of reference. The schools have adopted policies that strengthen and stabilize peer groupings by extending the time students remain together, both during the day and also over a period of several years. In Shoreham–Wading River and Noe, for instance, students may be in one wing for three years. Region 7 Middle School insists on a four-year middle school (grades 5–8) to establish early and then maintain a cohesive student body with a minimal amount of turnover. *Antisocial behavior that results from the randomness and brevity of student groupings in most secondary schools is substantially reduced in these schools.*

School climate, especially discipline, is tied to reward structures. In most secondary schools there are two routes to acknowledged excellence for students: academics and athletics. Students who do not excel in either of these two areas are excluded from scholastic rewards five days a week, 180 days a year. They therefore have few reasons to acquiesce to the norms, values, and expectations of the institution that does not value them. In successful schools the gate to praise is wide open.

Sports are very important in three of the four schools. Interscholastic team competition is valued because it allows students who might otherwise fall through the cracks to be stars. In addition, intramurals involve hundreds of students who would be excluded if sports were available only to rapid developers. As in any other school, students gain adult recognition through academic excellence. But the schools also take seriously the crippling burden of poor reading skills in these years when self-esteem is fragile while learning demands are more diversified than they were in elementary school. With reading programs based on individual continuous progress, especially in Region 7 Middle School and Noe, students are rewarded for their personal progress in a skill without whose mastery they can choose only to be outsiders.

Beyond athletics and academics, there are many routes to success. Students in Region 7 Middle School and Western Middle School are highly valued for their consideration, self-discipline, and general decorum. The arts are stressed in all the schools, with students winning accolades for musicianship, drama, crafts, sewing, and other areas of creative expression. Leadership is particularly valued. The community service program at Shoreham–Wading River Middle School gives students who have never excelled in anything else, as well as school "stars," a chance to be outstanding humanitarians. The variety of competitions and contests that students from Noe and Region 7 Middle School enter allows scores of students to shine. Special events like camping trips and simulations call upon skills from students who have never before gained recognition, giving them a chance to become equal to a new challenge.

Bill Kerewsky, the principal of Harper's Choice Middle School in Columbia, Maryland, cites two lines from Gwendolyn Brooks's "Boy Breaking Glass" to underscore the necessity for diverse means of expression in schools: "I shall create! If not a note, a hole./If not an overture, a desecration."[6] These schools challenge students to create "notes," "overtures," and much more, in the service of their own positive creativity and the integrity of the school fabric. Expecting students to conform to group norms need not lead to slavish conformity. Expecting them to adhere to communal conventions need not lead to conventionality. Diverse routes to success help students become diversely self-defined personalities. *Popular wisdom tells us a school has to be big to offer diverse opportunities for students. These schools are small or function in small units, yet they offer many roads to rewards. Diversity and intimacy are not mutually exclusive. As a result, large numbers of students who might otherwise be indifferent or alienated become bound to the school culture.*

Most early adolescent students in these schools are not helpful in analyzing the ease with which they consent and contribute to the schools' authority. "Why aren't you walking on the grass?" they are asked. "Because there's a path," they say, expecting their answer to be adequately explanatory. "Why are there no locks on the lockers?" "We try to show each other respect." (Yes, but *why?*) "Why are you talking so quietly in the corridors?" "So as not to disturb people in the media center." "How do you know what the rules are?" "You just know." The students' explanations appear to reflect an effortless internalization of adults' definitions of socially acceptable behavior. This appearance is fact in communities like Alamance County and Shoreham–Wading River, where the values of home and school blend into one set of expectations.

In other schools, especially Region 7 Middle School, conformity to school norms is less automatic and uninspected. Students express a more enthusiastic appreciation of authority than adults might anticipate because of the alternatives that the students know only too well. They value above all what their school gives them that no other school has: safety. Some also obey rules because they are anxious to preserve the tranquility of one of the few predictably orderly places in their lives. *In the schools with "difficult" students from disorganized neighborhoods there is the most passionate adherence to school norms. They have the most to lose.*

It is, nonetheless, possible that none of these schools draws so large a group of hostile students who reject out-of-hand the importance of schooling that they cannot be integrated into the mainstream culture of the school. If so, those who divvied up the children in the four districts are to be congratulated. More likely, the mix of students is a matter of luck. Schools like Noe and Region 7 Middle School see their practices, not luck, as responsible for their results. Were Noe to have ability tracking, for instance, the school would be likely to create a large subculture of school rejectors, as well might occur in Shoreham–Wading River, where the result would probably be a group of entitled but alienated suburban adolescents.

Unnoticed in most discussions about academic effectiveness and test scores is the attenuation of differences in some schools' behavioral results, an equally if not more exciting accomplishment. *Perhaps by remaining more elementary in tone and structure, in emphasizing fun and fantasy, and in personalizing every aspect of the school environment, these schools still appeal to the children within pseudomature adolescents. Being allowed to "leave it at home," as they say in Region 7 Middle School, students can reopen their not quite foreclosed childhoods and in so doing have a chance to grow into their early adolescence.* In addition, an inviting, diverse school program in a community whose rules they help set expands the possibilities for young adolescents' school acceptance. It is clear that, as Persell says, "Rather than lamenting the types of students they have, schools can analyze and perhaps redesign their social organization."[7] One is struck by how few students in these schools think they are bound to lose, how few "hard rocks" there are, to use the term Deairich Hunter learned in a Brooklyn, N.Y., school with adolescents who "have no worries, no cares. They're caught in the deadly, dead-end environment and can't see a way out."[8] It would appear that a combination of the luck of the draw and school practices carefully devised for specific school populations makes possible students' genuine commitment to these educational communities.

Teachers' Working Conditions

We spend a lot of time asking why adolescents buy into the culture of a school. The prior question is why teachers do. *Just as students need to be socialized into the goals, norms, and expectations of a school, so do teachers. Because in each school the principal chose either the entire staff from scratch or took a core group of teachers from his or her former school to the new assignment, a group with prior consensus about excellence in schooling for young adolescents established the school's norms.* Teachers hired subsequently have taken their cues from the tone that was established and have been directly or indirectly guided by the original core of teachers. Each school has a principal whose primary concern is instructional leadership, as seen not only in the principals' discussions about the schools but in the allocation of their time in a school week. Teachers see the principals as supporting their instructional goals and, in most cases, as deeply concerned about them as individuals in and out of school.

Boredom and idleness are rare commodities in these schools. This is as true for the teachers as the students. It is not clear how staff members of a school decide, if indeed they consciously do, on the level of adult effort that is the norm in their building. An unacknowledged norm, however, becomes apparent if one asks what would happen if the principal decided that the level of effort were to be increased or decreased by a given percentage. Teachers tend to agree that after several months of change, the school would slide back to its original level. The level of teacher effort in the four schools is very high. In part, it is required by some of the principals, who push incessantly for productive use of time. For the most part it is self-imposed. The psychic rewards for teaching in these schools are high. Aside from the personal and professional support of the principal, the teachers are gratified by administrative recognition of their professionalism. They are, in varying degrees in the various schools, curriculum builders, budget preparers, schedulers, and student advisors. They do not feel, as teachers do in so many schools, that they are at the bottom of the heap, powerless to effect change.

Most striking is the lack of adult isolation in these schools, unlike the experiences that so many of the teachers recount from their previous teaching assignments. Common planning and lunch periods, team meetings, and team teaching encourage constant communication and allow for high levels of companionship. *Teachers are not abandoned to their students, which is very important in working with this age group, with which daily experiences may not necessarily be rewarding.* The gratification of adult relationships in the schools can tide a teacher over the bad days when young adolescents go for the jugular, and can leave teachers open to enjoying the good times when they are the most enthusiastic, creative, and appreciative students one can teach.

The teachers are not harried despite all they do. They work very hard but are rarely frantic. Perhaps the lack of tension comes from administrative support and peer companionship. Perhaps it comes from a school organization where 150 young adolescents do not come at them in parceled lots every 48 minutes. Perhaps it is explained by the low number of discipline problems in the schools. This is not to say that the teachers do not become nervous or tired, but that they do not set the tone of their classes, and thereby a large measure of the students' school experience, by that nervousness and tiredness. The group norm is to be caring, involved, upbeat, and, in their students' terms, "cool." It is a style that people who work with young adolescents know to be effective. This norm contributes greatly to the climate of the school.

Beliefs and Expectations

Teacher expectations of student performance are an important aspect of school climate. In most school studies, student achievement is tied to high teacher expectations; yet, as we have seen in a school like Noe, teachers' behavior can run counter to their stated expectations for students' future aspirations and academic performance. This is a complex area not clarified by questions that ask teachers, for instance, whether their teaching objectives are the same for all, most, or some students.

What is the correct answer to such a question? If the teacher interprets "objectives" broadly, the answer will be "yes," to avoid the appearance that there are ceilings of expectations for anyone. If the teacher interprets the question as referring to individualization rather than equity, the correct answer will be that expectations are different for most students. The problem lies with the question and also with unrealistic, conflicting demands. It is impossible for teachers to have equally high and also individualized expectations for their students.

We lack an acceptable vocabulary for describing the differential expectations held by teachers that enhance students' capacity to learn. To say that teachers must have appropriate or realistic expectations is to use language redolent of racism, sexism, and elitism. But it is *not* reasonable that teachers should expect all students to learn, unless learning is a highly differentiated term. It *is* reasonable that their expectations not be tied to race, sex, or class so as to limit students' growth. It *is* reasonable that there be constant reassessment about structural barriers to learning.

It is important that teachers have high expectations for *themselves* and that they believe they are capable of making a difference in their students' learning. A surprisingly high number of teachers in all four schools feel that there is a great deal a teacher can do to ensure that all students achieve at a high level. In each school, a minority but still surprisingly high number also agree with the controversial view that evaluations of teachers should in some measure be tied to student performance. Most important, whatever else teachers say, they believe that all their students belong in their school rather than anywhere else.

When teachers say that they expect only some of their students to do well and graduate from high school or college, they have not necessarily established ceilings of expectations. Their expectation is based on experience in the classroom. *A teacher, like any other human being whose behavior is shaped by day-to-day experience, will not have the same objectives for everyone, especially with an age group so variable in development. In successful schools, the day-to-day experience is generally positive. Teachers are rewarded, for instance, by seeing test scores go up. They expect more from their students not because of biases about the inherent value of groups of students, but because their experience tells them that what they are doing works. Success breeds higher expectations, which leads to greater success. The expectations are as tied to teachers' assessment of their own performance as their students' performances.*

Teachers' behavior is not tied only to expectations. In these schools they put high levels of energy into their teaching because of many factors unrelated to the students, including a personal sense of mission, the esprit de corps of the staff, colleagues' expectations of teacher performance, the encouragement, supervision, and evaluation of esteemed principals, their sense of fighting for a cause, and the gratitude of parents and students. For many of these people, teaching is the central focus of their lives. Questions about equally held expectations barely begin to evoke the complexity of their commitment to their students' welfare.

Reciprocity

In many schools and school districts, the process of education is seen as being unidirectional, originating in the child. Contrary to the commonplace criticism that schools treat children like empty vessels into which they pour the wine of wisdom, schools more often see children as predefined, coming from backgrounds that determine classroom interaction. When asked to recommend schools in their districts to be visited as part of this study, high-level administrators, including district heads of educational research and evaluation, said: "Pick your neighborhood and you pick your school." All responsibility for school outcomes is thereby placed, through his or her family background, on the child. *The key factor in the climate of successful schools is their recognition of, indeed insistence upon, reciprocity in human growth and development. It is that, more than any other single factor, that accounts for the distinctive communities they have become.*

Curriculum and Instruction

Translating philosophy into curriculum is the most difficult feat for schools to accomplish. The translation to climate and organizational structure appears to be much easier for these schools than the translation of purpose into curriculum. The schools periodically assess their success in responding to young adolescents' developmental needs. They place strong emphasis on creating numerous opportunities for competence and achievement, self-exploration and definition, social interaction, and meaningful school participation. Opportunities for physical activity are not as numerous or frequent as three of the schools would like. This is an area they have identified as needing attention. The weakest area, in terms of responsiveness to developmental needs, is meaningful participation in the community. It is politically difficult for two of the schools to initiate community service programs. For the most part, though, the schools have not thought much about this area of early adolescent development. As a staff member from Shoreham–Wading River Middle School said: "It is interesting what schools don't see until someone shows them."

The strongest area of responsiveness is in providing diverse experiences for the students. Addressing the developmental variability of the age group is a constant struggle for schools, one which these four schools appear to do with ease. They meet the developmental diversity of the age group with comparable diversity in program. There are spectacular instances of curricular success in these schools, like the camping trip at Region 7 Middle School, Fifties Week at Noe, Circus Week at Western Middle School, and Authors' Week at Shoreham–Wading River Middle School. The four schools have learned the importance of flamboyance in schooling for young adolescents. The opening ceremony of the farm, an awards program for campers, WNOE, a Black History Week concert—all are examples of the school as theater. While in Shoreham–Wading River the spectacles are usually integrated into the daily curriculum, in the other schools these theatrical events take place mostly outside the regular instructional flow. These schools are dramatic impresarios. What looks at first like spectacle is also solid curriculum and pedagogy that derives from a confident, often intuitive understanding of what playful, group-oriented, curious young adolescents need.

The brilliant moments lend variety to otherwise uninspired, standard fare. It is not curriculum that raises these schools from the mundane. In fact, staffs' conversation betrays a surprising lack of emphasis on curriculum. Students reflect this lack of emphasis when asked what the school expects of them. Unless asked specifically about academics, their responses usually have to do with behavioral expectations. Aside from numerous discussions about special events, curriculum is not an issue that affects what a visitor observes in these schools.

This comes as a surprise. The schools have fought hard for curricular autonomy. They have put enormous amounts of energy into special areas like the farm and the arts at Shoreham–Wading River Middle School, schoolwide independent study time at Region 7 Middle School, a three-year social studies curriculum for multiaged teams at Noe, and the nature trail at Western Middle. The definition of "academics," however, is still very narrow. The need for articulation between elementary and senior high schools, the use of commercial textbooks, and the influence of state or district curriculum guides create uniformity of curricular content in the four schools. Certain teams in Shoreham–Wading River Middle School seem to be an exception to this observation. Even there, however, the comment of a teacher who is proudly insistent that under the surface there is a standard core curriculum is telling: "We're doing the same thing. It just looks different." Students would be able to transfer from one school to the next without suffering in the core academic subjects, especially reading and mathematics. What would surprise them would be the "delivery system."

Curricular similarity is not necessarily undesirable. It is important to the shared experiences of a generation to have a common understanding of its cultural and scientific heritage. It is striking, however, to hear principals and teachers talk about the school's attentiveness to the individual and group needs of its particular group of students and the age group in general, to see that attentiveness expressed in the school's organizational structure and climate, and then to see the same movie about the Salem witches in two schools within a period of four weeks. One gets the sense that if it is March, this must be Massachusetts. Despite all intentions to the contrary, there are, in two of these schools and in several classrooms at two others, to a greater extent than they acknowledge, the "graded expectations, graded standards, graded norms and the characteristics of curriculum, materials, and instruction that normally accompany the well-established, traditional graded school," as Goodlad and Klein observed in elementary schools.[9]

The quality of discourse in the classrooms is characterized by a surprising lack of intellectual rigor. While school administrators stress inquiry into ideas, teachers for the most part stress the transmission of facts. There is relatively little inquiry. The tone of classroom discussion reflects an assumption that young adolescents are developmentally incapable of grappling with concepts. At Noe and Shoreham–Wading River, this concrete approach to learning is a conscious decision based on personal experience and current popular research. Teachers and principals in these schools correctly criticize junior highs in which they have taught for curriculum that is too abstract for the cognitive maturity of most students. They buttress their empirical evidence with the results of Herman Epstein's research, the burden of which is that 12- to 14-year-olds are neurologically incapable of abstract thought because they are in a period of slow brain growth, or a plateau. They cannot process more complex information than they could when they were 10 to 12 years old and in a period of rapid brain growth. Slow mental growth "would explain some of the difficulties encountered in middle and junior high schools. Children should not be pushed to rise very much in cognitive level during these years but, instead, might be encouraged to develop and consolidate already initiated skills."[10]

This is not the proper forum for reviewing controversies about Epstein's work. It is noteworthy that, despite the schools' insistence on the diversity of young adolescents as to age in every other aspect of their growth, they have become ardent advocates of the uniformity of cognitive development. Most curricula for junior-high students are insensitive in their abstractness. However, two points are being overlooked in the stampede to concrete thinking and learning for all students. First, it is as much a failure to deny the diversity of development during early adolescence by making teaching predominantly concrete and atheoretical as by making it predominantly abstract. Second, sensitivity to the majority of students' limited capacity for theoretical ideation does not preclude the teacher from extracting general principles from the factual, making connections among concrete examples, or encouraging preliminary examination of ideas and values. Granted there are eighth-graders who cannot understand what, for instance, manifest destiny is, yet their social studies and literature courses expect them to. Teachers, as curriculum builders, need to become sensitive to "facts" that are actually prior concepts. They do not therefore need to excise concepts from their classrooms.

Interest in so-called brain growth theory, while building, is new and cannot account for the lack of intellectual discourse in so many classrooms. One explanation is the comparatively elementary, rather than secondary, definition of these schools. A principal who feels that good teachers can learn and teach any subject and who praises interdisciplinary pedagogy more vigorously than a single-discipline approach may be discouraging a passionate commitment to a subject area, which is often the keystone of outstanding instruction at the secondary-school level. Teachers with secondary-school backgrounds are more subject/area-oriented than teachers with elementary-school backgrounds. The principals lean toward the latter. The schools are walking a tightrope between elementary and secondary schooling while thoughtfully defining the level of schooling in the middle. Although their mastery in all other areas is secure, their balancing act in curriculum is still shaky.

Academic skills and standards are important. Demands for performance must be calibrated to the person's level, but not watered down. One of the skills is the ability to communicate orally and by written word. A second is coming to terms with how to deal with controversy. Academic content should not be *pap,* but be honest and detailed. Skills in learning how to evaluate material, to come to be aware that in many areas of life there are no right or wrong answers—there must be opportunity for such learning. [Irving E. Sigel, Educational Testing Service, letter to author, November 17, 1980.]

Another, and very troubling, argument can be made about intellectual rigor in schools. The Traditional School in Louisville, which accepts only students who have had no behavioral school problems and are willing to take two years of Latin, has adopted a management technique characteristic of many private schools by narrowing its clientele. It is less broadly responsive not only to the spectrum of early adolescent development but also to the heterogeneity of clientele that the school system serves. Shoreham–Wading River Middle School, with the least diverse school population, has the highest level of intellectual discourse, despite its enthusiasm about brain growth theory. Noe Middle School, with the most heterogeneous population, heterogeneously grouped in all but the Advanced Program classes, has the least *observable* level of intellectual discourse (partly because there is so little discourse at all in truly individualized, heterogeneously grouped classes). One of the finest discussions observed during a period of eight months was in Alexander Burger Intermediate School (I.S. 134) in the South Bronx, where in a homogeneously grouped social studies class, students were learning about the history of labor unions through American ballads. It is possible that homogeneous grouping through admissions policies or class assignment is necessary for substantive discourse in classrooms. Homogeneous grouping is a management response to diversity. Perhaps in schools that reject this response as socially harmful there is a substantial difference in the quality of discourse.

Most disturbing for educators who have continued to hope that schools can be the great academic if not social equalizer, excellence does not and cannot mean the same thing for all schools. Schools have limited resources, the most finite of which is time. When the principal of Region 7 Middle School decides to take 79 students on a camping trip to study ecology, he is also deciding that they will not be in their reading, math, science, social studies, language arts, and cultural arts classes. In addition to the defensible retort that the students may learn and retain more in all of these areas on one such trip than they will in weeks in the classroom, the argument supporting this use of preciously guarded time is tied to the nature of the school's student body. Many children from low-income neighborhoods spend years within the radius of a few blocks. As they become adolescents, they are increasingly deprived by the limitations of their neighborhoods. Schools like Region 7 Middle School see it as part of their mission to expand their students' frame of reference as much as possible, and to do so directly rather than vicariously whenever feasible.

The same argument might be made on behalf of students in suburban or exurban communities like Shoreham and Wading River, but one needs only to sit in the classrooms for several hours to hear that the students' frame of reference has been broadly expanded by family trips, reports at the dinner table about parents' occupational experiences, and excursions to museums and the theater. In addition, the majority of students in communities like Shoreham and Wading River do not enter middle school with the deficiencies in basic skills that Region 7 Middle School and Noe Middle School deal with. The time allocated to basic skills instruction is time not allocated elsewhere. These schools are effective in empowering their students to learn. Above-average scores on standardized achievement tests, while a remarkable academic achievement for some schools, are only minimal indicators of this empowerment for others. School effectiveness is tied to school clientele. These schools are the same in their adaptability to their clientele. Because they are the same, they are distinctly different, and so are their academic results.

A note about testing: *Standardized achievement tests appear to be playing a positive role in these schools.* In many districts, reading instruction stops, if not after third grade, certainly by sixth or seventh. Secondary teachers are generally ill-prepared to teach reading. The tests have documented the need for continued reading and math instruction and have required schools to commit time and staff to that task. They have helped document the effectiveness of schools that make this commitment. This documentation gives political protection to schools like Noe Middle School that are seen as too radical in organization and curriculum by powerful members of the community.

The tests need not restrict a school's program. Restriction is caused by schools' recognition of problems in basic skills areas and, in some cases, by a less-than-imaginative response to those problems. In fact, however, in schools like Noe and Western Middle, where a specific period of time is allocated to basic skills instruction in reading and math, the rest of teachers' and students' time is freed for other, more creative work. Standardized testing is limiting when used by limited people. The tests need improvement. Even so, as they are in these schools, when used as diagnostic tools for individual and group remediation and an indicator of instructional effectiveness, the tests can be an important pedagogical and political ally, contributing to and documenting the success of schools.

School Organization

None of the schools uses the same method of grouping students or of scheduling. A practice distinguishes each one, like a full period for Advisory at Shoreham–Wading River Middle School, multiaging in core subjects at Noe, rotating sets and schoolwide independent study time at Region 7 Middle School, and a variety of teaming options at Western Middle School. Each principal has been creative about fashioning the school organization and the school day to enhance communication, personalization, continuity in relationships, and individual choice. Each school's organizational structure has evolved over a period of years. None is the same as it was originally, and most have had at least one overhaul and many minor tune-ups. None of the principals is fully satisfied with the current arrangement; all anticipate further changes.

The lesson about structure is seen in words like organic *and* evolving. *The principals had a vision of what schooling should be like for young adolescents that did not start with teams or houses. Organizational decisions resulted from school philosophy. School philosophy was deeply influenced by sensitivity to the age group.* It was also influenced by the personalities of talented leaders and a core group of highly dedicated teachers responding to the clamorous demands of a group of students whose energies they enjoy and wish to promote.

Administrators often want answers to practical and seemingly simple questions, like whether multiaging or rotating class schedules make sense. Focusing directly and exclusively on these questions yields unsatisfactory results. It is not possible to deal successfully with the immediacy of schools without bearing in mind the deep historical roots of each school practice. Successful school organization has been achieved in these schools not by formula, mimicry, or short-term fixes, but through the evolving expression of vision, sensitivity, and personality in response to a particular social context.

The schools have in common an organic structure evolving in response to the staffs' evaluation of students' needs. Each school has made decisions that the other schools have rejected, like multiaged grouping, a day set aside for mini-courses, or self-contained graded classes. The particular decisions are less important than the process of decision making, which is collegial, and the basis for decision making, which is the academic and social well-being of the particular group of students and teachers.

All the schools have adopted a house and team structure so that groups of students live together for several hours of each school day, sometimes for two to three years. This minimizes size, personalizes the environment, increases communication among students and teachers, and reduces tension. The schools have all reduced the influence of subject-oriented departments in order to empower multidisciplinary teams. They have guaranteed teachers common planning periods so that every student is known predictably by a team of teachers who have time to consult with one another about his or her academic progress and general well-being. The common planning period also promotes collegiality and professionalism in curriculum development and review. In varying amounts, teachers in the four schools control the schedule of the school day so that they can allocate time to activities according to their natural flow and students' needs, interests, and attention spans. Finally, the schools are willing, indeed eager, to modify or overthrow the schedule for part of a day, a full day, a week, a session of the year, or for an ad hoc special event, to discourage the monotony of routine endemic to all schools.

Beyond these decisions, there is no indication from the experiences of these schools that one school's organizational decisions are superior to those the other three schools have adopted. They have no certainty that other practices, especially multiage grouping, contribute positively to learning or behavior, nor is there research to help them evaluate their experiences. The major unresolved area is ability grouping. While the schools resist homogeneous grouping, each has decided on some ability grouping, usually, but not always, in reading and math. Citywide reading programs like TRIP in Louisville and DORT in Detroit are so individualized that grouping is unnecessary. Individual study time in Region 7 Middle School minimizes the need for scheduled grouping. All the schools are resolutely opposed to tracking or to any attempt to refine grouping into multiple levels of classes. Teachers in three of the schools are not quite comfortable with the ability grouping they have adopted, either because they see the school as having too little or too much. Again, they find the research inconclusive about results of various methods of ability grouping at the middle-school level.

The area of greatest controversy in other communities appears to be resolved in these four schools: there is no dissension about the wisdom of their grade organization. There is consensus that the ninth grade belongs in the high school and that a 6–8 grade organization allows greater attentiveness to early adolescent needs and greater flexibility of program than a 7–9 organization. The only school to deviate from a 6–8 pattern, Region 7 Middle School, does so by retaining the fifth grade. Again, the reasoning is based on the nature of the school's clientele and the needs of the age group.

While the research is ambiguous, it provides some support to guide and buttress the schools on this issue. The research tells these schools that middle schools and K-8 schools have less alienation and victimization, higher student and parent satisfaction, and fewer disturbances in girls' self-esteem than junior high schools. (The research has yet to deal with what happens in the senior high to ninth-graders, our lost tribe in education. Preliminary indications are that they may experience more alienation and engage in more disturbed behavior, like substance abuse, in senior high than in junior high.)[11] Whatever the message from research, these schools are now unalterably opposed to any change in their grade organization. There appears to be absolute consensus that it works. An area of discord in other schools has been removed through a history of successful performance that may be accounted for more by the schools' clarity of purpose than grade organization. The debate will continue—but outside these schools.

The School in the Community

In 1953, in the beginning of a book on elementary-school objectives, Kearney wrote:

> Americans today are concerned about their schools. This interest springs from many sources. A high respect for education was evident in colonial days and has grown steadily since. It is based on the faith that through education one generation can help the next to live the good life, preserve the good values, improve as individuals, and promote the civic and economic welfare of all. One has to make only a casual survey to see on every hand evidence of this faith and this respect for education.[12]

Schools thrive or fail to thrive in particular community contexts. Almost thirty years later, the last sentence of Kearney's statement reads like sophomoric boosterism. At the same time, the rest of the statement continues to reflect the demands the public makes on schools. The demands persist while the faith and respect have corroded.

Kearney's statement is most appropriate to the community that supports Western Middle School in Alamance County, North Carolina, and least appropriate to Noe Middle School's community context in Louisville, Kentucky. *While each of the four schools functions in a different context, the key to each is the same. They are all responsive to their particular social and political milieu.* Western Middle School survives in Alamance County because of its strict discipline and substantial curricular predictability. Noe Middle School survives because it has turned inward, away from a contentious district. To maintain community support in Shoreham and Wading River, which are near the Brookhaven labs and Stony Brook University, their middle school must have strong science and math programs and prepare students for success on SATs. Only Region 7 Middle School fails to thrive. It is the one school that must choose between community (i.e., parent) and political support. Were the school less responsive to its clients, it would be guaranteed greater longevity. Its successful responsiveness to what it defines as its community is its undoing.

Neighborhoods or rational feeder patterns help schools, because the schools can belong to a self-identified constituency. Western Middle School and Shoreham–Wading River Middle School have this type of automatic community. Region 7 Middle School has a self-selected constituency in a large region. Because of gerrymandering and busing, Noe does not. The school would be less isolated and would have stronger parent support if it were part of a neighborhood. The school context does not have to be conducive to community support, as witness the success of Noe Middle School and the rocky history of Shoreham–Wading River Middle School. It does not have to have political support, as witness Region 7 Middle School. When it has this support, however, as Western Middle School and Shoreham–Wading River Middle School now do, energies are released within the school that can be invested directly in the school. Whatever their complex histories, each school is deeply embedded in its district. One way of ascertaining the strength of people's belief in them is to ask who would protest if the schools went out of existence. In each case, at the very least, staff, parents, and students would be up in arms. Through community education, successful performance, and an ability to stay within the (expanding) limits of community tolerance, the schools have been legitimized in their areas.

Parents are generally very apprehensive about the middle years of schooling. Junior high schools have been seen for many years as the least productive and most worrisome of public educational institutions. In these four schools, parent advisory councils are extremely active in communicating parental anxiety to the schools and in informing parents about school practices. The schools' administrators also stress constant openness with parents, both in the building and on the telephone. They all offer classes for parents on early adolescent development, aspects of peer relationships, and school life. This service, about which many parents are openly appreciative, binds them with loyalty to the school while helping them to understand family interactions and school practices they may have otherwise questioned. The reports of parents who participate in these school activities help set a tone that fosters school support in the community. And most important, *the most effective thing the schools do to relieve parental apprehension is to send home, day after day, happy children who are progressing well.*

The role of parents in these schools presents an unclear picture. Parent support for Region 7 Middle School has kept it alive. On the basis of the successful performance of this school, it is easy to conclude that parent support is a vital antidote to political chicanery. The situation looks quite different in Louisville, however, where citywide parental pressure for additional schools like the Traditional School leaves the staff at the Noe Middle School grateful for the relatively high level of parental apathy in their district. In the past, parent activism has endangered the progress of Shoreham–Wading River Middle School. Only strong parent support from one faction, with an element of fratricidal warfare, enabled the school to continue in its present form when another faction's indignation threatened to uproot the school's foundation. Parent activism is not always present, nor does it always take the same form in the lives of these schools. The picture becomes clearer if a distinction is made between parent activism and participation, which tends to take the form of activities that directly support the schools' programs. Parent participation, through the advisory councils, volunteering, attendance at school functions, and other signs of unity with the schools' purposes, bolsters staff morale and appears to help some students identify with the purposes of schooling.

Again, however, the picture is uncertain. Young adolescents, while seeking increased autonomy from parental supervision, are often embarrassed by their parents' participation in school activities. Principals in predominantly middle-class schools complain that parent pressure, which is almost exclusively for academic performance, can be disruptive of the school's social purposes while also academically inappropriate. It appears, however, that in communities where adolescents are bucking the antischool mores of the peer group, direct parent participation in the school is an important factor in their being school-oriented. In a study of Michigan elementary schools, Brookover and his colleagues found that parent involvement was negatively associated with mean school achievement in basic skills in White middle-class schools and positively associated in Black schools. "Any conclusion concerning the effect of any school characteristic outcomes may therefore be in error unless it is examined in the context of its function in the school social system," they conclude.[13] The relationship between the nature of early adolescent development and the nature of parental involvement is unclear. Parent activism and participation have not been studied in several varied community contexts at the intermediate level of schooling.

Schools do not seem to be thought of as objects that it might take a long time, many hands, and even more that one generation to come to understand. Individual schools do not seem to be thought of as individual in character. They are thought of, perhaps, as "urban," "inner-city," or the like; but mostly they seem to be thought of as equivalent settings for the interaction of certain recurrent variables—principals, teachers, pupils, curricula, and methods of instruction. . . . It is usually difficult to recover from educational studies the information about the context that would enable one to characterize it.

If this impression is correct, then the knowledge of schools in the United States is about one hundred years behind knowledge of American Indian kinship. [Dell H. Hymes, "Educational Ethnology."]

If effectiveness meant the same thing across different populations of students, schooling would be an easier enterprise. There is no more powerful example of the contextual demands on schools than the first half hour of a visit to I.S. 139 in the South Bronx. The police are in the front office because of two separate thefts the previous night. One is of typewriters, not an uncommon occurrence in many schools. The nature of the other theft is uncommon: the entire school lunch has been stolen. The ham and ground beef have been cleaned out. School lunches are marketable on the streets of the South Bronx. The principal's day begins with a search for food. Meanwhile, an incoherent woman carrying two shopping bags stuffed with clothes comes lumbering up the front stairs of the school, accompanied by a police officer. Under duress, she is returning clothes that belong to the school. John Quinn, the enterprising principal of the school, collects clothes that are unclaimed at dry cleaning establishments in the area. As the buildings in the area are set afire by arsonists, he gives the dispossessed families of the burned-out buildings some clothing. This woman has taken clothes under false pretenses and has given them to her brother, who is selling them at a profit in his neighborhood thrift shop. Students in the school have reported her, just as they will report where the school lunch cartons are found later in the day. As he is rounding up a motley combination of canned foods for the day's lunch, Mr. Quinn is listening to the woman's unintelligible explanation of why she took the clothes. In his office is a sign: "When life gives you lemons, make lemonade."

The question is not only whether school effectiveness and success can mean the same things across diverse populations, but also in what ways they do and should mean something different. Successful schools are responsive to particular social contexts. They contribute, as a result, to greater diversity rather than homogenization in American schooling. While this is an overstatement, given the curricular similarities in the schools, it is not a misstatement. The distinctiveness of each school is the result of the interplay between a coherent concept of schooling for the age group, particular personalities, and the constraints and demands of a social context.

The differences in these successful schools, however, are predictable, not random. It is predictable that schools successfully serving students who are severely handicapped in reading, writing, and mathematics will focus intently on these skills. It is predictable that schools successfully serving well-read students with cosmopolitan backgrounds will focus intently on enhancing their skills of interpretation and synthesis. The schools must start at different points on the same continuum of academic expectations.

It is also predictable that schools responsive to early adolescent development will reduce the size of focus groups, personalize the quality of adult-student relationships, give ample room for peer groups to flourish, acknowledge diverse areas of competence, involve students in participatory activities, emphasize self-exploration and physical activity, and encompass all these in a clearly defined, structured environment. *While academic expectations may differ, the schools' behavioral expectations are the same.* Their practices for encouraging desired social behavior vary according to the cultural background of the student body and community tolerance.

Nonetheless, these schools do not make radical departures from some of our most automatic expectations about schools. No one would doubt that they are schools. They have classes, schedules, rules, tests. They transmit information in standard packages of English, math, social studies, and science. Adults spar with students about chewing gum, running in the halls, and getting homework in on time. But these schools snatch diversity from the jaws of uniformity, and it is the basis for doing so that distinguishes them. *The schools are inextricable from their constituents, both students and adults, both present and past. Were they less responsive to their communities, they would be more homogeneous and directly transportable.*

Conclusion

Successful schools for young adolescents adapt creatively to the extreme differences in biological and social maturation of their students. Their success raises questions about other schools. Why, for instance, do other schools not give students opportunities for community engagement, the way Shoreham–Wading River Middle School does? Why is it so difficult for other schools to arrange for week-long simulations involving 150 students at a time, the way Noe Middle School does? What stops other schools from having exciting interdisciplinary curricular units, the way Western Middle School does? Why are other schools unable to establish times when students exercise their own judgment in choosing classes, the way Region 7 Middle School does? Traveling from school to school, one hears school officials explaining why the very practices one has observed elsewhere are structurally impossible for schools to adopt. In fact, such explanations are engendered by a failure of conviction.

There are harder questions. Why, for instance, cannot many other schools have unlocked lockers, interracial seating in the cafeteria, caring relationships, well-behaved students and teachers intent on learning, and parents who are informed about and support the schools' purposes? There are no set formulas for achieving school success. *Extracting school practices from an entire school culture and replicating them elsewhere may make a bad school mediocre. To become a good middle-grade school requires a change in vision about the possibilities of educating young adolescents.*

The teachers in the four schools do not see their schools as unique, partly because they feel uncomfortable about being considered radically different, but mostly because they want other schools to emulate them. They are frustrated by school board members, principals, and teachers from other schools who dismiss their experience as idiosyncratic or totally dependent on one principal's talents. They resent other schools' willingness to learn from pallid examples of schooling while rejecting their examples as unique.

When asked what is special about their school that could be replicated elsewhere, the teachers emphasize four areas. First, any school can have a coherent philosophy about the environment in which young adolescents learn. Second, any school can establish a climate characterized by consistency of expectations, a positive attitude about young adolescents, and a high level of energy in job performance. Third, teachers must be acknowledged as the professionals they are, especially in the area of instruction. Fourth, organizational ingenuity is possible in any school, reducing isolation by allowing for the small student focus groups and joint teacher planning time that characterize the four successful schools. Teachers see underlying all these factors one essential ingredient that is not always replicable but should be: they must want to be where they are.

There are many factors these schools do not hold in common. Student population, union contracts, hiring policies, financial resources, school plant, parent involvement, school board support, court orders, citywide reading programs—these differ from school to school. There *are* aspects held in common and, contrary to the teachers' arguments, may be replicable only under conditions that are not widespread in American schooling. Each school's first principal (in Noe, its second) has been a driven, energetic worker, committed to establishing the best possible school environment for the age group. Each principal seized the opportunity—any opportunity—to incorporate a philosophy of schooling for young adolescents into the defining concept of the school, whether it was a part of the school's charge or not. Each was able either to hire his or her own staff in toto or transfer a core group of teachers into the school. Except for Noe, each school was involved in lengthy planning and sometimes bitter fights at the outset, which helped establish clarity of definition and unified, strong supporters. Each has been able to establish diversity of curricular offerings, whatever the district or state requirements. Each has been masterful at selling the school to the community.

Since these factors in the experiences of the four schools appear to be of such importance, policy setters can take heed and make more widespread the conditions that appear to account for school success at this level. Otherwise, we will continue to founder because of a dangerous attitude that sees mediocrity as replicable but excellence as unique. This excellence far surpasses the accomplishments of many other institutions. The federal government has mandated that schools, more than any other public or private institution, respond to the noblest impulses of American public policy for social justice, especially in the areas of equity for the handicapped, all races, and both sexes. The four schools address with clear conviction and administrative ease these potentially divisive mandates. They are far ahead of other social institutions in their communities. Certainly, no church in Alamance County is as desegregated as Western Middle School, nor are the area's private schools, nor is public higher education. No other agency draws Whites back into Detroit the way Region 7 Middle School does. No corporation mainstreams the handicapped the way Noe Middle School does. Few public or private institutions can rival Shoreham–Wading River Middle School in affirmatively providing equal opportunities to both sexes.

The principals and their staffs make these policies work the way they make everything else work. They are thoughtful about implementing regulations that many others prefer to ignore or find overwhelming. Every table, class, or foursome in square-dancing must be integrated at Region 7 Middle School. Handicap Awareness Day and daily responsibilities for their fellow students are an integral part of school life at Noe. Staff members at Shoreham–Wading River Middle School actively recruit boys into traditionally female activities and vice versa. Students at Western Middle School are carefully assigned to houses to maintain racial balance at all times. An important function of advisories at Noe and Western Middle School is encouraging communication about these issues. However deep the schools' commitment to social justice, though, and it is usually very deep, the commitment is to quality schooling for each child. Equality follows from that commitment, prodded and buttressed by federal regulations and court orders.

At a time when the role of government in public education is being challenged, it is important to note that the federal government has legitimized these educators' best social impulses. It has established an atmosphere conducive to social equity. While there have been deeply divisive unintended effects as a result of these policies elsewhere, the federal government's ability to initiate public commitment to specific areas of equity has been central to the quality of the social fabric of these schools.

Are these schools exceptional or representative of a larger number of schools for young adolescents? On the basis of this investigation it is not possible to speculate about how prevalent such schools are. Similarly, no conclusion can be drawn about how broad a spectrum of school types there is at the intermediate level. This investigation did not uncover a broad array of public institutions, ranging from paramilitary to experiential schools. These four schools take an experiential approach to schooling. Whether they are representative of the central tendency in successful schools for young adolescents cannot be determined by this investigation. On the basis of numerous school visitations, however, it seems reasonable to speculate that these are maverick schools that are representative of the most prominent but extremely limited trend in successful middle-grade schooling.

These schools tell us that diverse groups of young adolescents can learn together with one another and with adults in peaceable school communities. They tell us that schooling can be enjoyable and productive for adults and students in the middle grades. They tell us that contrary to prevalent assumptions, young adolescents need not be experienced by adults as an emotionally and physically assaultive age group to be placed on "hold" until they "grow out of it." They tell us that it is possible to gather large numbers of young adolescents together in one building for many hours to satisfy adult expectations about behavioral and intellectual growth. They tell us that it is possible for schools to set norms that young adolescents come to value equally with adults. They tell us that so-called dichotomies like social versus intellectual development and equity versus quality need not be mutually exclusive.

These schools tell us that despite the insufficiency of schools in compensating for societal inequities, middle-grade schools can be effective in releasing the stranglehold of social class on academic performance. And despite massive differences during early adolescence in rates of biological, psychological, and intellectual growth, schools can be positive environments for social development. The challenge of these four schools is that, with diverse means and in diverse circumstances, some schools are both. These schools tell us, in other words, that schooling for the age group is viable, that schools can be breeding grounds for academic *and* social excellence, and that, with all its unreasonable and discouraging aspects, the social and political expectation for equitable public education is reasonable and valuable.

Notes

1. Joan Lipsitz, *Growing Up Forgotten: A Review of Research and Programs Concerning Early Adolescence* (New Brunswick, N.J.: Transaction, 1980):124.
2. Seymour B. Sarason, *The Culture of the School and the Problem of Change* (Boston, Mass.: Allyn & Bacon, 1971):14.
3. Vito Perrone, "Adolescents in School," *Conference Proceedings: The Time of Early Adolescents* (Grand Falls, N.D.: University of North Dakota Center for Teaching and Learning, 1980):30.
4. B.R. Clark, "The Organizational Saga in Higher Education," *Administrative Science Quarterly* (1972):178–84. Cited in Terrence E. Deal's review of *Organization without Authority* by Ann Swidler, *Harvard Educational Review* 50 (May 1980):297.
5. Michael Rutter et al., *Fifteen Thousand Hours: Secondary Schools and Their Effects on Children* (Cambridge, Mass.: Harvard University Press, 1979):126–27.
6. Gwendolyn Brooks, *The World of Gwendolyn Brooks* (New York: Harper & Row, 1972):408–9.
7. Carolyn Hodges Persell, "Fifteen Thousand Hours" (review), *Harvard Educational Review* 50 (May 1980):290.
8. Deairich Hunter, "Ducks vs. Hard Rocks," *Newsweek* (August 18, 1980):14–15.
9. John I. Goodlad and M. Frances Klein and Associates, *Behind the Classroom Door* (Belmont, Cal.: Wadsworth, 1970):86–87.
10. Herman T. Epstein, "Learning to Learn: Matching Instruction to Cognitive Levels," *Principal* 60 (May 1981):28.
11. See Dale A. Blyth, John P. Hill, and Charlotte Smyth, "The Influence of Older Adolescents: Do Grade Level Arrangements Make a Difference in Behaviors, Attitudes, and Experiences?" *Journal of Early Adolescence* 1 (Spring 1981); Dale A. Blyth, Roberta G. Simmons, and Diane Bush, "The Transition into Early Adolescence: A Longitudinal Comparison of Youth in Two Educational Contexts," *Sociology of Education* 51 (July 1978):49–62; Dale A. Blyth and Elizabeth Lueder Karnes (eds.), *Philosophy, Policies, and Programs for Early Adolescent Education: An Annotated Bibliography* (Westport, Conn.: Greenwood, 1981); National Institute of Education, *Violent Schools—Safe Schools: The Safe School Study Report to the Congress*, vol. 1 (Washington, D.C.: U.S. Government Printing Office, January 1978).
12. Nolan C. Kearney, *Elementary School Objectives*. Report Prepared for the Mid-Century Committee on Outcomes in Elementary Education (New York: Russell Sage Foundation, 1953):14.

13. W.B. Brookover, "Effective Secondary Schools." Report prepared for Research for Better Schools (mimeographed, n.d.): 7.

Appendix: Protocol for Site Visits

Effective schools are well defined as to their goals and desired outcomes. They establish their programs and practices on the basis of a clear sense of purpose. The translation of program to practice, however, is very difficult to achieve. The framework for each school observation therefore included questions ranging from broad purposes to particular instances of instruction, the reification of a school's dreams, goals, and rhetoric. The questions then move outward to the larger community. Each case study was structured by nine categories for observation and discussion:[1]

1. *Purposes, goals, definitions.* The items ask what the underlying rationale or purpose of this school is. For instance, are there stated goals? Where? By whom? For whom? Are there structured priorities? Is there conflict in the school? About what? Is there consensus among the staff about the school's goals? Is this seen as an elementary or secondary school or neither? What do staff and others cite as five characteristics of effective middle-grade schools? Who talks about the purposes of middle-grade schooling? What makes this level so hard? What is done to make it easier? Is this seen by staff as being an effective school? By what standards? "Schools have a choice in the norms they select"—Do respondents say this is true?

2. *School climate.* The items attend to norms, beliefs, and expectations; responsiveness to developmental needs; academic purposefulness; learning expectations; behavioral norms; working conditions; the physical setting; and socialization for discipline and order. Examples are: How does this school "feel?" How does the school respond to developmental diversity? Are decisions made specifically because of the population of the students? What are the expectations for students? For teachers? For the principal? Are there discipline and joy? Is there a "collective ideology?" What one thing symbolizes this school? Do students and teachers relate informally? Are people nice to each other? Can they express their feelings and opinions without fear of ridicule or embarrassment? Do they like this school? Do teachers want to be here? What do teachers talk about in the lounge? Is the staff diverse in terms of abilities, interests, teaching styles, age, race, sex? When students and

teachers have a problem in school, to whom do they speak? Are there work and service opportunities for students? Do people trust one another? Are there times when it is okay just to "mess around"? What is very important to students? Does it have a place in school? Do students think that school makes a difference? What do they say are the academic expectations? Is there a subgroup of students indifferent to academic success? How is the academic emphasis created? How much deadly routine is there for students and teachers? How long do the teachers feel they can continue doing what they are doing? What do teachers say sustains them? Is it easy to be a good teacher in this school? Is the building neat, clean, and in good repair? Is the space exciting and inviting? Flexible? Are there places for quiet and privacy? For noise? Is there room in the corridors to move around? Is the space personalized by teachers and students? Can one tell who lives and works here? How do students learn what is good and bad in this school? To whom does this school belong, according to the students? Can they make a difference in this school? Why do they obey rules? What would they like to change? How would they go about it? Are they ever afraid in school? According to teachers, students, and the principal—what happens when a rule is broken? Why do people break rules here? When can students go to the bathroom? How much praise do they say they get? What is special about this school that could be replicated elsewhere? What is unique and nonreplicable?

3. *Organization.* The items attend to responsiveness to developmental needs, graded or multiaged organization, staff organization, scheduling, grouping, and open or contained classroom structure. Examples are: Are structural decisions made in response to the nature of the school population? Are students in self-contained classes, do they change classes with the same group, or do they change as individuals from class to class? Is there parental choice about grade assignment? Is instruction delivered by departments? Do people think it should be? Is the schedule flexible, including some block scheduling? Do people think it should be? Is there a variety of teaching arrangements that includes teams, departments, and self-contained grades? Should there be? Is there an advisory system? How does the school structure deal with school size and variable development?

4. *Curriculum.* Items attend to issues of curricular balance, articulation with elementary and senior high schools, and thoughtfulness about adaptation to the nature of the school population, including the needs of young adolescents. Examples, not tied to particular subject areas, are: What is the balance between basic skills, areas of organized knowledge, the arts, vocational exploration, physical activity, and personal understanding? Is there an array of schooling options responsive to the needs and diversity of the age group? The school population? Do respondents think an emphasis on "back to basics" and academic

success leaves little room for social development? What do the feeder elementary schools think of the school? What does the district high school think of it? How much do/should students' interests, needs, and tastes determine the curriculum? How successful are attempts at interdisciplinary curricula? What skills do staff and administration expect students to master? How is agreement on this determined? Are decision-making and problem-solving skills incorporated into the curriculum? How? What proportion of time is focused on self-understanding? What disciplines are considered fundamental knowledge? Can the "exploratory" be incorporated into the core disciplines? Should it be? Are there electives? How does the curriculum accommodate different rates of learning and levels of ability? What is the staff's understanding of "continuous progress?" Do they emphasize this? Do students help develop special interest courses and make other contributions to the curriculum? Does the schedule of special interest courses vary over time? Are this year's offerings the same as last year's? Do teachers get to teach at least one thing they are vitally interested in? Does a wide variety of clubs and activity groups meet during school hours? Are art, drama, and music part of the regular curriculum? Does the school provide community service opportunities for students? Are people in the community involved in the school program? How are the needs for self-exploration and definition, competence, meaningful participation, structure, social interaction, physical activity, and diversity met in the school program? Are there clear curricular expectations? How are they established? Does the school have a curricular specialty? What areas do staff say the school is particularly strong in? Weak in?

5.   *Instructional practices.* Items attend to responsiveness to developmental needs, the work process, how objectives are identified and accepted, student choice, allocation of time, rewards, and assessment. Examples, not tied to specific subjects, are: Does the classroom reflect teachers' adaptations to learners' differing levels of maturity and ability? Are students actively involved in their learning? Are instructional methods varied (direct, open, activity, labs, small group, individualized, large group, field trip, interdisciplinary, etc.)? How is intensity created? Do teachers reflect on what they teach? How? Do teachers think about the process of learning? Does the principal appear in the classroom to lend authority to teachers' instructional purpose? Does the subject matter grip the students? Where do ideas come from? Is there emphasis on inquiry? Are there ceilings of expectations? How are students' strengths and weaknesses diagnosed? Does this diagnosis direct instruction? Is progress monitored? How? Are groupings flexible, short-term, and often based on criteria other than academic ability? What decisions do teachers make about teaching arrangements and strategies? What say do teachers have in instructional decisions made by the principal? How do teachers respond to new ideas and techniques? Is

good teaching rewarded? How? Do teachers greet students when they enter the classroom? Are instructions clear? Is a high percentage of class time spent on learning? Can students say what they are doing and why it is important? Do they move around freely? Do they use each other as resources? Do teachers frequently praise students' good work? Do pictures, posters, instructional materials, and practice represent various racial and ethnic groups realistically and sensitively? Do pictures, posters, and displays reflect boys and girls engaged in non–sex-stereotyped behavior? Can girls take all courses that boys do? Does each classroom have a mini-library? Are there many students using the media center or library most of the time? Are books checked out to teachers or classrooms? Are teachers teaching "at the top of their bent"? Is there anything particularly striking or compelling? Is the instruction deadly dull? Are there incentives for teachers to experiment? To cooperate with each other? What in-service staff development activities were offered last year? This year? Will be offered next year?

6. *Leadership.* The items address the principal as leader, how authority is established and norms are set, and the principal as the translator of the school for the community. Examples are: What would happen if the principal left? Does school excellence all come down to the principal? What does the principal say is the role of luck? According to the principal—what does this school stand for? How does a school manage self-renewal? What does everyone see as the principal's role here? Who sets the budget? How much budgetary discretion does the principal have? How much control does the principal have over curriculum, staff development, materials? What else does the principal want control over? What are the barriers to good leadership? What political considerations does the principal take into account in making decisions about the school? Does "effectiveness" mean something special here, to this principal? Does the principal think deeply about reducing achievement differences among poor and middle-class students? How does the principal account for the school's success in meeting the nonnegotiable threshold criteria? How does the principal know if he or she is doing a good job? What does the school reward? How? Why?

7. *The community context.* Items address the external pressures that impinge on the school, its history, the role of parents in the school, and the school's response to its local context. Informants include the principal, superintendent, school board members, community leaders, and parents. Examples of questions asked of them are: Is this a good school? What are its strengths? What improvement is needed? What were the intentions that influenced the original decisions about the school? What role did parents play? Historically, what made this school come about and endure? What gives it "staying power?" Are there important splits in the community? Was there a key event that

legitimized the school in the community? Has luck played a part? Would this school work anywhere? How important is the community context? Does "effectiveness" mean something special here? What political decisions have to be taken into account in running this school? What kind of school do parents want? How are their concerns voiced? Heard? When one thinks about the history of the school, were there changes in purpose, leadership, funding, staff, community support? Did they help? What changes hurt the school? Why do people believe in this school?

8. *Public policy questions.* These items address issues at large that affect schools. Examples of questions asked include: Are there things that boys do that girls should not, do not, or will not? And vice versa? Do both sexes have full access to everything offered? How was desegregation handled? How successful is integration? In classes? Lunchroom? Among teachers? Is there a plan to integrate the student body more successfully? Does anyone think deeply about attenuating differences in achievement based on race or social class? What has the school's response been to Public Law 94–142, which mandates placing handicapped students in the least restrictive environment? Is it possible to have quality schools that have equal access to all? Does this school need more money? What could it do with more? Could it be as good with less? What needs to be reformed in middle-grade education? Is this school optimizing what is best in standard American education or is it moving far away from it?

9. *Self-evaluation.* An assumption was made that successful schools engage in a good deal of self-scrutiny. Items asked include: Is this a good school? How do you know? What needs to be changed? Can it be? How? What criteria do you set by which to judge effectiveness? How do you know if you have done a good job? Is there an ongoing process for study, evaluation, and planning for this school? Who is involved? What changes have occurred in the past two years as a result of this process? How has this school improved recently? Does being developmentally responsive change achievement levels? Is working in or running a school an initiation into the limits of choice?

The questions and observation items were many times more numerous in order to get as rich an impressionistic picture of each school as possible. In addition, a short informal instrument for gathering demographic information was used at each site.

Note

1. The questions come from many sources, including, but not exclusively, Wilbur Brookover et al., *Social Systems and Student Achievement:*

Schools Can Make a Difference (New York: Praeger, 1979); Gayle Dorman, *Middle Grades Assessment Program* (Chapel Hill: Center for Early Adolescence, University of North Carolina, 1981); Ronald R. Edmonds, "Some Schools Work and More Can," *Social Policy* 9 (March-April 1979):28–32; Nicholas P. Georgiady, Jack D. Riegle, and Louis G. Romano, "What Are the Characteristics of the Middle School?" in *The Middle School: Selected Readings on an Emerging School Program,* ed. Louis G. Romano, Nicholas P. Georgiady, and James E. Heald (Chicago: Nelson-Hall, 1973):73–84; John I. Goodlad and M. Frances Klein and Associates, *Behind the Classroom Door* (Belmont, Cal.: Wadsworth, 1970); Charity James, *Beyond Customs: An Educator's Journey* (New York: Schocken, 1974); Gordon Lawrence, "Do Programs Reflect What Research Says about Physical Development?" *Middle School Journal* 11 (May 1980):12–14; George B. Redfern, "Classroom Observations: What to Look for," *NAESP Communicator* 10 (January 30, 1981):3–6; Michael Rutter et al., *Fifteen Thousand Hours: Secondary Schools and Their Effects on Children* (Cambridge, Mass.: Harvard University Press, 1979); letters from numerous correspondents to questions from the author; and discussions with Michael Cohen, Bruce Haslam, Tommy Tomlinson, and Saul Yanofsky at the National Institute of Education, and Terry Saario, then deputy assistant director at the Department of Education.

Bibliography

Alexander, William M., and George, Paul S. *The Exemplary Middle School.* New York: Holt, Rinehart, & Winston, 1981.

Alexander, William M., and Kealy, Ronald P. "From Junior High School to Middle School." In *The Middle School: Selected Readings on an Emerging School Program,* ed. Louis G. Romano, Nicholas P. Georgiady, and James E. Heald. Chicago: Nelson-Hall, 1973.

Ausubel, David P., and Ausubel, Pearl. "Cognitive Development in Adolescence." *Review of Educational Research* 36 (October 1966):403–13.

Bamber, Chrissie. *Student and Teacher Absenteeism.* Phi Delta Kappa Fastback 126. Bloomington, Ind.: Phi Delta Kappa, 1979.

Blyth, Dale A., Hill, John P., and Smyth, Charlotte. "The Influence of Older Adolescents: Do Grade Level Arrangements Make a Difference in Behaviors, Attitudes, and Experiences?" *Journal of Early Adolescence* 1 (Spring 1981):85 –110.

Blyth, Dale A., and Karnes, Elizabeth Lueder (eds.). *Philosophy, Policies, and Programs for Early Adolescent Education: An Annotated Bibliography.* Westport, Conn.: Greenwood, 1981.

Blyth, Dale A., Simmons, Roberta G., and Bush, Diane. "The Transition into Early Adolescence: A Longitudinal Comparison of Youth in Two Educational Contexts." *Sociology of Education* 51 (July 1978):149–62.

Bronfenbrenner, Urie. "Toward an Experimental Ecology of Human Development." *American Psychologist* 32 (July 1977):513–31.

Brookover, Wilbur B. "Effective Secondary Schools." Report prepared for Research for Better Schools. Mimeographed, n.d.

Brookover, Wilbur B., Beady, Charles H., Flood, Patricia K., Schweitzer, John H., and Wisenbaker, Joseph M. *Social Systems and Student Achievement: Schools Can Make a Difference.* New York: Praeger, 1979.

Brookover, Wilbur B., Schweitzer, John H., Schneider, Jeffrey M., Beady, Charles H., Flood, Patricia K., and Wisenbaker, Joseph M. "Elementary School Social Climate and School Achievement." *American Educational Research Journal* 15 (Spring 1978):301–18.

Brooks, Gwendolyn. *The World of Gwendolyn Brooks.* New York: Harper & Row, 1972.

Brundage, Diane (ed.). *The Journalism Research Fellows Report: What Makes an*

Effective School? Washington, D.C.: Institute for Educational Leadership, 1980.

Carnegie Council on Policy Studies in Higher Education. *Giving Youth a Better Chance: Options for Education, Work, and Service.* San Francisco: Jossey-Bass, 1980.

Carney, Maureen F. *Inservice Education for Desegregation: A Review of the Literature.* Rand Note N-1331-NIE. Santa Monica, Cal.: Rand, 1979.

Clark, B.R. "The Organizational Saga in Higher Education." *Administrative Science Quarterly* (1972):178–84. Cited in Terrence E. Deal, review of Ann Swidler, *Organization without Authority. Harvard Educational Review* 50 (May 1980):295–99.

Cohen, Donald, and Frank, Richard. "Preadolescence: A Critical Phase of Biological and Psychological Development." In *Mental Health in Children,* vol. 1, ed. D.V. Siva. Westbury, N.Y.: PJD, 1975.

Cohen, Jere. "High School Subcultures and the Adult World." *Adolescence* 14 (Fall 1979):491–502.

Cohen, Michael. "Policy Implications of an Ecological Theory of Teaching: Toward an Understanding of Outcomes." *Ecological Theory of Teaching.* San Francisco: Far West Lab for Educational Research and Development, 1980.

Community Relations Service, U.S. Department of Justice. *"Human Relations: A Guide for Leadership Training in the Public Schools—Summary Report on a Project with the Syracuse, N.Y. School System.* Washington, D.C.: U.S. Government Printing Office, 1980.

Cramer, Jerome. "The Latest Research on Brain Growth Might Spark More Learning in Your Schools." *American School Board Journal* 168 (August 1981):17–20.

Cremin, Lawrence A. *The Transformation of the School: Progressivism in American Education, 1876–1957.* New York: Knopf, 1961.

Dorman, Gayle. *Middle Grades Assessment Program.* Chapel Hill: Center for Early Adolescence, University of North Carolina, 1981.

Duckworth, Kenneth E. "Schools as Student Work Organizations: Report of the First Year of Research." Eugene, Ore.: Center for Educational Policy and Management, mimeographed, 1979.

Edmonds, Ronald R. "Some Schools Work and More Can." *Social Policy* 9 (March-April 1979):28–32.

Eichhorn, Donald M. "The School." *Toward Adolescence: The Middle School Years—The Seventy-Ninth Yearbook of the National Society for the Study of Education,* part 1. Chicago: University of Chicago Press, 1980.

Epstein, Herman T. "Learning to Learn: Matching Instruction to Cognitive Levels." *Principal* 60 (May 1981):25–30.

Epstein, Herman T., and Toepfer, Conrad F. "A Neuroscience Basis for Reorganizing Middle Grades Education." *Educational Leadership* 35 (May 1978):656–60.

Epstein, Joyce Levy (ed.). *The Quality of School Life.* Lexington, Mass.: Heath, 1981.

Erikson, Erik. *Identity: Youth and Crisis.* New York: Norton, 1968.

Feuerstein, Reuven. *Instrumental Enrichment: An Intervention Strategy for Cognitive Modifiability.* Chicago: University Park Press, 1980.

Firestone, William A. "Images of Schools and Patterns of Change." *American Journal of Education* 88 (August 1980):459–87.

First, Joan McCarty, and Mizell, M. Hayes. *Everybody's Business: A Book about School Discipline.* Capitol Station, Columbia, S.C.: Southeastern Public Education Program, 1980.

Fisher, Dorothy. "It Can Be Done: The Five Year Story of an Integrated, Innovative, Alternative Middle School." Detroit: Region 7 Middle School, mimeographed, 1976.

Garbarino, James. "Some Thoughts on School Size and Its Effects on Adolescent Development." *Journal of Youth and Adolescence* 9 (1980):19–31.

Garbarino, James. "The Role of Schools in Socialization to Adulthood." *Educational Forum* 42 (January 1978):169–81.

Georgiady, Nicholas P., Riegle, Jack D., and Romano, Louis G., "What Are the Characteristics of the Middle School?" In *The Middle School: Selected Readings on an Emerging School Program,* ed. Louis G. Romano, Nicholas P. Georgiady, and James E. Heald. Chicago: Nelson-Hall, 1973.

Glasman, Naftali S., and Biniaminov, Israel. "Input-Output Analyses of Schools." *Review of Educational Research* 51 (Winter 1981):509–39.

Goodlad, John I., and Klein, Frances M. and Associates. *Behind the Classroom Door.* Belmont, Cal.: Wadsworth, 1970.

Gottfredson, Gary D., and Daiger, Denise C. *Disruption in Six Hundred Schools: The Social Ecology of Personal Victimization in the Nation's Public Schools.* Center for Social Organization of Schools Report No. 289. Baltimore: Johns Hopkins University, 1979.

Hamilton, Stephen. "Educational Outcomes in Ecological Perspective." San Francisco: Far West Lab for Educational Research and Development, mimeographed, 1980.

Hill, John P. *Understanding Early Adolescence: A Framework.* Chapel Hill: Center for Early Adolescence, University of North Carolina, 1980.

Hill, John P. "Secondary Schools, Socialization, and Social Development During Adolescence." Paper prepared for the National Institute of Education, U.S. Department of Health, Education, and Welfare, Washington, D.C., 1978.

Hunter, Deairich. "Ducks vs. Hard Rocks." *Newsweek* (August 18, 1980):14–15.

Hymes, Dell H. "Educational Ethnology." *Anthropology and Education Quarterly* 11 (Spring 1980):3–8.

Ianni, Francis A.J., and Reuss-Ianni, Elizabeth. "School Crime and the Social Order of the School." *IRCD Bulletin* 14 (Winter 1979).

James, Charity. *Beyond Customs: An Educator's Journey.* New York: Schocken, 1974.

Kaeser, Susan C. "Suspensions in School Discipline." *Education and Urban Society* 2 (August 1979):465–84.

Katz, Michael. "Reflections on Metaphors of Educational Reform." *Harvard Graduate School of Education Association Bulletin* 25 (Fall 1980):4–9.

Kearney, Nolan C. *Elementary School Objectives: A Report Prepared for the Mid-Century Committee on Outcomes in Elementary Education.* New York: Russell Sage, 1953.

Klitgaard, Robert E., and Hall, George R. *A Statistical Search for Unusually Effective Schools.* Rand Report R-1210. Santa Monica, Cal.: Rand, 1973.

Kozberg, Geraldine. "Left Out Kids in a Left Out School." *Harvard Graduate School of Education Association Bulletin* 25 (Fall 1980):24–26.

Lawrence, Gordon. "Do Programs Reflect What Research Says about Physical Development?" *Middle School Journal* 11 (May 1980):12–14.

Lipsitz, Joan Scheff. "Adolescent Psychosexual Development." In *Adolescent Pregnancy: Perspectives for the Health Professional,* ed. Peggy B. Smith and David M. Mumford. Boston: G.K. Hall, 1980.

Lipsitz, Joan Scheff. "The Age Group." In *Toward Adolescence: The Middle School Years—The Seventy-Ninth Yearbook of the Society for the Study of Education,* part 1. Chicago: University of Chicago Press, 1980.

Lipsitz, Joan. *Growing Up Forgotten: A Review of Research and Programs Concerning Early Adolescence.* Lexington, Mass.: Heath, 1977.

Lounsbury, John H., Marani, Jean Victoria, and Compton, Mary F. *The Middle School in Profile: A Day in the Seventh Grade.* Fairborn, Ohio: National Middle School Association, 1980.

Marshall, Kimbrough. "How Effective Is Our School?" *Harvard Graduate School of Education Association Bulletin* 25 (Fall 1980):27–32.

McPartland, James M., and Karweit, Nancy. "Research on Educational Effects." In *Educational Environments and Effects,* ed. Herbert J. Walberg. Berkeley: McCutcheon, 1979.

Metz, Mary Haywood. *Classrooms and Corridors: The Crisis of Authority in Desegregated Secondary Schools.* Berkeley: University of California Press, 1978.

National Institute of Education. *Violent Schools-Safe Schools: The Safe School Study Report to the Congress,* vol. 1. Washington, D.C.: U.S. Government Printing Office, 1978.

National Institute of Education Research on Instruction Team: "Instructionally Effective Schools: Research Area Plan." Mimeographed, n.d.

Newmann, Fred M. "Research Prospectus: The Potential for Generating Collective Identity in Secondary Schools: Implications of Research on Adolescence." Madison: University of Wisconsin, mimeographed, April 1980.

Persell, Caroline Hodges. "Fifteen Thousand Hours" (review). *Harvard Educational Review* 50 (May 1980):286–91.

Perrone, Vito. "Adolescents in School." *Conference Proceedings: The Time of Early Adolescence.* Grand Forks: University of North Dakota Center for Teaching and Learning, 1980.

Peterson, Penelope L. "Direct Instruction Reconsidered." In *Research on Teaching,* ed. Penelope L. Peterson and Herbert J. Walberg. Berkeley: McCutcheon, 1979.

Phi Delta Kappa. *Why Do Some Urban Schools Succeed? The Phi Delta Kappa Study of Exceptional Elementary Schools.* Bloomington, Ind.: Phi Delta Kappa, 1980.

Redfern, George B. "Classroom Observations: What to Look For." *NAESP Communicator* 10 (January 30, 1981):3–6.

Report on Educational Research. "Public Trust in Schools Increasing, Gallup Poll Finds." Vol. 12 (August 20, 1980):4.

Romano, Louis G., Georgiady, Nicholas P. and Heald, James E. (eds.). *The Middle School: Selected Readings on an Emerging School Program.* Chicago: Nelson-Hall, 1973.

Rutter, Michael. "School Influences on Children's Behavior and Development: The 1979 Kenneth Blackfan Lecture, Children's Hospital Center, Boston." *Pediatrics* 65 (February 1980):208–20.

Rutter, Michael, Maughan, Barbara, Mortimore, Peter, and Ouston, Janet. *Fifteen Thousand Hours: Secondary Schools and Their Effects on Children.* Cambridge, Mass.: Harvard University Press, 1979.

Sarason, Seymour B. *The Culture of the School and the Problem of Change.* Boston: Allyn & Bacon, 1971.

Scanlon, John (ed.). *The Turbulent Years.* New York: Academy for Educational Development, 1980.

Schofield, Janet Ward. "Complementary and Conflicting Identities: Images and Interaction in an Interracial School. In *The Development of Friendship: Description and Intervention,* ed. Steve Asher and John Gottman. Cambridge: Cambridge University Press, 1981.

Schofield, Janet Ward. "The Impact of Positively Structured Contact on Intergroup Behavior.: Does It Last under Adverse Conditions?" *Social Psychology Quarterly* 42 (1979):280–84.

Simmons, Roberta G., Blyth, Dale A., Van Cleave, Edward F., and Bush, Diane Mitsch. "Entry into Early Adolescence: The Impact of School Structure, Puberty, and Early Dating on Self-Esteem." *American Sociological Review* 44 (December 1979):948–67.

Sizer, Theodore R. *Places for Learning, Places for Joy: Speculations on American School Reform.* Cambridge, Mass.: Harvard University Press, 1973.

South Carolina Department of Education, Division of Administration and Planning. *Rankings of the Counties and School Districts of South Carolina 1978–79.* Columbia: South Carolina Department of Education, 1980.

Tikunoff, William J., and Ward, Beatrice A. "Conducting Naturalistic Research on Teaching: Some Procedural Considerations." *Education and Urban Society* 12 (May 1980):263–90.

Timpane, Michael. "View from America: Current Research on Effective Schools." *Harvard Graduate School of Education Association Bulletin* 25 (Fall 1980):14–15.

Tomlinson, Tommy M. "Student Ability, Student Background, and Student Achievement: Another Look at Life in Effective Schools." Paper presented at the Conference on Effective Schools sponsored by the Office of Minority

Education, Educational Testing Service, mimeographed. New York, May 27–29, 1980.

Weber, George. *Inner-City Children Can Be Taught to Read: Four Successful Schools.* Occasional Papers no. 18. Washington, D.C.: Council for Basic Education, 1971.

Wynne, Edward A. *Looking at Schools: Good, Bad, and Indifferent.* Lexington, Mass.: Heath, 1980.

Yanofsky, Saul M. *A Report on the External Programs of the Pennsylvania Advancement School, 1968–1971.* Philadelphia: Pennsylvania Advancement School, mimeographed, June 1972.

Index